The Puritan Tradition
in Revolutionary,
Federalist, and Whig
Political Theory

Major Concepts in Politics and Political Theory

Garrett Ward Sheldon
General Editor

Vol. 13

PETER LANG
New York • Washington, D.C./Baltimore • Boston
Bern • Frankfurt am Main • Berlin • Vienna • Paris

Dean Hammer

The Puritan Tradition in Revolutionary, Federalist, and Whig Political Theory

A Rhetoric of Origins

PETER LANG
New York • Washington, D.C./Baltimore • Boston
Bern • Frankfurt am Main • Berlin • Vienna • Paris

Library of Congress Cataloging-in-Publication Data

Hammer, Dean.
The Puritan tradition in revolutionary, Federalist, and Whig
political theory: a rhetoric of origins / Dean Hammer.
p. cm. — (Major concepts in politics and political theory; 13)
Includes bibliographical references.
1. Political science—United States—History. 2. Puritans—New
England—History. 3. Puritans—United States—History. I. Title.
II. Series: Major concepts in politics and political theory; vol. 13.
JA84.U5H33   320.5'5'0973—dc21   97-11669
ISBN 0-8204-3821-9
ISSN 1059-3535

Die Deutsche Bibliothek-CIP-Einheitsaufnahme

Hammer, Dean:
The Puritan tradition in revolutionary, federalist, and Whig political
theory: a rhetoric of origins / Dean Hammer.
–New York; Washington, D.C./Baltimore; Boston; Bern;
Frankfurt am Main; Berlin; Vienna; Paris: Lang.
(Major concepts in politics and political theory; 13)
ISBN 0-8204-3821-9 Gb.

Cover design by James F. Brisson.

The paper in this book meets the guidelines for permanence and durability
of the Committee on Production Guidelines for Book Longevity
of the Council of Library Resources.

To Shirley and Carl,
my mother and father

Acknowledgments

Over the years, I have accumulated many debts. I would like to express my gratitude to a number of different people. At the inception of this project, Norman Jacobson, Mitchell Breitwieser, Hannah Pitkin, and Michael Rogin provided important guidance. As the project took on new directions in subsequent years, I have profited from the help of Richard Ellis, Kyle Pasewark, Aaron Wildavsky, Major Wilson, the student assistance of Elizabeth Pika and Susan Strandberg, and the financial support of the Berkeley Regents, the Augustana Research Foundation, and Franklin and Marshall College. Parts of Chapter One appeared as "Cultural Theory and Historical Change: The Development of Town and Church in Puritan New England," in *Politics, Policy & Culture*, eds. Dennis Coyle and Richard Ellis (Boulder: Westview Press, 1994). Significant portions of Chapter Five appeared as "The Puritans as Founders: The Quest for Identity in Early Whig Rhetoric," *Religion and American Culture: A Journal of Interpretation* 6 (Summer 1996): 161-194. A special note of gratitude goes to Andrew Janos, whom I have never managed to adequately thank, and to Carol for her love.

Table of Contents

INTRODUCTION   xi

CHAPTER 1 PURITANISM AND THE
                  SPACE OF DISCOURSE   1
           Self and Society   3
                  The Insular Individual   3
                  The Hierarchical Community   6
                  Reconciling Authority Claims:
                      The Practice of Theory   18
                      i. Church Membership   19
                      ii. The Antinomian Affair   21
                      iii. Suffering the Worldly Spirit   23
           The Individual and Creation   29

CHAPTER 2 CRAFTING A PURITAN INHERITANCE   49
           The Origins of a Puritan Origin   50
           The Institutional Transmission of a
                  Puritan Inheritance   54
           The Great Awakening   58
                  Creation   60
                  Self and Community   63
           The Years of War   70
           Crafting a Founding Legacy:
                  Eighteenth-Century Historiography   72

CHAPTER 3 THE PURITANS IN REVOLUTIONARY
                  DISCOURSE   93
           Liberalism   98
           Republicanism   105
                  The Radical Whigs and the
                      Rhetoric of Corruption   107

A Republican Inheritance   110
Liberalism and Republicanism:
    The Space of Authority   115

CHAPTER 4 THE FEDERALISTS AND THE
            MODERATION OF PASSION   135
The Reinterpreting the Revolution   142
The Party Spirit   147

CHAPTER 5 THE WHIG RHETORIC OF FOUNDING   167
The Rise of Commerce   172
    A Commercial Republic   174
    The Bonds of Commerce   177
The Puritan Basis of Whig History   184

EPILOGUE   RHETORIC WITHOUT MEANING   201

INDEX   213

Introduction

In Puritan scholarship, one cannot be agnostic about one's stand on the nature and extent of a Puritan legacy in American culture. One must be willing to perish in the flames of conviction. My conviction is that there is a Puritan legacy, but it is one that has been largely misconceived. Studies claiming to identify such a legacy, and likewise, scholarship that has refuted such a legacy, have been guided by a search for continuity that is premised on a notion of a Puritan essence. By this, I mean that the legacy of Puritanism was understood as the transmission forward into American culture of particular genetic characteristics, whether psychological, rhetorical, thematic, theological, or ethical, that in some way were rooted in and definitive of a Puritan past. I will cite three examples, important because they suggest the general contours of the field, though hundreds more could be listed. The first is Perry Miller, to whom we owe our contemporary appreciation of the Puritans. Miller rescued the Puritans from the parodies of the Progressive era by locating in American Puritanism an "Augustinean strain of piety" that would become a part of the New England and then colonial mind.[1] Perhaps Miller's most influential argument that served as the framework for Puritan studies for years was what has become known as the "declension thesis": that the history of Puritanism was seen, both at the time and by subsequent historians, as the falling away from a religious and communal ideal.[2]

Alan Heimert's work, with a title suggestive of this search for continuity, *Religion and the American Mind: From the Great Awakening to the Revolution*, traced the legacy of Jonathan Edwards and the New Lights to Jeffersonian and Jacksonian democracy. For Heimert, "the American tradition—of Populists and rank-and-file Jacksonians and Jeffersonians—was hardly the child of the Age of Reason. It was born of the 'New Light' imparted to the American mind by the Awakening and the evangelical clergy of colonial America."[3] Although the book received some scathing reviews at the time, it exerted a significant influence over Puritan scholarship for the next two decades, cited and quoted widely.

Finally, Sacvan Bercovitch, perhaps the most influential scholar of the Puritans since Miller, has sought "to demonstrate the richness of the seventeenth-century New England imagination through a study" of what he sees as "a central aspect of our Puritan legacy, the rhetoric of American identity." What the Puritans gave to America, writes Bercovitch, was "the status of visible sainthood," a status expressed as a nationalist spiritual biography: "American dream, manifest destiny, redeemer nation, and, fundamentally, the American self as representative of universal birth."[4] In subsequent works, Bercovitch has pushed this thesis still further, identifying the "hegemonic" influence of Puritan rhetorical forms and images that has infiltrated all aspects of American life. So the jeremiad, a type of Puritan sermon in which the sins of the current age were enumerated in great detail, serves for Bercovitch as "a powerful vehicle of middle-class ideology," a civil religion for the bourgeoisie.[5]

The assault on these studies of Puritanism has occurred on two fronts. On one front was a scholarly debate, at times acrimonious if for no other reason than the frustrating nature of the enterprise, about the definition of Puritanism. The search was ultimately about finding some Puritan essence, something that uniquely captured what it meant to be Puritan.[6] To the extent that such an essence could not be found or was no longer identifiable in American culture, Puritanism could be declared dead. So, in discounting a Puritan legacy, Stephen Foster argues that not only does the Puritan community disappear but the "Puritan social ethic in America . . . increasingly dissolves into unrelated, often irreconcilable parts."[7] Those studies that clung to a notion of a traceable essence appeared increasingly unpersuasive as they attributed to Puritanism such broad cultural expressions as providentialism, American exceptionalism, and American civic virtue, expressions that could easily claim multiple parentage.

On the second and more recent front, a series of regional and local historiographies have questioned the penetration of Puritanism into society outside of New England and have identified, instead, a number of other factors influencing the development of American culture. Jack Greene, for example, has sought to demonstrate that the declension thesis for Puritan New England, rather than serving as the developmental model for the nation, was actually a regional anomaly. Greene carefully argues for the importance of other regional influences, particularly the Chesapeake, to understand American development.[8]

Yet, there is something that does not quite sit right in all these formulations. We say we cannot define a Puritan essence, but we still talk about Puritanism. And we agree that Puritanism was overstated as a developmental model at the expense of a wealth and variety of local histories. But Puritanism looms, nevertheless. It shows up in the ambivalent commemoration of the tricentennial of the Salem witch trials, in the Thanksgiving legacy of the Pilgrims, in the rhetoric of the "city on a hill,"[9] and serves as part of our daily parlance in describing everything from American work habits to sexual repressiveness. We are left marginalizing intellectually what we participate in daily.

Part of the difficulty arises because in seeking a Puritan essence we strip away the patina of history that has given to Puritanism its richness of meanings. Puritanism does not mean one thing; it never did. It does not even mean one consistent set of things, however we want to define those things. Instead, it is a legacy that itself was constructed, transformed, and reformulated by subsequent individuals and groups, a struggle to identify the meaning of this legacy that had begun before the passing of the first generation of Puritan settlers.

This has significant implications for how we approach the study of Puritanism. We are directed away from causal interpretations in which the Puritans are seen as generating a set of meanings or attitudes that are then transmitted to subsequent generations. Instead, our attention is directed toward a more hermeneutic understanding of Puritanism, which locates meaning in its use. I am at this point drawing on Wittgenstein who, in rejecting a notion of language in which words carry specific meanings that label objective phenomena, argues that the "meaning of a word is its use in the language."[10] Our understanding of words, for Wittgenstein, is not traceable to discerning some essence within the word; rather, understanding is a matter of knowing how to use language to express ideas, make references, and convey experiences. How we learn to do this is itself constituted by the activity of using language. We learn the meaning of words by learning what they can do, and this is done not through the mastery of carefully articulated principles but through an accumulation of understandings acquired through a conglomeration of concrete examples and experiences.[11] In using a term, then, one is engaged in an interpretation of its meaning as one places it in a particular context and associates it with particular words and activities.[12]

Our understanding of words is not a random event, though. Our activity of speech always occurs within a particular context, which Wittgenstein refers to as "language games" or a "form of life." A "form of life" consists of a pattern of "rules" (or a "grammar") that define both the uses and meanings of words.[13] Thus, language is tied back to a cultural system in which words do not correspond to an objective world but to conceptual understandings of how things operate, of how we are to perceive the world, and of how we are to act. These understandings do not rely upon a conscious articulation by the participants any more than we can provide a *"clear view* of the use of our words.—Our grammar," like the traditions of which we are a part, "is lacking in this sort of perspicuity."[14] But individuals do develop a "practical consciousness," an accumulation of understandings of how and why to act acquired through our interaction with others, even without having to give verbal expression to this conduct.[15]

Wittgenstein's understanding of the nature of language is suggestive of how we might understand the cultural legacy of Puritanism. For what is suggested here is that Puritanism does not have a discrete meaning or set of meanings; rather, these meanings are constituted as this past is invoked. Rather than speaking of a "form of life" that consists of "rules" for the uses and meanings of words, we will speak of a "political culture," which we can define as a "system of beliefs, attitudes, and techniques for solving problems."[16] To understand these meanings, one must look to the associations, meanings, and interconnections of words, images, ideas, and experiences made "not 'in the head' but in that public world where 'people talk together, name things, make assertions, and to a degree understand each other.'"[17] For that reason, we will direct our attention to public rhetoric, specifically to invocations of this Puritan past. For it is through the sermons and writings as well as the often over-looked political orations that we can begin to identify the grammar of a culture, or what Jürgen Habermas refers to as a "life-world": "a culturally transmitted and linguistically organized reservoir of meaning patterns" of the participants."[18] We see in public rhetoric attempts to convey ideas in a publicly accessible language.[19] In part intended to persuade, in part to shape, such rhetoric draws upon cultural referents shared by the audience, answers to common concerns, and confirms shared orientations toward economic, political, and social life.

The approach of this study differs in an important way from other efforts to trace a Puritan legacy. I have not attempted to associate Puritanism or a Puritan legacy with any thematic continuities or persistent dualisms, since such themes do not have easily traceable genealogies. Nor have I sought to demonstrate that a Puritan legacy could be conceived of as a particular "form of life" whose grammar shapes subsequent political discourse. Like attempts to trace a Puritan essence, this causal reading of a Puritan past risks miscasting the nature of a Puritan legacy by paying attention to what Puritanism "does" and not to how it is "used." My focus, instead, unlike that of any other study of Puritanism in American culture, will be on specific invocations of the Puritans in public rhetoric. By allowing those at the time to speak for themselves as they invoked a Puritan past, we avoid both the overbroad identification of the American psyche with the Puritan soul and the overly rigid requirement that one must be a Puritan to claim such an inheritance.

The image that gets created here as we look at specific invocations of a Puritan past is that of a web, with Puritanism at its center.[21] The web does not have fixed or clearly defined boundaries.[22] Instead, the dimensions of the web, which I will refer to as a "space of discourse," are constituted by the associations made as a Puritan past is used. As I focus on the Puritans, I will not be making any claims that this was the only, or even the dominant, cultural referent. That is, a web with Puritanism at its center does not serve as a template for American culture. Focusing on this Puritan web, though, yields two different types of insights. First, we can see how a Puritan legacy was defined and constructed *as* it was related to other aspects of American life. This stands in contrast to the premise that has governed scholarly debates, a premise that identifies such a legacy only to the extent that Puritanism, itself, shapes the meaning of these aspects of American life. Second, using Puritanism as a starting point, we can begin to reconstruct the web of meanings that comprise what we will identify as distinct political cultures. That is, in the process of identifying a Puritan legacy, we are engaged in an examination of different "forms of life" in which the meaning of Puritanism is "woven."[23] This is a study, then, not of the decline of Puritanism nor of the resurrection of its soul, but of the construction of a Puritan rhetorical community.

From the beginning of their landing in New England, the Puritans were engaged in an interpretive exercise to define themselves. This interpretative exercise has been treated extensively in scholarship on the Puritans. One thinks, for example, about Robert Middlekauff's enduring study of the Mather generations, Virginia Anderson's discussion of the creation of the symbol of the "Great Migration," Stephen Innes's placement of the creation of a commonwealth within the context of commercial development, and Stephen Foster's contributions in giving to Puritan development a trans-Atlantic perspective.[24]

What I have sought to do in the opening chapter is not to provide some definitive statement about the nature of Puritanism but to identify what I see as an irresolution in two critical aspects of their own self-definition: one involving the relationship of the self to society and the other, a more ontological question of one's relationship to creation. The Puritans affirmed the authority of the insular individual, yet tried to place this individual within a hierarchical, organic community. Of creation, the Puritans conveyed the deepest sense of despair about a corrupt world, yet embraced a notion of redemption that demanded immersion in that very world. Though Puritan scholars will immediately recognize these tensions, what I have sought to identify is how this irresolution created what J. David Greenstone, in his discussion of American liberalism, calls "boundary conditions,"[25] boundaries that defined the domain of legitimate discourse in Puritan New England. Identifying these boundary conditions yields two results. First, they give shape to the debates within the Puritan community by framing the struggle of the Puritan elite to define, and then maintain, their own identity in an environment that they saw as fundamentally challenging these boundary conditions. Second, though the Puritan maintenance of these boundaries was often conducted with a dogmatic rigidity, the boundaries themselves, ironically, yielded a series of polarities. These polarities were not necessarily transmitted to future generations; rather, they provided considerable latitude in interpretation as subsequent generations could locate themselves in, and in turn reconstitute, different parts of this space to claim a Puritan legacy as their own.

Chapter 2 focuses on the cultural mechanisms by which a Puritan legacy was crafted in the seventeenth and early eighteenth centuries. What we find is that the theological developments of the Great Awakening as well as later historiographic works drew on, modified, and expanded the nature of a Puritan discursive space. This expansion occurred geographically as a Puritan founding legend was transmitted outside of New England. And this expansion occurred ideologically as the Puritans were made more palatable through their association with a Whig rhetoric of liberty. These subsequent interpretations were not "Puritan," as such, particularly as they became less theological and more political and sociological in their focus. This does not mean, though, that we should read such religious invocations as merely gratuitous or disingenuous manipulations in which there was little meaning to the images used. We can understand this transformation as a process in which religious concepts spread beyond their "specifically metaphysical contexts" to provide "a recommended attitude toward life, a recurring mood, and a persisting set of motivations."[26] We see the Puritans invoked, then, as groups engaged in debates about particular ways of life, including questions of the nature of the self, of social relationships, and of the basis of political authority.

Chapter 3 focuses on invocations of the Puritans in revolutionary discourse. This chapter addresses a central debate in colonial scholarship; namely, the extent to which colonial rhetoric and thought was framed by a Lockean or a civic republican language. By focusing specifically on the images that were associated with the Puritans in sermons, pamphlets, and newly emerging political orations of the time, I argue against a notion of either a Lockean or civic republican "paradigm." What we discover as we look at invocations of the Puritans is neither a consistent ideological framework nor contested paradigms, as has been argued by J. G. A. Pocock. Instead, we find a complex association of words and meanings, of a Lockean "right of soil" and a republican language of civic virtue and corruption, both given a Puritan inheritance and both contributing to an ambivalence in revolutionary rhetoric toward the nature of authority. It is an ambivalence that is often missed in attempts to read a Puritan past forward to look for its "impact" or its "contribution" to later revolutionary developments.[27]

Chapter 4 explores how the Federalists used the Puritan past not in service to the cause of liberty but as a force of moderation. The Federalists were placed in the untenable position of wishing neither to repudiate the Revolution nor to affirm what they saw as its outgrowth, made worse by the terror in France; namely, the subjection of the social body to convulsions of passion. In interpreting the Federalists' rejection of the egalitarian implications of the American Revolution, though, we too easily dismiss their political theory as disingenuous and cynical. We can account for some of the tone of Federalist rhetoric as revealing a deeply felt anxiety about how the emerging cultural institutions would be defined. And we can demonstrate a coherence to concerns of the Federalists as they interpreted the revolutionaries as heirs of Puritan moderation and saw in Puritanism a social theory that would protect liberty through the control of human passion.

In all of this the Federalists were ultimately unsuccessful. But, as we see in the final chapter, the Federalists would lay the groundwork for a Whig reinterpretation of America's Puritan past. In a history-conscious age, the Whigs fashioned for the nascent commercial republic a founding legend that gave America a voice in the conversation of history. The Whigs read into the American past the moral basis for their economic and political vision, a vision in which the individual remained closely tied to a corporate order. At a time in which an individualist ethos was penetrating American economic, social, and political life, the Puritans served as a reminder for the Whigs that the individual did not exist apart from the community nor the community from history.

It is notable that the final two chapters end not with the winners in history but the losers. Perhaps it is no accident that those groups who most sought to ground their understanding of American life in an historical past, whether real or constructed, would vanish from the American political scene. In the Epilogue, I take up precisely this point, showing how a rhetoric of meaning has been replaced by a rhetoric of suspicion in which the Puritans have come to represent anything that binds us. In casting something as Puritan, we are doing more than denouncing a Puritan past; we are rejecting any notion of action that arises from a shared pursuit of purpose or a notion of collective responsibility. And we are embracing, in its place, a vocabulary of freedom whose very essence is that it has neither grounding nor direction beyond our immediate needs or desires. This book, then, supplements Robert Bellah's important discussion of an American covenant as he describes what he sees as the dissolution of a "myth of origin," of shared symbols in American political life.[28]

Notes

1   Perry Miller, *The New England Mind: The Seventeenth Century* (1939; reprint ed. Boston: Beacon Press, 1961), chapt. 1.

2   For the most extended development of the declension thesis, see *The New England Mind: From Colony to Province* (Cambridge: Belknap Press, 1953).

3   Alan Heimert, *Religion and the American Mind: From the Great Awakening to the Revolution* (Cambridge: Harvard University Press, 1966), 15.

4   Sacvan Bercovitch, *The Puritan Origins of the American Self* (New Haven: Yale University Press, 1975), ix, 108.

5   Bercovitch, *The American Jeremiad* (Madison: University of Wisconsin Press, 1978), 28. See also Bercovitch, *The Rites of Assent: Transformations in the Symbolic Construction of America* (New York: Routledge, 1993).

6   For an overview of the rather heated controversy about how one can identify Puritanism, see Richard L. Greaves, "The Nature of the Puritan Tradition," in *Reformation, Conformity and Dissent: Essays in honour of Geoffrey Nuttall*, ed. R. Buick Knox (London: Epworth Press, 1977), 255-7. A number of approaches have been taken to depicting Puritanism. For an example of understanding Puritanism through its orientation to ecclesiastical and civil polity, see Paul Christianson, "Reformers and the Church of England under Elizabeth I and the Early Stuarts," *Journal of Ecclesiastical History* 31 (October 1980): 463-482. Examples of understanding a Puritan "essence" as primarily theological can be found in J. F. H. New, *Anglican and Puritan: The Basis of their Opposition, 1558-1640* (1964) and Basil Hall, "Puritanism: the Problem of Definition," in *Studies in Church History*, ed. G. J. Cuming (London: Ecclesiastical History Society, 1965), vol. 2. For examples of identifying Puritanism by its soteriology, see Miller, *New England Mind: The Seventeenth Century*; L. J. Trinterud, "The Origins of Puritanism," *Church History* 20 (March 1951): 37-57; Darrett Rutman, *American Puritanism: Faith and Practice* (New York: J. B. Lippincott, 1970); Charles E. Hambrick-Stowe, *The Practice of Piety: Puritan Devotional Disciplines in Seventeenth-Century New England* (Chapel Hill: University of North Carolina Press, 1982); and Harry S. Stout, *The New England Soul: Preaching and Religious Culture in Colonial New England* (New York: Oxford University Press, 1986). Examples of the class basis of Puritanism include Christopher Hill, *Society and Puritanism in Pre-Revolutionary England* (New York: Schocken: 1964) and Michael Walzer, *The Revolution of the Saints: A Study in the Origins of Radical Politics* (Cambridge: Harvard University Press, 1965). And examples of depicting Puritanism by its particular spiritual characteristics include G. F. Nuttall, *The*

Holy Spirit in Puritan Faith and Experience: The Puritan Spirit (Oxford: Basil Blackwell, 1946); Alan Simpson, *Puritanism in Old and New England* (Chicago: University of Chicago Press, 1955); Greaves, "Puritan Tradition"; Ian Breward, "The Abolition of Puritanism," *The Journal of Religious History* 7 (1972-3): 20-34; William Lamont, "Puritanism as History and Historiography: Some Further Thoughts," *Past and Present* 44 (1969): 133-46; and Charles Cohen, *God's Caress: The Psychology of Puritan Religious Experience* (New York: Oxford University Press, 1986). For examples of writings that attempt to locate Puritanism on a spectrum that combines these different categories, see Michael G. Finlayson, "Puritanism and Puritans: Labels or Libels?" *Canadian Journal of History* 8 (1973): 203-23 and Patrick Collinson, "A Comment: Concerning the Name Puritan," *Journal of Ecclesiastical History* 31 (October 1980): 483-88.

7   Stephen Foster, *Their Solitary Way: The Puritan Social Ethic in the First Century of Settlement in New England* (New Haven: Yale University Press, 1971), xiv.

8   See Jack P. Greene, *Pursuits of Happiness: The Social Development of Early Modern British Colonies and the Formation of American Culture* (Chapel Hill: University of North Carolina Press, 1988). See also his *Imperatives, Behaviors, and Identities: Essays in Early American Cultural History* (Charlottesville: University Press of Virginia, 1992).

9   This is the central theme, for example, in Mario Cuomo's well-received keynote address at the 1984 Democratic National Convention.

10   Ludwig Wittgenstein, *Philosophical Investigations*, trans. G. E. M. Anscombe (New York: The Macmillan Company, 1953), §43. See my discussion of Wittgenstein and tradition in "Meaning and Tradition," *Polity* 24 (Summer 1992): 551-567 and the extension of Wittgenstein to a study of political culture in J. David Greenstone, *The Lincoln Persuasion: Remaking American Liberalism* (Princeton: Princeton University Press, 1993).

11   Wittgenstein's *Philosophical Investigations* is filled with examples of this argument. See also Paul Ziff, *Semantic Analysis* (Ithaca: Cornell University Press, 1960).

12   Wittgenstein, *Philosophical Investigations*, §201.

13   See Wittgenstein, *Philosophical Investigations*, §23.

14   Wittgenstein, *Philosophical Investigations*, §122.

15   The term is from Anthony Giddens, *Central Problems in Social Theory: Action, Structure and Contradiction in Social Analysis* (Berkeley: University of California Press, 1979), xxii-xxiii, 9, 129-30. See also Giddens, *The Constitution of Society: Outline of the Theory of Structuration* (Berkeley: University of California Press, 1984), xxii-xxiii, 3, 9, 41-92. The

idea of implicit knowledge is developed in Jürgen Habermas in *Theory of Communicative Action*, vol. 1: *Reason and the Rationalization of Society*, trans. Thomas McCarthy (Boston: Beacon Press, 1984); and in Wittgenstein, *Philosophical Investigations*, §156.

16   Daniel Walker Howe, *The Political Culture of the American Whigs* (Chicago: University of Chicago Press, 1979), 2.

17   Clifford Geertz, "Ideology as a Cultural System," *The Interpretation of Cultures* (New York: Basic Books, 1973), 213. Quoting W. Percy, "The Symbolic Structure of Interpersonal Process," *Psychiatry* 24 (1961): 39-52.

18   Jürgen Habermas, *Theorie des kommunikativen Handelns*, 2 vols (Frankfurt-Main: Suhrkamp, 1981), quoted in Fred R. Dallmayr, *Critical Encounters Between Philosophy and Politics* (Notre Dame: University of Notre Dame Press, 1987), 82. For a discussion of the notion of the life-world, see also Habermas, *The Theory of Communicative Action*, vol. 1: *Reason and the Rationalization of Society*, 70-1, 82-3, 335-7. See Wittgenstein, *Philosophical Investigations*, §337, for his discussion of how "the use" of a word is "embedded in its situation, in human customs and institutions." This notion of a "reservoir" has resonance with Gadamer's notion of a "reservoir of meaning." See Hans-Georg Gadamer, *Truth and Method* (New York: Crossroads, 1986); "On the Scope and Function of Hermeneutical Reflection," in *Philosophical Hermeneutics*, trans., ed., David E. Linge (Berkeley: University of California Press, 1976); "Hermeneutics as Practical Philosophy," in *Reason in the Age of Science*, trans. Frederick G. Lawrence (Cambridge, MA: The MIT Press, 1981); "What is Practice? The Conditions of Social Reason," in *Reason*; and Paul Ricoeur, "Hermeneutics and the Critique of Ideology," in *Hermeneutics and Modern Philosophy*, ed. Brice R. Wachterhauser (Albany: SUNY Press, 1986).

19   For a discussion of the importance of oratory to reach the common people, see Harry S. Stout, "Religion, Communications, and the Ideological Origins of the American Revolution," *The William and Mary Quarterly* 34 (October 1977): 519-541. Merle Curti also suggests that the oration "epitomized the whole pattern of American patriotic thought and feeling" (*The Roots of American Loyalty* [New York: Columbia University Press, 1946], 140-1). That rhetoric and oratory were no longer conceived of as "stylistic ornaments" but were intended for "persuasion broadly understood as the active art of moving and influencing the passions" is argued by Jay Fliegelman, *Declaring Independence: Jefferson, Natural Language, & the Culture of Performance* (Stanford: Stanford University Press, 1993), 30.

20   This would certainly be one strategy to pursue. Greenstone, for example, in *The Lincoln Persuasion* applies this Wittgensteinian notion

of a grammar of culture to examine the bipolar nature of American liberalism.

21 I draw, in part, on Hannah Arendt's notion of the "web of relationships," which "consists of deeds and words and owes its origin exclusively to men's acting and speaking directly *to* one another" (*The Human Condition* [Garden City, NY: Doubleday, 1959], 162-3).

22 See Wittgenstein, *Philosophical Investigations*, §69.

23 See Wittgenstein, *Philosophical Investigations*, §7.

24 Robert Middlekauff, *The Mathers: Three Generations of Puritan Intellectuals, 1596-1728* (London: Oxford University Press, 1971); Virginia DeJohn Anderson, *New England's generation: The Great Migration and the formation of society and culture in the seventeenth century* (New York: Cambridge University Press, 1991); Stephen Innes, *Creating the Commonwealth: The Economic Culture of Puritan New England* (New York: W. W. Norton, 1995); and Stephen Foster, "English Puritanism and the Progress of New England Institutions, 1630-1660," in *Saints and Revolutionaries: Essays on Early American History*, eds. David D. Hall, John M. Murrin, and Thad W. Tate (New York: W. W. Norton, 1984).

25 Greenstone, *Lincoln*, 42.

26 Clifford Geertz, "Religion as a Cultural System," *The Interpretation of Cultures* (New York: Basic Books, 1973), 123-4. See also Max Weber, "The Social Psychology of the World Religions," *From Max Weber: Essays in Sociology*, trans. and eds. H. H. Gerth and C. Wright Mills (New York: Oxford University Press, 1958).

27 See, for example, John M. Murrin, "No Awakening, No Revolution? More Counterfactual Speculations," *Reviews in American History* 11 (June 1983): 161-71. In assessing the "impact" of the Great Awakening on independence, Murrin concludes, "Without the Great Awakening and its successors, there would have been a revolution in 1775, but in all probability, no Civil War in 1861" (161, 169). More problematic, Murrin suggests that New Divinity men "lopsidedly supported the other side - the Federalist, Antimasonic, Whig, Know-Nothing, and Republican parties" rather than the Democratic party, as suggested by Heimert (169). If we start from the Great Awakening, we read a straight line through to the Civil War. If we look, instead, to the invocations by these groups, specifically the Federalists and Whigs, of this Puritan past, we discover not a continuous thread but the emergence of distinct political cultures that give shape to this Puritan past as they talk about the present.

28 Robert Bellah, *The Broken Covenant: American Civil Religion in Time of Trial* (New York: Crossroad, 1975), 4.

Chapter 1

Puritanism and the Space of Discourse

Scholars have seen in Puritanism everything from the antici-
pation of bourgeois capitalism to a primitivist attempt to restore a biblical commonwealth. And the Puritans have been
credited with providing the civil basis for a democratic politics as well as contributing to a notion of American exceptionalism that is viewed as giving rise to everything from jin-
goism to both imperialism and isolationism. Earlier generations
saw in the Puritans both enlightened defenders of liberty and
somber, hypocritical persecutors of dissent. What is striking
in these testimonies to a Puritan legacy is not only the number
of different images that become associated with this Puritan
past but how at important points these images fundamentally
conflict with each other. We could, as many scholars have done,
enter into an argument about whose interpretation is most historically precise. But that does not do justice entirely to the
nature of this historical curiosity, for we leave untouched the
question of how the Puritans, a group who, in the words of
one historian, created a "totalitarianism of true believers,"[1]
would provide the space for such a range of subsequent and
often contradictory interpretations of their legacy. In approach-
ing this question, the place to begin is not by recounting moments of Puritan dogmatism, though there are plenty of such
instances, but by looking at aspects of irresolution in their own
understanding of the world.

We may use the shorthand "world view" to describe this
understanding of the world, a view that encompasses concepts
of nature and of self and society. World views provide an orientation: they give shape to the world by lending meaning and

positing relationships.[2] In answering how the Puritans viewed their world, we are soon confronted with a problem, though. For in mapping the space in which the Puritans oriented themselves, we find that at critical junctures the map points in conflicting directions. Of creation the Puritans embraced a world that was made by God, but saw its goodness everywhere corrupted by sin. It was a view that lent itself to a particular ethos, or attitude toward this world, namely, that of an anxiousness, as the Puritan was to be "in" the world but not "of" it. Of self and society, the Puritans affirmed the authority of the insular individual in one's relationship to God and initially envisioned society as composed of a natural bond of saints. But experiences in the early years of settlement, in which insularity threatened to dissolve this bond, resulted in a redefinition of the basis of community life. As we trace the political and ecclesiastical developments through these first decades, we see a struggle in which the commonwealth continued to affirm the authority of the insular individual, but endeavored increasingly to place this individual within a hierarchical, organic community.

It is not remarkable that the Puritans used categories of sin and grace to describe their religious experience: every Christian group, to understate the case, does so in various ways. Nor is it particularly noteworthy that the Puritans had to wrestle with contending notions of authority. Rather, my suggestion is that these polarities, and in particular the inability to resolve decisively any one of these polarities, served to shape the space of discourse in the Puritans' struggle to define themselves. What we encounter is not a univocal Puritanism but, as Janice Knight has recently suggested, "alternatives and oppositions *within* the Puritan mainstream."[3] These alternatives, which involved "definitions of sainthood and citizenship, relations of anxiety to confidence, and discipline to piety,"[4] often appeared as rhetorical shadings in Reformed theology but became increasingly the site of a struggle over cultural identity. This irresolution, I am suggesting, created a space in which Puritanism as a rhetorical image could be subsequently located and reinterpreted. Before we get too far ahead of ourselves, though, we must return to the Puritans and see the dimensions of this discursive space in Puritan rhetoric and action.

Self and Society

On the face of it, in Puritanism there appears to be nothing but hostility toward the self: sermon after sermon decried the corruption of the body, the sins of pride and vanity, and the evil of selfishness. The focus of individual life, so the Puritan thought, should be directed toward God and the community. Despite such fervent exhortations for selflessness, though, the Puritans never quite managed to purge the self. The reason for this was not want of effort or sincerity, but a profound ambivalence to selfhood. While abhorring any emphasis on the importance of the self, the Puritans could never escape the centrality of this self to their doctrine and the assertion of the self in their practices and institutions. It is not that the Puritans recognized in some banal way that the individual was important. Instead, the Puritans advanced a notion of a sphere of individual insularity from the secular world. Within this realm resided the individual's relationship with God and one's will. The sphere was not absolute: the community could and did exercise some dominion over the individual in many different ways. But in certain important respects the community was proscribed from penetrating this sphere of the self.

The Insular Individual

The religious experience of the Puritans centered on the individual. As children of the Reformation the Puritans' primary concern was to insure that nothing obstructed the relationship between the individual and God. It was the assertion of the insularity of the individual's relationship with God that served as the basis for the Puritans' dispute with the Anglican Church. The institution, as it had come to be in England and as it intruded into the insular sphere of the individual, was a hindrance to the religious experience. The word of God, most clearly expressed in the Bible, had become obscured by vestments, ornamentation, fancy language, the rights and ceremonies of the Book of Common Prayer, and an elaborate hierarchy. As Increase Mather pointed out, Christ "is the only Head of his Church: . . . no Officers, no Ordinances, no Sacraments, or Religious Ceremonies ought to be there, besides what Christ himself has appointed."[5] The individual could not even begin the first step toward conversion, that of attentiveness to God's word, if His word were lost in the rituals and ceremonies of a corrupt church.

Once these institutional impediments were removed, attention could turn to the human will. For those, like John Cotton, who placed more emphasis on a doctrine of free grace, the activation of the will followed the inward reception of grace so that the individual could respond to God's love with affection. John Cotton, in a famous sermon, defined the "efficacy of the spirit of Grace" as wading "in the rivers of God his grace up to the ankles, with some good frame of spirit; yet but weakly, for a man hath strength in his ankle bones. . . and yet may have but feeble knees." The Christian was to wade out further "and get more strength to pray, and to walk on in [his] callings with more power and strength" until finally he "shall swimme."[6] For what became the dominant ideology in Puritan Massachusetts, grace was to be actively pursued, not passively received. Even though grace was outside the province of human control, "that men hear not Gods voice is none of Gods fault, but the fault of their own *Wicked Wills*. 'Tis very vain to pretend they *cannot*, for their *Cannot* is a *Will-not*."[7] Wrote Thomas Hooker, "Know, that by thy dayly continuance in sin, thou dost to the utmost of thy power execute that Sentence upon thy soul: It's thy life, thy labor, the desire of thy heart, and thy dayly practice to depart away from the God of all Grace and Peace, and turn the Tomb-stone of everlasting destruction upon thine own soul." It was not human "distresses" that so much upset God; God's wrath ensued "when the heart becomes like the Stomach, so weak it cannot help itself" or even be helped, when there is only "a faint and feeble kind of opposition against sin."[8]

Though the individual was integrated into a matrix of devotional practices, ultimately the Puritan was to follow a "path of free spiritual expression and initiative," a path in which the ministers were to provide a model of prayer independent of established forms of worship. Where "the Catholic practicer was rarely encouraged to assume individual responsibility for his or her own spiritual development," manuals on Puritan worship "located responsibility for devotional practice in heads of households and ultimately in individuals."[9] We might as-

sume that such insularity would foster a tranquillity as the individual could carry on a private relationship with God. But
for a people consumed by a sense of their own depravity, such
insularity "took away the props of convention and the pillows
of custom" and "it demanded that the individual confront existence directly on all sides at once, that he test all things by
the touchstone of absolute truth, that no allowance be made
for circumstances or for human frailty."[10] How troubling, indeed, as the Puritans were told of their utter depravity while
still being held responsible for striving toward grace. George
Goodwin, in a popular poem of the seventeenth-century, revealed some of the anxiety that arose out of this struggle:

> I sing my SELF; my *Civil Warrs* within;
> The *Victories* I howrely lose and win;
> The dayly *Duel*, the continuall Strife,
> The *Warr* that ends not, till I end my life.
> And yet, not Mine alone, not onely Mine,
> But every-One's that under th' honor'd Signe
> Of Christ his Standard, shal his Name enroule,
> With holy Vowes of Body and of Soule.[11]

This struggle was not resolved neatly by the Puritans, even
through such theological maneuvers as an emphasis on the
covenant of grace. Unlike the covenant of works, the original
covenant between God and Adam which regulated conduct
according to the laws of nature (laws that could be known by
uncorrupted humanity), the covenant of grace carried no such
expectation about conduct. Since the Fall, humans were unable to fulfill God's law. Recognizing this, God introduced the
covenant of grace, though the nature of that covenant remained
the subject of ongoing dispute. At issue was whether the covenant was a unilateral and absolute expression of God's unconditional love or a reciprocal and conditional expression
that rested on some human initiative.[12] In either case, there
was preserved a realm of individual insularity. For those who
spoke of unconditional grace, as we saw with Cotton, the experience of grace was an individual one in which faith was
nurtured through a close, even intimate, relationship with God.
For the "preparationists" who emphasized human initiative,
sin directed individuals inward to confront their own depravity and to labor to give up their sins in the hopes of preparing

themselves for God's grace. Although the Puritan ministers insisted to the end that there was nothing the individual could do to bring about grace, the emphasis on human responsibility in "preparationist" theology revealed "the turn inward and earthward of a theology progressively focused on human agency."[13]

At the center of this ambivalence toward the self was the simultaneous affirmation by the Puritans of both the insular and sinful individual. Without a claim to insularity the individual could be subsumed easily enough into the corporate body. Without the concern with sin, insularity would pose little danger.[14] What emerged in Puritan practice was an attempt to incorporate this insular individual within a hierarchical community. This is not simply the suggestion that Puritan society displayed aspects of individualism and hierarchy. Rather, the argument is that individual insularity and hierarchy were both essential and largely incompatible aspects of Puritan life.

The Hierarchical Community
To understand the transformation that occurred in Puritan society toward a more hierarchical basis of social organization, we must trace back briefly the Puritan migration to its European beginnings. Reacting to both the traditional hierarchical order of the Anglican church and the disorder brought about by rural depopulation, urbanization, religious decay, and the decline of traditional feudal social organization, disenchanted elements of English society constructed not only an alternate explanation of the world around them but created a corresponding method of organizing their social relations. It was this new social organization that Michael Walzer refers to as a Calvinist politics, an essentially egalitarian cadre of saints.[15] Indicative of an egalitarian association, the Puritans in England required a total dedication on the part of the saint as they sought nothing less than a remaking of society. Prospective as well as current members had to exhibit continually a "commitment and zeal" that "must be tested and proven." Members were subject to constant and intense examination to insure the ideological purity of the group. And this "voluntary association of the holy" erected clearly defined boundaries that separated communicants from non-communicants and sought to exclude the latter.[16]

As the English Puritans sought to clearly define themselves as distinct from the unregenerate, so they strove to eliminate gradations of authority within the organization. The saints replaced the old hierarchy with a collective organization founded on the equality of all men "within the band of the chosen." Rather than given status differentiation, members were "measured by their godliness and by the contributions they can make to the work at hand." This organization maintained a tight discipline, but one self-imposed.[17] To the extent that authority was exercised by others, it was exercised collectively rather than by one individual over another. Ultimate sanction for the "unrepentant excommunicant," as it was exercised in the name of the group, "was exile," a form common to egalitarian organizations since they do not have available to them a variety of methods for enforcing prescriptions.[18]

As the Puritans moved across the Atlantic, from a country in which the "primary task" of the saints "was the destruction of traditional order" to a colony in which these saints became the traditional order, the nature of Puritanism as a social organization changed. For the Puritans of England there was minimal conflict between claims of corporate and individual authority since both the community and the individual defined themselves in opposition to first Catholicism and then Anglicanism. The American Puritans, on the other hand, found themselves defending two systems of authority: one born, at least in part, of their opposition to established authority, the other developed as they became the established authority, as they found themselves engaged in a struggle within their own community about who would define the nature of their emerging cultural institutions. The result was no longer a Puritanism with an egalitarian basis of authority but one that sought increasingly to place the insular individual within a hierarchical community.[19]

Because not much was written by the Puritans during their first years of settlement, it is tempting to fill in these silences by focusing on later forms of Puritan political organization. Evidence for Richard Bushman's emphasis on the Puritan's concern with order, for example, comes from laws and sermons after 1637.[20] More recently, Theodore Dwight Bozeman's claim that John Winthrop and other Puritan leaders had clearly defined assumptions about "official prerogatives and acts of political officers" rests almost entirely on debates and journal entries that occur after 1636.[21]

There have been scholarly accounts that have noted a transformation in early Puritan social organization, but these accounts suffer from overly broad interpretative categories. Michael Zuckerman, for example, argues that the increasingly repressive strictures of the Puritan community, and indeed, the simultaneous individuation within the community, were part of a more general reaction across all colonial settlements to modernity. Writes Zuckerman, "few of these dispositions and disjunctions" to "simultaneously . . . individuate and aggregate" were "unique to the New England Puritans." Zuckerman points to the Quaker community in which personal revelation was placed in a system of church control "with a thoroughness the Puritans never imagined."[22] More recently, Adam Seligman has identified the transformation in the early decades of New England settlement in Weberian terms as the result of the "institutionalization of charisma."[23]

The categories of "individual" and "community" that Zuckerman sees existing in tension with each other and the process of routinization that Seligman identifies do not allow us to distinguish different ways in which communities organize (or routinize) their social relations. Zuckerman and Seligman seem to use two characteristics for identifying the "authoritative" nature of "community": that the community establishes boundaries between insiders and outsiders and that the community imposes strict controls on its members.[24] What is missed in this rendering of community is the nature of these controls, namely, whether social regulations operate to minimize internal role differentiation or whether the social regulations serve to differentiate, and perhaps even stratify, roles.[25] A failure to identity these different bases of social regulation is significant in this case for two reasons: First, we are left unable to distinguish between the egalitarianism of the consensual basis of authority that one can observe in Quakerism from the more hierarchical basis of authority that emerges in Puritanism; and second, we are left unable to identify changes in authority relations that occur within Puritanism, particularly, as I will argue, within this first decade of settlement.

This leads us to a second set of issues raised by Zuckerman and Seligman, that of explaining both the reasons for and the timing of this change in Puritan organization. Zuckerman chooses the "stresses" that arise from the uprooting effects of modernity as leading to pronounced tensions between individuality and community.[26] Seligman identifies the change as resulting from the "structural and organizational imperatives of institutional building," imperatives which work to circumscribe the individual expressions of free grace upon which the charismatic community was originally premised.[27] Certainly, the long-term development of any community at this time must be read against the backdrop of modernity and the need to institutionalize, but neither modernity nor routinization are sufficient to explain the form of social organization that emerges. Modernity and routinization might be better understood as providing particular conditions or imperatives to which individuals and communities then must react. And, indeed, communities may react in a number of ways, from moving toward the more individualistic, bourgeois culture that Sacvan Bercovitch identifies to a hierarchical response that we see with the American Whigs to the maintenance of an egalitarian organization as we see with the Quakers to some mix of these different elements.

Two questions about Puritan development, thus, remain to be answered: First, why do Puritan communities move toward embracing more hierarchical aspects of "community" whereas other groups, like the Quakers, move toward (or maintain) a more egalitarian basis? And second, why do we see such a rapid change in the basis of Puritan social organization within the first decade of settlement? At least part of the explanation for both the timing and nature of Puritan development lies in what might be called "shocks" to the Puritan community that came at a critical time in Puritan self-definition. The argument draws its insight from organizational theory, which views organizations as both defining for themselves particular tasks and, in turn, modifying these tasks and the form of organization necessary to accomplish these tasks in response to environmental changes.[28] This allows us to move beyond attributing the increasing "direction from the center" to "the necessity of governing and the temptation of power"[29] (which presumably all communities would encounter) to identifying how the necessity to govern was itself reinterpreted in the face of increasing challenges to the Puritans' own self-definition. What I am arguing is not that we can define a Puritan identity, as such. Rather, my suggestion is that we can read these first decades of settlement as a struggle by the Puritans (and particularly the Puritan elite) to define, and then maintain, their own identity in an environment, both outside and then inside their community, that they saw as increasingly hostile.

The Puritans came to New England having given little thought to the internal structure of the community. There was "no preconceived plan of town organization to guide them in forming a body politic."[30] Certainly the Puritan leaders looked to Biblical communities in creating the commonwealth. But the Bible was at best an indeterminate guide for wrestling with the practical exigencies of creating a community. While initially the General Court, the central governing body, assumed control over the direction of the Massachusetts Bay Colony, as the Assistants found themselves overwhelmed by commonwealth business they quickly delegated much of their authority to the nascent towns and their representatives, even though these towns had no legal status.[31] "Each town, each leader, was on his own."[32] In the establishment of Sudbury, for example, the General Court did not define the administrative powers of the town leaders "with any precision" to allow the town to adjust to new situations.[33] One historian even goes so far as to note that "New England society" in these early years "was politically flexible."[34] There is support for this conclusion given Winthrop's ruling principle at this time that "in the infancy of plantations, justice should be administered with more lenity than in a settled state, because people were then more apt to transgress, partly of ignorance of new laws and orders, partly through oppression of business and other straits."[35]

In the early years of settlement, members of the new communities were left to improvise as needs arose. William Bradford, in writing about the election of Assistants in Plymouth in 1624, spoke of the need for a change in persons occupying these positions. If being an Assistant was an "honour or benefit, it was fit others should be made partakers of it"; if, on the other hand, "it was a burthen," then "it was but equal others should help to bear it."[36] In the first years of the formation of Sudbury, one sees a similar diffusion of authority. Like the early Boston settlement, the Sudbury government was "still flexible and experimental." Authority was granted to individuals sparingly, and then "for a limited time, at most a year." Power resided with the townspeople, who exercised this authority through monthly town meetings. Rather than there being officially prescribed roles, "When specific jobs had to be done," the nature of these jobs being impossible to predict too far into the future, "the townsmen looked around the meetinghouse to see who was there and who would assume the responsibilities." Over these initial years of town creation, the citizens of the town invariably held a variety of posts—field surveyor, tithingman, highway surveyor, fence surveyor—shifting "from one type of job to another quite readily."[37]

The dispersion of authority resulting from this inattention to internal structure could be seen in such important community issues as the legal authority of the towns and the allocation of land. Not until 1636 did the Massachusetts commonwealth finally codify the authority of the town. The first bylaws were recorded in Sudbury only after a year of settlement. Land allocation was made without central direction, even when such direction was intended at the outset. Early land arrangements were often informal, "characterized by inexactness in distribution, inattention to recording, and neglect of the most basic statutory requirements of occupancy and fencing." This "hastily contrived" land system was "one born of convenience and necessity" due to needs for prompt cultivation, uncertain residential patterns, and lack of customs to guide behavior.[38]

This early political organization was not an individualistic one, though, as the community was closely bound together. Religious boundaries served as an important source of demarcation between those included and those excluded from the body politic. That there was a desire to create a tightly knit community is evidenced by early regulations by the General Court that no dwelling could be built more than one-half mile from the meetinghouse. Such actions, even as they failed, "revealed the lingering force of the communal paradigm" as the leaders of the Massachusetts Bay Colony attempted to maintain a cohesive, disciplined community.[39] Efforts were also made to establish barriers to entrance into the political community. In the Dedham Covenant signed by the founders of the community in 1636, the exclusivity of the community was made clear: "That we shall by all means labor to keep off from us all such as are contrary minded, and receive only such unto

us as may be probably of one heart with us. . . ."[40] The goal was
not a pluralistic community, but one founded upon a unity of
purpose and belief.

Though egalitarian features persisted in Puritanism throughout the seventeenth-century, egalitarianism becomes less useful in explaining Puritan social organization after the mid-
1630s. Although the group remained tightly bound together,
perhaps increasingly so, the internal structure of the group
underwent significant changes. The fluid authority born of an
equality of saints gave way to oligarchical authority and hierarchical patterns of social relations as it became evident to
certain critical members of the elite that all Puritans were not
of one mind about the direction of the community. This concern was not the result of any one event but grew out of a
number of seemingly unrelated occurrences. Throughout the
1630s there had been growing disillusionment among the leaders, for example, with the handling of land settlements.
Alarmed by the social problems in England caused by increasing land rents and forfeitures, the leaders of the Massachusetts Bay desired a just community in which all had access to
land. By 1634 Winthrop expressed concern that the poor were
being forced off their land, notable members of the community were hoarding corn to sell it when it became scarce, and
land speculation was on the rise. Having emigrated in the belief it was English institutions that caused the pettiness they
found all around them, the Puritans viewed with great concern the persistence of this pettiness in their new community.[41]

The most significant harbinger of the dangers posed by what
was seen increasingly as a deviant population was the
Hutchinson affair, an event whose resolution was to have an
impact beyond the Boston settlement.[42] Anne Hutchinson was
to dramatically challenge the Boston leadership in her claim
that the Puritan ministers preached a covenant of works rather
than grace and that religious authority rested ultimately with
private revelation. There was a perceptible shift, particularly
in Boston, in the Puritan understanding of the environment
after the Hutchinson affair. Where before the Puritan elite had
placed some faith in the judgment of communicants, there
emerged a growing sense that even those within the group
could not be trusted. As Andrew Delbanco notes, in "reduc-
ing" Anne Hutchinson "the Puritan community was repudiat-

ing not so much an external threat as an uprising part of itself."[43] This anxiety arose because the people were seen as too easily fooled and too easily misled by corrupt principles. Winthrop noted, for example, how the people sympathized with Anne Hutchinson and her supporters and how quickly they condemned the true Puritans (Pastor John Wilson, in this case, whose continuance as pastor of the First Church of Boston had come under attack by the Hutchinsonians).[44]

A substantial number of Puritan leaders, John Winthrop among them, came to see themselves as involved in a sustained effort to prevent these corrupt social patterns and cultural orientations from exercising a significant influence over the definition of emerging social institutions. Winthrop's *Journal* entries, for example, changed from talk of Indians, fortifications, and the administrative task of setting up new churches, to a preoccupation with corruption within the community.[45] And tellingly, in *A Short Story*, which was Winthrop's explanation to an English audience of the struggle against the Antinomians, the task facing the Puritan community was portrayed as having changed from surviving the external threats of "persecuting Prelates, and the dangers at Sea" and the "wildernes troubles in our first plantings in New-England" to a new "plague." This plague, as the image suggests, threatened the community from within. "Multitudes of men and women, Church-members and others, having tasted" the "unsound and loose opinions" of the Antinomians, wrote Winthrop, "were eager after them, and were streight infected before they were aware, and some being tainted conveyed the infection to others." The result was "disturbances, divisions, contentions they raised amongst us, both in Church and State, and in families, settling division betwixt husband and wife!"[46] Although depravity had always been central to a Puritan understanding of human nature, hope had been entertained that a community of saints could be established based on a voluntary gathering of God's elect. No longer convinced of this possibility that human nature was in some way retrievable, it became increasingly difficult to resist the hierarchical argument for institutional restraints.[47]

An increasing concern with corruption did not end with the exile of Hutchinson and her followers. Instead, this anxiety was reinforced, as Stephen Foster has argued, by increas-

ingly militant Puritans arriving in the late 1630s who were dis-
illusioned by the failure of the Church of England to respond
to their demand for radical ecclesiastical reforms. The concerns of this new group of Puritan exiles with constructing a
purified, exclusive church separate from England reinforced
the changing attitudes of the Massachusetts leaders. Adding
to this increased anxiety was an influx of what was seen as an
"English contagion" of Quaker, Baptist, and Anglican ideas.
The Massachusetts Bay authorities, consequently, sought to
"construct a theological cordon sanitaire around the inhabitants" that "began at times to approach the obsessive." The leadership, furthermore, attempted to "export its anxieties" to its
neighbors by putting pressure on outlying towns to tolerate
less dissent.[18] The institutions, at a most vulnerable point, were
awash in a sea of corruption.

In Winthrop's words alone one can see a change toward a
more hierarchical view. Governor Winthrop had downplayed
early efforts to establish a strict internal order. But in 1636, in
the face of rising dissension, Thomas Dudley attacked Governor Winthrop for his "lenity" in administering the commonwealth. Dudley's view would prevail; Winthrop would from this
point adopt a more hierarchical stance. Whether he was leading or following this tide, Winthrop was clearly in agreement
with the most influential segments of the Puritan community
in making this transition. In time, he became one of the most
articulate spokesmen for the new oligarchy.

We see emerging after this conflict the first significant attempts to centralize the authority of the commonwealth, to
create a visible body of leaders who could control the development of civil institutions. Within this centralized body was a
call for the unity of delegates to the General Court, motivated
by a concern that dissension would weaken their authority.
Delegates were to "express their difference in all modesty," or
to express their difference as a question, or even to postpone
the issue until time might bring all to agreement (or at least
until the issue was no longer relevant). There was to be "more
strictness used in civil government and military discipline."
Importantly, and more instructive of this move toward central-
ization, were the injunctions for secrecy. Out of the Court the
magistrates "should not discuss the business of parties in their

presence, nor deliver their opinions," nor should any dissent in Court be shown to others, either "publickly or privately." Secrecy provided an important insulation of the elite from the rest of the group, allowing the Court to make and enforce laws without having to answer to public concerns. So important was secrecy for maintaining state control that less than a year later the ministers of the commonwealth would agree that no church officials should publicly question a magistrate for a speech made in the Court because "the court may have sufficient reason that may excuse the sin, which yet may not be fit to acquaint the church with, being a secret of state."[49]

The General Court, concerned with the dispersion of power and substantial discretion the towns had acquired, sought to consolidate their authority through the Town Act of March 3, 1636. The Act, argues David Konig, was meant to carefully limit the powers of the towns. Even the powers that were granted to the towns in the Town Act would be overseen by the commonwealth government. "As a way of maintaining control over the towns and of being assured that they would not use their legal powers to gain too much autonomy, the General Court passed the famous Town Act (Order No. 285) only *after* it had created a supervisory level of magistratical government above the towns earlier that same day."[50]

The move toward a more centralized commonwealth authority was met with resistance, most notably by the town deputies who had previously exercised substantial discretion. The town deputies saw as a "great danger to our state" the "want of positive laws" that might allow the magistrates to "proceed according to their discretions." The deputies thus proposed that "some men should be appointed to frame a body of ground of laws" that should be treated as "fundamental laws," laws that would presumably limit the arbitrary control of the magistrates. Six years later, in 1641, after a series of committees had worked on drafting just such a code, the *Body of Liberties*, which spelled out both protections and a range of punishments for different offenses, was finally enacted into law over the opposition of Winthrop.[51]

In developing the *Body of Liberties* still more debate arose about the extent of discretion that should be allowed judges in meting out punishments. In 1644 the ongoing dispute between

the magistrates and deputies was taken to the elders "to reconcile the differences." Of utmost importance was whether
the standing council composed of the magistrates could act in
place of the General Court when the Court was not in session.
After answering in the affirmative, the elders undertook a
delicate balancing act with the remaining questions. With some
revisions the recommendations of the elders were accepted by
the Court but, in the words of Winthrop, for a "few leading
men (who had drawn on the rest) [who] were still fixed upon
their own opinions. So hard a matter it is, to draw men (even
wise and godly) from the love of the fruit of their own
inventions."[52]

Less than one year later, in May 1645, this concern of the
deputies with the arbitrary power of the magistrates was to
directly involve Winthrop. Accused by the town of Hingham
of exceeding his authority in dealing with a mutiny against an
unpopular Court-imposed militia officer, Winthrop (in his eyes)
placed himself on trial. The controversy, as Winthrop saw it,
was that "Two of the magistrates and many of the deputies
were of opinion that the magistrates exercised too much power,
and that the people's liberty was thereby in danger; and other
of the deputies (being about half) and all the rest of the magistrates were of a different judgment, and that authority was
overmuch slighted, which, if not timely remedied, would en-
danger the commonwealth, and bring us to a mere democracy."[53] The different sides may have framed their argument
in the language of the Bible, as suggested by Theodore
Bozeman, but the debate reflected a more generalizable conflict between the egalitarian suspicion of authority and the
hierarchical interest in central control.[54]

Having been "acquitted" of the charges, Winthrop made
clear in his speech before the Court what was at stake if the
discretion he had earlier allowed were permitted to continue.
In this speech Winthrop provided the understanding of magisterial authority that would be revised only with the overthrow
of the Andros regime in 1689. Winthrop announced that the
magistrate's authority is from God and that in all but clear
cases of error magisterial proclamations must be obeyed or, in
his words, "yourselves must bear it." Of fundamental importance for Winthrop was bridging the opposition between lib-

erty and authority. Winthrop declared that moral liberty (as opposed to the license of a beast) depended upon "subjection to authority." Listen to Winthrop's example of the proper model of such submission: "The woman's own choice makes such a man her husband; yet being so chosen, he is her lord, and she is to be subject to him, yet in a way of liberty, not of bondage; and a true wife accounts her subjection her honour and freedom, and would not think her condition safe and free, but in her subjection to her husband's authority." We are, as brides of Christ, to "cheerfully submit" to the "yoke" of authority.[55] Gone is the "communitarian" hope of the *Arbella* sermon; in its place is a pronouncement of the need for the central authority of the magistrates.[56] Without such authority the Christian commonwealth risked collapsing from its own sinfulness.

Depicting Winthrop as a transitional figure between an older, traditional time of deference and a more modern, "entrepreneurial" climate, as does Sacvan Bercovitch, is problematic because Winthrop became increasingly hierarchical even as he presumably became more modern.[57] The "direction" toward free enterprise that Bercovitch sees as "unmistakable" in the utterances of the likes of Winthrop is disputed by the increasing internal prescriptions enacted in the commonwealth. Land was distributed to maintain social distinctions.[58] So, too, a variety of social regulations, from "the order on school and college class lists, the seating in many churches, and the use of honorifics ranging from 'goodman' upwards to 'esquire' all registered an individual's place in the social scale, and both the Massachusetts and Connecticut governments lent a hand by passing sumptuary legislation restricting fine apparel to men of quality."[59] We also see the entrenchment of a political elite in which the high turnover in office gave way to an established pattern of the same people being reelected to the same posts.[60]

In the continuing effort to enforce distinctions in the community, the Massachusetts General Court in 1653 sought to regulate lay preaching, which had been a customary practice, by establishing a strict licensing system. In defending the act the Court revealed its anxiety that "persons of bolder spirits and erroneous Principles may take advantage to vent their errours, to the infection of their hearers and the disturbance of the peace of the country." In the face of heavy resistance the Court repealed the act only to come back in 1658 to a milder restriction with, in the words of Stephen Foster, "a solemn and awful preface."[61]

To help secure the safety of the group from outside infiltration, group boundaries not only remained high but were enforced with a new harshness. After the Hutchinson affair, in which Anne Hutchinson would attract a following that included those outside of Boston through her claims that religious authority rested ultimately with private revelation, restrictions were placed on how long strangers could remain in the town. No household could entertain a stranger for more than a couple of weeks without consulting town authorities, nor could one receive a stranger who had an intent to reside in the town without consent of a member of the General Court or two other magistrates. Anabaptists were identified in colonial law as "infectors of persons" and were whipped.[62] In 1649 and 1650 the Massachusetts leadership was able to convince the Plymouth Colony to suppress "a newly formed Baptist church at Rehoboth, and in the next few years the colony whose deputies had approved universal toleration in 1645 proceeded to put its first comprehensive set of repressive laws on its statute books." In 1658 the Massachusetts General Court passed a law with a penalty of death to punish any non-resident Quakers in Massachusetts. Plymouth, New Haven, and Connecticut would follow with their own anti-Quaker laws.[63] In 1661, after horror was expressed over the execution of four Quakers, the law was repealed and in its place was substituted the Cart and Whip Act. Only marginally more humane but entirely consistent with efforts to purify the commonwealth, the Act provided that Quakers be whipped and carted out of Puritan jurisdiction.

Reconciling Authority Claims: The Practice of Theory
There is the suggestion that the voluntaristic basis of Puritan civil and religious life, whether it be membership in the church or the consensual basis of marriage, was indicative of the egalitarian aspects of Puritan life. Such voluntary arrangements might suggest the fundamental opposition of the Puritans to the hierarchical bonds of feudalism.[64] But it was precisely through these voluntary elements of Puritan society that the

Puritans attempted to join the insular individual to a hierarchical collective. A voluntary joining was necessary since only the individual could properly exercise the will. Once consent was exercised, the individual submitted to the hierarchy of functionally differentiated, unequal parts serving the corporate whole. Where in a Rousseauean social contract a good government was one based on consent, for the Puritan contract the good society was premised on consent to a well-ordered civil and ecclesiastical system.

What appeared to be reconciled rhetorically was less easily resolved in practice. One sees in Puritan society a continual tension between the authority of the insular individual and the hierarchic community.[65] Three examples from Puritan life suggest the dimensions of this tension. The first, the issue of church membership, points to the inseparability and even mutual dependence of the notions of the insular individual and hierarchic community for Puritan self-definition. The second example, the Antinomian controversy, highlights the tension in these conceptions. Anne Hutchinson and her allies posed such a threat to the Puritans because, while playing upon the individual basis of authority implicit in Puritan culture, they were seen as fundamentally undermining the communal basis of a Puritan identity. The third example, the Puritan's ambivalent response to the rise of a merchant class, appears as a confirmation of and then confrontation between overlapping notions of the insular individual. What was at stake, ultimately, was the dissolution of the bonds of community as spirituality gave way to claims of material interest.

i. Church Membership

Although the Puritans were reacting against what they saw as the establishment of an "objective church" in England, a church seen as standing between the individual and God, the Puritans were unwilling to relinquish completely corporate involvement in the most private of events, grace. The Puritans, unlike the Baptists and Quakers, placed great emphasis on the validation of the individual experience of grace by the community of believers embodied in the church. Richard Wait, for example, pleaded for readmission to the church because he believed he could never receive God's mercy without membership. John Cotton had told Wait when he was excommunicated that "If God hath shut up any of the brethren's hearts from you, then know God also shut up his heart from you." This intertwining of God's grace with the fellowship of the church was reiterated by Pastor Wilson at the same occasion. Wilson, though on shaky theological grounds, told Wait he should think as follows: "I see my repentance is not sound, the church doth not accept it; therefore, God hath not accepted it."[66] It was through the church pulpit that one heard the Holy Spirit spoken, it was through the church that one could be aided in discovering the depth of one's own sinful nature, and it was through the church that one was baptized to Christ and shared in the Communion.

A clear expression of this relationship between individual insularity and corporate involvement can be seen in the requirements for church membership that emerged in the 1630s. Public proof of one's saving faith (or, for women, a private demonstration to the minister) became a requisite for church membership. The "authenticity" of individual grace had to be ratified by the community, with the attendant communal religious and civil privileges following from proof of this private experience. Although the community validated the individual's experience, the group's own authenticity rested precisely on it being composed of saints, a status achieved through one's private relationship with God. "The essence of the Congregational idea," was "the autonomous church, limited to visible saints and founded on a covenant of their profession, which meant deliberate exclusion of the townsfolk who submitted to (and paid for) the rule of the righteous."[67] Thus, Thomas Shepard, in stopping a proposed new church at Dorchester in 1636 on the grounds that the founders had not given sufficient proof of conversion, suggested, "'Tis not faith, but a visible faith, that must make a visible church, and be the foundations of visible communion."[68] Neither the insular individual nor the hierarchic community was sufficient in itself; both drew their legitimacy from the other.[69]

Not surprisingly, there were questions raised within the Puritan community by this practice of church admission, a tension founded on this dual basis of legitimacy. Public proof of one's grace was seen by some, notably Solomon Stoddard, as untenable because assurance of one's grace, though possibly available to the individual, was inaccessible to the community. Conversion, wrote Stoddard, "cannot be made evident by experience to the world, because the world cannot certainly know." For that reason Stoddard allowed all church congregants, which was practically the whole Northampton community, to participate, without evidence of saving grace, in the Lord's Supper. It was not that Stoddard opposed hierarchical authority; he did not.[70] Nor did Stoddard downplay human depravity. Fear and hope were a constant element of his sermons: "to have fear without hope, or hope without fear, they are like a ship that goes outside the Channel, and is in danger to be broken to pieces; a mixture of fear and hope makes men diligent."[71] Despite what appeared to be Stoddard's radical departure from Puritan practice, in this regard, he did not place himself outside the Puritan community. Through his acceptance of this dual basis of authority Stoddard continued to speak from within a Puritan discursive space.[72]

ii. The Antinomian Affair

While Stoddard remained a Puritan in his attempt to straddle this tension, Anne Hutchinson and her supporters placed themselves outside Puritanism by rejecting the hierarchical basis of authority in favor of individual insularity. Beginning in the mid-1630s Anne Hutchinson, influenced by the teachings of John Cotton, began holding religious sessions in her home. Hutchinson made two significant claims of interest to us here. First, Hutchinson suggested that only through faith—and not works—was one saved. In the minds of the ministers, Hutchinson's suggestion appeared as an accusation. As Winthrop noted in his recounting of the proceedings of the General Court against Hutchinson and her allies, "Then the Court laid to her charge, the reproach she had cast upon the Ministers, and Ministery in this Country, saying that none of them did preach the Covenant of free Grace, but Master *Cotton*, and that they have not the Seale of the Spirit, and so were not able Ministers of the New Testament."[73] What made Hutchinson's claim so difficult for her accusers to dispute was that the foundation of her argument was consistent with the notion of individual insularity advanced by Puritan theology. John Cotton, who had preached similar ideas, was accepted and, in fact, seen as an authority, by the mainstream ministers.

The difficulty of denying Hutchinson's claim was evidenced in a meeting of the General Court on October 25, 1636. The session took place against the backdrop of increasing attacks by the Hutchinsonians on Pastor Wilson of the church of Boston. John Wheelwright, whom the Hutchinsonians wanted called as a teacher at the church of Boston, and John Cotton were present at the meeting. Regarding the question of whether sanctification (works) was any evidence of justification, both Wheelwright and Cotton readily agreed that it was, but Cotton added that "the essential witness of salvation lay in the immediate testimony of the Spirit." The ministers of the Court, eager to claim Cotton "for their own . . . slurred over the qualifier and professed their agreement on this issue."[74]

What the Hutchinsonians claimed, moreover, was that religious authority rested on private revelation.[75] This claim, perhaps more than any other, led to the downfall of Anne Hutchinson. By appealing to the absolute authority of the self in communion with God, Hutchinson placed herself outside the boundaries of the Puritan discursive space. She had unequivocally resolved the basis of one's identity by locating authority in the self, a contention she lost in Massachusetts but won in history. Although the ministers could go along with Hutchinson's critique of a covenant of works, they could not countenance the abolition of communal authority. Claims to private revelation certainly contradicted the Puritan doctrine that the age of revelation ended with the writing of the Bible. But the social issue of authority and order became much more prominent in the trial of the Hutchinsonians. What was at stake was whether the private experience of Scripture would be privileged against the contention that Biblical interpretation was a communal concern. Of John Wheelwright the Court declared that "All things are turned upside down among us." As for Anne Hutchinson, the Court accused her of "the utter subversion both of Churches and civill state. . . ." Winthrop wrote "that her opinions and practise have been the cause of al our disturbances, & that she walked by such a rule as cannot stand with the peace of any State; for such bottomlesse revelations, as either came without any word or without the sense of the word, (which was framed to humane capacity) if they be allowed in one thing, must be admitted a rule in all things. . . ."[76]

The insularity of the self, which in the instance of church membership served to legitimate the Puritan community, now threatened to undermine its authority. And it did so, thought Winthrop, because actions undertaken by the authority of the insular self often intruded into the public realm. Stated Winthrop in response to Anne Hutchinson's claims to be obeying her conscience, "Your conscience you must keep or it must be kept for you."[77] The problem with this dual basis of authority, as Winthrop recognized, was that the respective realms invariably overlapped.

To help keep the Hutchinsonians' consciences, Winthrop moved in 1636 to purge the General Court of Hutchinson supporters and was able to win election for governor over Henry Vane, a Hutchinson sympathizer, at least in part by moving the election out of Boston. In 1637, contrary to the charter, Winthrop dissolved the General Court and held a special election intended to strengthen his support on the Court. The move worked. The first act of the new Court was to unseat and disenfranchise two Hutchinson deputies from Boston, William Aspinwall and John Coggeshall. Despite similar efforts, the Court was unable to force out another Hutchinson deputy, William Coddington. With new-found resolve, the Court moved against other Hutchinson supporters, requiring any strangers to obtain Court permission if they were in the colony for more than two weeks (to prevent the Antinomians from adding to their numbers) and ultimately disenfranchising and banishing the leaders of the movement.

To further deprive communal infection of its requisite nourishment, the assembly of churches meeting in 1637 in Cambridge agreed that large assemblies should be prohibited and questions in church condemned. Lack of church attendance would serve as the basis for church censure and, importantly, would be an indication to the local leaders to help or compel a person to be present.[78] As the Hutchinsonians made clear the danger of the insular individual, the community sought to assert its authority.

iii. Suffering the Worldly Spirit

A central issue that scholarship on the Puritans has sought to address is the ambivalence of the Puritan ministerial and political elite toward the rise of an entrepreneurial merchant class. We see on the one hand a continual interest on the part of Massachusetts Bay to promote economic prosperity. To that end, the General Court advertised for local shareholders to attract English capital and provided various economic incentives, including licenses, subsidies, and tax relief to local enterprises.[79] Encouragement came from religious quarters, as well, as ministers often spoke of a pious life in economic terms. Thomas Shepard sounded a common theme when he pointed out the wonder of "a commonwealth erected in a wilderness, and in so few years brought to that state that scarce the like can be seen in any of our English colonies in the richest places of this America after many more years standing."[80] Edward Johnson wrote about the spiritual rewards for hard work:

> For great is he thee to this work assign'd,
>   Whose pleasure is, heavens Crown shall be thy pay.

And in even more glamorous terms he observed that "the people are laborious in the gaining of the goods of this life, yet they are not unmindful also of the chief end of their coming hither, namely, to be made partakers of the blessed Ordinances of Christ, that their souls might be refreshed with the continual income of his rich grace. . . ."[81] God was almost like an investment, a metaphor of which Cotton Mather made use in *Bonifacius*, in which the investor would be made wealthy.

Yet the wealth to which Shepard, Johnson and Mather pointed was spiritual vitality, not material well-being, although both tended to accompany hard work. This brings us, then, to the other aspect of the Puritan ambivalence toward entrepreneurial activities, namely, an anxiety about the loss of spiritual vigor. This anxiety found expression in not only sermons of the day but laws, such as restrictions on labor movement, that sought to maintain the purity of the commonwealth at the expense of entrepreneurial interests. These anxieties arose as the Puritans, in following their callings, were to pursue worldly business with diligence and partake in the wonders of the universe, yet were beckoned to be "*Strangers* in the World!"[82] Richard Mather remarked early on about the difficulties of balancing involvement in the world with this detachment. Although all must conduct themselves in worldly business "for the maintenance of your selves & your families. . . experience shews that it is an easy thing in the middest of worldly business to lose the life and power of Religion, that nothing thereof should be left but only the external form, as it were the carcass or shell, worldliness having eaten out the kernell, and having consumed the very soul & life of godliness."[83]

In explaining this ambivalence, we must account as much for what was attractive as for what was unattractive to the Puritan elite about entrepreneurial activity. My suggestion here is that what allowed the Puritans to appeal to this nascent class was an intersection in their views of authority. The legitimacy of entrepreneurial capitalism rested on the insular individual, an individual left to succeed or fail by his or her own initiative, discipline, and work. So too, the insular individual, particularly in regard to the pursuit of one's calling, served as an important basis of authority in the Puritan community. These were more than passing similarities as many early entrepreneurs came out of and shared a Puritan orientation and many of the Puritan leaders, including Simon Bradstreet, Richard Saltonstall, Jr., and John Winthrop, Jr., were sympathetic to promoting such economic activity.[84] The point of conflict was not so much over economic activity, then, but over perceived threats to a corporate identity as merchants pushed to expand the sphere of the insular individual.

We see this conflict emerge early on as Robert Child, an entrepreneur and Presbyterian, linked the future prosperity of New England to "liberty of conscience." Without such liberty, he expected "nothing to thrive."[85] Such concerns would take the form in 1646 of a Remonstrance to the General Court, in which Child and six other petitioners claimed that there was "too much unwarranted power and dominion on the one side, and perpetual slavery and bondage on the other." The petition called for expanded protections to individuals to secure a "sure and comfortable enjoyment of our lives, libertyes, and estates." Such proposed reforms would allow for "civill liberty and freedom . . . to all truely English" (which would include such disenfranchised Englishmen as Child), eliminate the impressment of servants in service to the war with the Narragansett Indians, and remove the imposition of "undoe oaths."[86] To such challenges, the General Court responded that the Remonstrants were seeking to "lift ye up yourselves above the congregation of the Lord."[87] When Child pressed the case still further, seeking to appeal the response of the General Court to Parliament, he was arrested for sedition, fined, and placed under house arrest.[88] Issues of "conscience," as we saw in the Hutchinson affair, were not negotiable.

The Puritan leadership, though, would later make some concessions, including an extension of the political franchise to non-church members. Rhetorically, as well, accommodations would be made to economic interests as ministers slid toward a more overt association of piety and material wealth. The community, it was suggested, could expect prosperity if it cleaved to God. "Mark here, *that as Godliness has the Promise of the life that now is*, so the most High God, takes great pleasure in the Prosperity of his *Israel* . . . and he delights to prove them with long Life, Health and Strength, Peace & Safety, Plenty and Power, in this World. . . ."[89] As John Whiting reminded his audience, "*The Lord was with* Joseph, *and made all that he did to prosper*. To have God with us, is the way to have all go well; His favourable presence, brings outward prosperity, in what measures he sees meet."[90] That prosperity was God's reward for righteousness could be seen in not only the Bible but New England's own history. In an image that would become a staple of later political rhetoric, John Danforth spoke of how the Puritan forefathers had come to an unknown wilderness, a "Land not Sown," and, armed only with the knowledge of the Lord, "turned a Desert into a Land of Fourscore and Seven Towns, in about Fourscore Years," changed "a barren Land into Fruitfulness," and "gave the Harvest of the Sea, and the sweet Cane, and the Wine and the Oyl, the Silver and Gold of other Countrys, to assist and encourage them in his [Christ's] service."[91] There were not only community but individual benefits, as well, as Christianity "hath a natural tendency to promote civil Peace and Order; to make a People prosperous in their trade & business."[92] Christian honesty in the case of William Phips caused him to receive less from his salvage of a Spanish wreck; yet, "As an acknowledgment of which *Honesty* in him, the Duke of *Albermarle* made unto his Wife, whom he never saw, a present of a *Golden Cup,* near a Thousand Pound in value."[93] Honesty was indeed the best policy, particularly when golden chalices were the reward.

A clear indication of such a move toward a more overt connection of religion and wealth can be seen in Cotton Mather's *Magnalia Christi Americana.* Mather cited a letter by John Winthrop to his son, John Winthrop, Jr., in which the father explained that with the inheritance gone, as well as the rest of the family, "you only are left to see the Vanity of these *Temporal things,* and learn *Wisdom* whereby, which may be of more use to you, through the Lord's Blessing, than all that *Inheritance* which might have befallen you: And for which this may stay and quiet your Heart, *That God is able to give you more than this:* and that it being spent in the furtherance of *his Work,* which hath here prospered so well, through his Power hitherto, you and yours may *certainly expect a liberal Portion in the Prosperity and Blessing there of hereafter. . . .*" Winthrop's emphasis was primarily on the godly rewards, the richness of the heart that came from devoting one's life to God. Yet, at the conclusion of the letter Mather chose to point to the material rewards alluded to by Winthrop. Mather concluded that "the good Providence of God Recovered this Worthy Gentleman and his Family, so the *Monitory Part* of it was most Exemplarily attended in his Holy and Useful Conversation."[94] Whereas previously it had been unquestioned that wealth was meaningless unless accompanied by grace (that is, grace justified wealth), prosperity now was a reward for, perhaps even an inducement to, piety. Outward well-being, the growth of the population, the acquisition of territory, the accumulation of wealth, and the display of strength all appeared as rewards of God's glory.

We can speculate as to the reasons the ministers would take this tact. The Puritans, for one thing, were acutely aware of their audience: people abroad who thought the Puritan mission doomed to failure and those at home who, from the beginning, were interested in making money and less interested in church. Boston had early on taken its place in the world as a thriving trading center, which in turn propelled the rest of the economy. Boston had become, as one historian termed it, an "economic beacon" to the rest of the world. With the continued prosperity of Boston in the 1630s and 40s, "those attracted to Boston had in mind the material opportunities awaiting them, not thoughts of heaven and hell."[95] By playing upon the ambiguity of the religious message, the Puritans might hope to speak to both their international and domestic audiences.

To those overseas they could point to Puritan economic and political success as a sign that they were on the right path, that they were God's chosen people. To those at home interested in profit, the church could appeal by speaking in a language they could understand.

What is of interest to us here, though, is how the Puritan language of insularity, which could accommodate itself to an emerging entrepreneurial ethos, would conflict so fundamentally with a Puritan language of community. The same ministers who would speak of the material rewards of piety would decry, as Richard Mather had predicted, the undermining of the communal basis of Puritan identity.[96] In spelling out this threat, ministers would look back to, and provide an interpretation of, the founding of the commonwealth. Reverend John Higginson of Salem, for example, reminded his congregation, "My fathers and brethren, this is never to be forgotten, that New-England is originally a plantation of religion, not a plantation of trade. Let merchants and such as are increasing cent per cent remember this. Let others that have come over since at several times understand this, that worldly gain was not the end and design of the people of New England, but religion."[97] John Danforth, who spoke of the material rewards to the Puritan community, noted how earlier generations prospered because they "followed the Lord in a Wilderness, a Land not Sown," whereas the new spirit that had emerged from this prosperous climate promoted the "Self" as an "Idol, and the Oracle that men will hear *nothing* against." We hear in this language a concern that claims of insularity had become so prominent that they threatened to undermine the hierarchical basis of authority. In a telling statement, Danforth noted how there were now even "bitter Contentions about Seating" in the churches.[98]

Samuel Wigglesworth looked with horror at how prosperity was undermining the religious basis of the commonwealth:

> I shall only now add, That the *Powerful Love of the World, and Exorbitant Reach after Riches*, which is become the reigning Temper in Persons of all Ranks in Our Land, is alone enough to awaken our concerns for abandon'd, slighted and forgotten Religion. 'Tis this that takes up our Time, seizes our Affections, and governs our Views: Straitens our Hands; respecting Works of Charity, and pusheth us into the most wicked Schemes and Methods. 1*Tim* 6.9,10. This *Worldly Spirit*

has in a great measure thrust out Religion, and given it a *Wound* which will prove *Deadly* unless infinite Mercy prevent.[99]

And for Cotton Mather, though prosperity glorified God, the "private spirit" that had emerged threatened to destroy the "Whole People" as they are knit together in a sacred bond. The sense of Christian community, of watching over one's brother, was endangered by the private spirit. "They would not care tho' the *Houses* of their Neighbours were Burnt, if their own *Apples* might be Roasted at the Flame." Just as the body was threatened by the corruption of its parts, so New England faced perils because of this private spirit. "It is *this* [Private Spirit] that has a more Dismal Aspect upon our *own* Land, than all the other things that Bode ill unto us. We read in 2 *Tim.* 3.1,2. *In the last Days Perillous Times shall come; for men shall be lovers of their own selves.*"[100]

This transformation, even perversion, of the calling raised an outcry as the Puritan leaders struggled to reclaim a communal basis of individual identity. What before had been warnings about the dangers of pride erupted into jeremiads on self-ishness. The new economic age shook to its very foundations the communal basis of a Puritan identity and left the Puritan ministers scrambling to answer a nagging question: "Have we become them?"

The Individual and Creation

Far less controversial in Puritan scholarship, but no less important for understanding the unresolved nature of Puritan self-definition, was their view of the nature of creation. Fundamental to this view is one's understanding of human nature since this is the most immediate and salient experience of creation. There are a number of ways for individuals to respond to this issue, from the Augustinean loathing of the body and the ascetic withdrawal from earthly life to a utopian socialist vision of the perfectibility of humankind.

Traditionally, Christianity has responded to this question by establishing the duality of sin and grace, a duality that the Puritans embraced with vigor. They both loathed and loved, were engulfed in sin and yet exulted in God's creation. Even as there was revulsion toward the world around them, the Puritans were not inclined to mysticism or a retreat from earthly slime.[101] There was a great difference in knowledge, observed Hooker, between the traveler who "hath taken a view of many coasts, passed through many countries . . . hath been an eyewitness of the extreme cold and scorching heats, hath surveyed the glory and beauty of the one, the barrenness and meanness of the other," and the person who "sits by his fireside and happily reads the story of these in a book, or views the proportion of these in a map."[102] Winthrop noted in his diary how the Christian must confront existence. He who

> would have sure peace and joy in Christianity, must not aim at a condition returned from the world and free from temptations, but to know that the life which is most exercised with trials and temptations is the sweetest, and will prove the safest. For such trial as fall within compass of our callings, it is better to arm and withstand then to avoid and shun them.[103]

The world, though—and this is the heart of the ambiguity in the Puritan's relationship to creation—was not simply something to be endured, a ritual punishment for one's own evil, but was to be enjoyed. To retreat from the world would be to turn away from the joy and the harmony of God's work. The Puritans, consequently, delved into earthly life. From fulfilling one's calling to exploring the wonders of the universe through a telescope and microscope to writing on the cross-fertilization of corn and the developing science of inoculation, the Puritans were attracted to the beauty of a world. Thomas Brattle, for example, recorded the elliptical path of a 1680 comet (which helped Newton prove that gravity determined the path of comets). Increase Mather wrote of his studies of comets in his 1683 books, *Kometographia*, and Cotton Mather, a member of the Royal Society, published a paper on cross-fertilization of corn and was quite knowledgeable of the new science of inoculation. Paul Dudley wrote on the habits of whales, earthquakes, the making of maple syrup, cross-fertilization of corn, and other topics.[104]

The Puritans could stare out at the natural world to demonstrate the beauty of God's creation, but when they peered into their own nature there was no such certainty about their place in God's plan. It was with despair that the Puritans realized that they were separated from God; yet, it was out of this deep sense of affliction that the individual was made ready for the gift of grace. By humbling the self one cleansed the soul, removing those elements (pride, love of the world, covetousness, etc.) that impeded the working of grace. After many had died in New England, including the Lady Arbella (for whom the flagship had been named), John Winthrop wrote to his wife, Margaret,

> Thus the Lord is pleased still to humble us; yet he mixes so many mercies with his corrections, as we are perswaded he will not cast us off, but, in his due tyme, will doe us good, according to the measure of our afflictions. He stayes but till he has purged our corruptions, & healed the hardness & error of our hearts, & stripped us of our vaine confidence in his arme of flesh, that he may have us relye wholly upon himselfe.[105]

After Margaret fell ill, John wrote to his son, John, "Thus the Lord is pleased to kepe us under" so that "he may weane us from this world, and drawe our hearts more after Christ Jesus, and those riches, which will endure to eternity."[106] In his critique of other views of the psychological experience of being a Puritan, Cohen writes, "The portrait of the evangelical style, wonderfully evocative of personalities writhing in the throes of constricted self-abnegation, omits the joy that sometimes broke through their ordeal and misses the sense of power that humiliation brought."[107] From the humiliation of sin would come the joy of God's presence.

Not only was exultation experienced during times of intense humility, but only in the light of grace would one's true degradation be realized. For the sinner was blind to sin and refused to raise himself or herself up from earthly depravity. Grace, however, by engulfing the individual in God's presence, allowed that person to catch a glimpse of absolute perfection, of absolute harmony and justice, of absolute goodness and happiness. Through this experience one came to see just how depraved his or her existence actually was.

Such anxiety translated into communal concerns, as well, as vividly portrayed in the jeremiads, the practice of rhetorical self-flagellation in which the Puritans catalogued the backslid-

ing of their community.[108] Unlike the original Jeremiah, who
was charged with blasphemy, beaten, and stoned by the people
of Judah, the jeremiad in New England thrived because it made
sense to a people torn between sin and glory. That the Puritans had entered into covenant with God meant that there would
be covenant-mercies as well as covenant-afflictions. That New
England was the New Israel suggested that the Puritans could
follow the path to glory of the spiritual Israel or the way to
degeneracy of the secular Israel. That they were a chosen
people meant that their failures would bring about both more
shame and harsher punishment by the sword of God's ven-
geance. "Would we sink, or would we swim in this Sea of trouble
that is a coming?" asked Increase Mather. "If we break, we shall
sink; if we divide, we perish, and are like to be an undone
people: But if we be *whole*, if we unite, we shall *swim*, our heads
will then be above water, let what troubles can come. . . ."[109] As
one body New England could survive to bask in God's glory;
as individuals, as a body torn apart, New England was doomed.

The contradictory impulses of hope and despair and the
corresponding irresoluteness of the Puritan sense of identity
can be seen clearly, almost painfully, in the recounting of the
most important moment in the life of the Puritan: the conversion narrative. What one discovers in these narratives is neither a linear pilgrimage from sin to grace nor a gradual less-
ening of despair but a continual anxiety about one's own
relationship to creation. "Considered in the abstract," notes
one historian in his discussion of the Puritan conversion experience, "conversion could be charted precisely, its steps checked
off in logical order, but shifting perspective to the flesh made
an exact reckoning impossible." Joy was "drowned" by sadness
as the "spirit move[d] human beings by fits and starts."[110] And
this anxiety was exhibited across the social spectrum. A maid
of John and Elizabeth Russell, for example, revealed how after
hearing a sermon by John Rogers that "the just shall live by
faith," she had an "abundance of comfort from the word and I
blessed the Lord for that condition. But afterward I questioned
whether it was possible the Lord should have mercy upon me,
and so I heard a poor creature may question his condition.
And so I doubted whether I was humbled or no." Thinking
she was "humbled enough," Katherine felt she had fallen "into

a temptation of blasphemous thoughts of slighting the Lord and hence prayed that He would put His fear into my heart."[111]

Deadness of the heart was always to be feared. The shipmaster William Andrews "sought to God to give peace and searched after promises that He would take away stony heart." But the comfort which Andrews sought, and apparently received, was as much a cause of concern as his deadness to God. Andrew's greatest joy came not when he gained material comfort but when, in a storm, he lost his ship "and so lost my sin," the temptation of success.[112] The anxiety of the Puritan life is conveyed poignantly by Nathaniel Sparrowhawk, a prominent member of the Cambridge church. Desiring one fast day to "bewail my condition . . . the Lord revealed Himself so as never before with abundance of the sweetness of Himself, which rejoicing made me to break out to weeping and hardly could I refrain from speaking to others and let them see what Lord had done." Sparrowhawk found his "heart locked up most when he thought to find Lord nearest." There is never resolution in Mr. Sparrowhawk's narrative. "But the assurance of Lord's love I have not found."[113] Patricia Caldwell, in her discussion of the conversion narrative, writes that Mr. Sparrowhawk "describes what seems to have been a genuine religious experience while he was still in Old England. . . . Yet he undercuts it at once and nothing in the subsequent narrative returns to this pitch of spiritual joy. Instead, the rest of Mr. Sparhawk's relation unravels in a string of rather sad, confused emotions connected with the move to New England. . . ." This pattern of "limp and irresolute endings" was repeated by other New England narratives and, notably, was "a far cry from the reassuring conclusions of the English conversion stories."[114]

We can get some sense of the irresoluteness of the Puritan conversion experience by comparing it to that in the Quaker conversion narratives. The pattern in these Quaker writings is not one of irresolution but of a progression from ignorance and sin to knowledge and grace. Journal after journal of the Quakers' starts with the individual in a state of sin, leading a life of corruption. And each journal moves to a realization of and discontent with this condition, a search for the means to move beyond this condition, and ultimately resolution. In this moment of resolution there is none of the anxiety portrayed by the Puritan narrative. George Fox recalled how in his conversion "I was come up in spirit through the flaming sword, into the paradise of God." Life was completely altered. "All things were new; and all the creation gave unto me another smell than before, beyond what words can utter." With conversion came a decisive change in one's understanding of and relationship to creation: "I knew nothing but pureness, and innocency, and righteousness; being renewed into the image of God by Christ Jesus, to the state of Adam, which he was in before he fell. The creation was opened to me; and it was showed me how all things had their names given them according to their nature and virtue."[115] John Woolman, in a fairly typical Quaker journal entry, wrote, "As I lived under the Cross and simply followed the openings of Truth, my mind from day to day was more enlightened. . . ."[116]

This difference of resolution becomes quite clear when we compare the journal entries of a Puritan, Samuel Sewall, with John Woolman at a similar time in their life: their entrance into the church. Sewall writes that "since I had thoughts of joining to the Church, I have been exceedingly tormented in my mind" for, among other reasons, his feelings of his "own unfitness and want of Grace." Despite such misgivings, Sewall offered himself to the church and (it is interesting to note his depiction of acceptance in the negative) "was not refused." Where we would expect some joy we get more despair: "now that Scruple of the Church vanished" Sewall "began to be more afraid" of himself. So Sewall looked to the community for validation of his experience, but found more cause for anxiety. Sewall noted how he ran into Goodman Walker, one of the founders of the South Church of which Sewall had just become a member, "who used to be very familiar with me. But he said nothing of my coming into the Church, nor wished Good to show me grace therein, at which I was almost overwhelmed, as thinking that he deemed me unfit for it." Sewall's depiction of the irresolution of his experience of grace is almost painful to read:

> And I could hardly sit down to the Lord's Table. But I feared that if I went away I might be less fit next time, and thought that it would be strange for me who was just then joined to the Church, to withdraw, wherefore I stayed. But I never experienced more unbelief. I feared at

least that I did not believe there was such an one as Jesus Xt., and yet was afraid that because I came to the ordinance without belief, that for the abuse of Xt. I should be stricken dead; yet I had some earnest desires that Xt. would, before the ordinance were done, though it were when he was just going away, given me some glimpse of himself; but I perceived none.[117]

Compare this torment at a presumably happy moment in Sewall's life with the satisfying resolution of Woolman's experience. After saying "some words in a meeting" Woolman became "sensible of my error, I was afflicted in mind some weeks without any light or comfort, even to the degree that I could take satisfaction in nothing." But that despair did not remain: "I then felt forgiveness for my offense, and my mind became calm and quiet, being truly thankful to my gracious Redeemer for his mercies. And after this, feeling the spring of divine love opened and a concern to speak, I said a few words in a meeting, in which I found peace." Where Sewall's doubts only increased, Woolman's "understanding became more strengthened to distinguish the language of the pure Spirit which inwardly moves upon the heart. . . ." And where Sewall looked to the community for validation of his experience, Woolman "found it safest for me to live in private and keep these things sealed up in my own breast."[118]

Woolman hints at a critical difference between Puritan and Quaker conversion. Though for the Puritans there was never assurance of grace, for the Quakers such certainty was experienced. Fox provided the model for such assurance: "Thus when God doth work, who shall hinder it? and *this I knew experimentally*."[119] Francis Howgill gave a fairly typical statement of this certitude. Displaying none of the Puritan equivocation, he wrote, "For I have obtained mercy through his free grace, from Christ, who is risen from the dead, and saw no corruption; and by which grace I am saved from sin, and cleansed from unrighteousness, after long and sore labor and travail. . . ."[120] Such certainty by a prospective church member would have been treated with suspicion by a Puritan church membership, and would have likely been grounds for refusing admission.

For the Puritan, one's travels were fraught with travail, a travail that had no earthly end. In struggling with their own self-definition—through decisions of civic and religious organization, in their responses to external and internal threats to the community, and in their own self-narratives—the Puritans created a discursive space that maintained, unresolved, conflicting understandings of creation and of self and society. It was a space, as we will see, that would continue to be redefined as later groups would claim this Puritan space as their own.

Notes

1 Michael Zuckerman, *Peaceable Kingdoms: New England Towns in the Eighteenth Century* (Westport: Greenwood Press, 1970), 6.

2 See Clifford Geertz, "Ethos, World View, and the Analysis of Sacred Symbols," *The Interpretation of Cultures* (New York: Basic, 1973), 126-41.

3 Janice Knight, *Orthodoxies in Massachusetts: Rereading American Puritanism* (Cambridge: Harvard University Press, 1994), 5. See also Bruce Daniels, *Puritans at Play: Leisure and Recreation in Colonial New England* (New York: St. Martin's Press, 1995), who suggests that "Puritan society was profoundly ambivalent—partly because of divisions between individuals but even more because of unresolved conflicts *within* them" (16). These tensions were created by contradictions between "conformity to doctrine" and "liberty of conscience," between working for "material prosperity" and wanting to "avoid worldly temptations," and by prizing "social communalism" but asserting "economic individualism" (16).

4 Knight, *Orthodoxies*, 74.

5 Increase Mather, *David Serving His Generation. . .* (Boston: B. Green & J. Allen, 1698), 21, reprinted in *Increase Mather: Jeremiads*, ed. Sacvan Bercovitch (New York: AMS Press, Inc., n.d.).

6 John Cotton, *The Way of Life* (London: L. Fawne and S. Gellibrand, 1642), 104-5.

7 John Danforth, *The Vile Prophanations of Prosperity by the Degenerate Among the People of God* (Boston, 1704), 7, reprinted in *The Puritan Sermon in America, 1630-1750*, 4 vols., ed. Ronald A. Bosco (Delmar: Scholars' Facsimiles and Reprints, 1978), vol. 1. See also, Increase Mather, "Awakening Truths Tending to Conversion" (Boston, 1710), in *The Puritans*, eds. Perry Miller and Thomas H. Johnson (New York: Harper & Row, 1963), 337.

8 "The Application of Redemption By the Effectual Work of the Word, and Spirit of Christ, for the bringing home of Lost Sinners to God. The Ninth and Tenth Books," 2nd ed. (London, 1659), in *Puritans*, eds. Miller and Johnson, 298-300.

9 Charles E. Hambrick-Stowe, *The Practice of Piety: Puritan Devotional Disciplines in Seventeenth-Century New England* (Chapel Hill: University of North Carolina Press, 1982), 50, 47.

10   Perry Miller, *The New England Mind: The Seventeenth Century* (1939; reprint ed. Boston: Beacon Press, 1961), 45.

11   George Goodwin, *Auto-Machia*, J[oshua] S[ylvester] (trans.) (London, 1607), no pagination, quoted in Sacvan Bercovitch, *The Puritan Origins of the American Self* (New Haven: Yale University Press, 1975), 19.

12   See Knight, *Orthodoxies*, chapt. 4.

13   Knight, *Orthodoxies*, 103.

14   For a discussion of how a view of human nature as sinful serves to reinforce hierarchical social relations, see Michael Thompson, Richard Ellis, and Aaron Wildavsky, *Cultural Theory* (San Francisco: Westview Press, 1990), 34-5.

15   Some defense needs to be made for classifying the English Puritans as egalitarian. This can be done by using a typology of cultural organization proposed by the anthropologist Mary Douglas. Douglas suggests that there are a finite number of ways individuals organize themselves. These ways can be depicted using two dimensions of sociality: grid and group. Group is defined as the extent to which the individual's life is "absorbed in and sustained by group membership." Organizations with a high group dimension ascribe considerable importance to membership and involvement in the organization. Entrance into the group is often difficult, and clear boundaries are drawn between members and nonmembers. Grid refers to the "degree to which an individual's life is circumscribed by externally imposed prescriptions." Significant role differentiation and regulation would be indicative of groups with a high grid. An egalitarian association would have high group boundaries and low grid regulations. Other forms of social organization include fatalism (high grid, low group), collectivism/hierarchy (high grid, high group), individualism (low grid, low group), and autonomy. See Douglas, *Cultural Bias*, occasional paper No. 34 (Royal Anthropological Institute of Great Britain and Ireland, 1978) and Thompson, Ellis, and Wildavsky, *Cultural Theory*, 5.

16   Michael Walzer, *The Revolution of the Saints: A Study in the Origins of Radical Politics* (Cambridge: Harvard University Press, 1965), 318, 221.

17   Walzer, *Revolution of the Saints*, 318, 56-7, 170, 312.

18   Thompson, et al., *Cultural Theory*, 6; Walzer, *Revolution of the Saints*, 55.

19   We are talking about neither clean breaks nor pure social systems here. Rather, my suggestion is that we can identify a change in Puritan social organization from one organized more along egalitarian lines to one increasingly hierarchic. Hierarchical cultures, according to Aaron Wildavsky, justify "inequality on grounds that specialization and division of labor enable people to live together with greater har-

mony and effectiveness than do alternative arrangements" ("Choosing Preferences by Constructing Institutions: A Cultural Theory of Preference Formation," *American Political Science Review* 81 [March 1987]: 6). For an excellent discussion of notions of Puritan order, see Stephen Foster, *Their Solitary Way: The Puritan Social Ethic in the First Century of Settlement in New England* (New Haven: Yale University Press, 1971), 11-40.

20 Richard Bushman, *From Puritan to Yankee* (New York: Norton and Company, 1967).

21 Theodore Dwight Bozeman, *To Live Ancient Lives: The Primitivist Dimension in Puritanism* (Chapel Hill: University of North Carolina Press, 1988), 158.

22 Michael Zuckerman, "The Fabrication of Identity in Early America," *Almost Chosen People: Oblique Biographies in the American Grain* (Berkeley: University of California Press, 1993), 45.

23 Adam Seligman, *Innerworldly Individualism: Charismatic Community and Its Institutionalization* (New Brunswick: Transaction, 1996), 1.

24 See Zuckerman, "Fabrication of Identity," and Seligman, *Innerworldly Individualism*, chapt. 3.

25 See Douglas, *Cultural Bias*, and Thompson, Ellis, and Wildavsky, *Cultural Theory*. For an argument that egalitarian societies may depend on rules systems that are "more expansive and complex than those required for hierarchical society," see Steve Rayner, "The rules that keep us equal: complexity and costs of egalitarian organization," *Rules, Decisions, and Inequality in Egalitarian Societies*, eds. James Flanagan and Steve Rayner (Aldershot: Avebury: 1988), 21.

26 See Zuckerman, "Fabrication of Identity," 32.

27 Seligman, *Innerworldly Individualism*, 75.

28 See Philip Selznick, *Leadership in Administration: A Sociological Interpretation* (New York: Harper & Row, 1957). For an application of this approach to the development of Leninist regimes, see Kenneth Jowitt, "Soviet Neotraditionalism: The Political Corruption of a Leninist Regime," *Soviet Studies* 70 (July 1983): 275-97.

29 Zuckerman, *Peaceable Kingdoms*, 10.

30 Darrett Rutman, *Winthrop's Boston: A Portrait of a Puritan Town, 1630-1649* (Chapel Hill: University of North Carolina Press, 1965), 41.

31 See John Winthrop, *The History of New England from 1630 to 1649*, 2 vols., ed. James Savage (New York: Arno Press, 1972), 1: 128-9, 132. See also David Thomas Konig, *Law and Society in Puritan Massachusetts. Essex County, 1629-1692* (Chapel Hill: University of North Caro-

lina Press, 1979), 21. Darrett Rutman traces the rise of the town in *Winthrop's Boston*, 62-4.

32 Sumner Chilton Powell, *Puritan Village: The Formation of a New England Town* (Middletown, Conn.: Wesleyan University Press, 1963), 5.

33 Ibid., 80.

34 T. H. Breen, *The Character of the Good Ruler* (New Haven: Yale University Press, 1970), 37.

35 Winthrop, *History*, 1: 178. See also 1: 85.

36 William Bradford, *Of Plymouth Plantation*, ed. Samuel Eliot Morison (New York: Alfred A. Knopf, 1952), 140.

37 Powell, *Puritan Village*, 98-9. Also see Robert Emmet Wall, Jr., *Massachusetts Bay: The Crucial Decade, 1640-1650* (New Haven: Yale University Press, 1972), 24. For an excellent discussion of Winthrop's accommodation to this changing environment, see James G. Mosely, *John Winthrop's World: History As A Story; The Story as History* (Madison: University of Wisconsin Press, 1992), chapt. 2.

38 David Thomas Konig, "Community Custom and the Common Law: Social Change and the Development of Land Law in Seventeenth-Century Massachusetts," *The American Journal of Legal History*, 18 (1974), 137-8. For an excellent discussion of land distribution policies, see Rutman, *Winthrop's Boston*, 42-3, 46.

39 Konig, *Law and Society*, 30.

40 Kenneth A. Lockridge, *A New England Town: The First Hundred Years, Dedham, Massachusetts, 1636-1736* (New York: W. W. Norton, 1970), 5.

41 Andrew Delbanco, *The Puritan Ordeal* (Cambridge: Harvard University Press, 1989), 77, 80. This situation is not what Winthrop had in mind when he suggested aboard the *Arbella* that there "must be rich some poore." This early statement certainly contains hierarchical elements, but we must be careful to place this statement within Winthrop's more egalitarian notion of charity in which "noe man is made more honourable then another or more wealthy etc., out of any perticuler and singuler respect to himselfe . . ." (Winthrop, "Modell," 195-6).

42 For a documentary history of the Hutchinson affair, see David D. Hall, ed., *The Antinomian Controversy, 1636-1638* (Middletown, Connecticut: Wesleyan University Press, 1968). For a discussion of Anne Hutchinson, see Emery Battis, *Saints and Sectaries: Anne Hutchinson and the Antinomian Controversy in the Massachusetts Bay Colony* (Chapel Hill: University of North Carolina Press, 1962).

43 Delbanco, *Puritan Ordeal*, 138. Marilyn J. Westerkamp has suggested that "In fact, Massachusetts Bay was still working out its salvation when

Hutchinson became popular, and it might be argued that the defeat of Hutchinson marked the beginning of the stable, homogeneous society that has come to be known as New England Puritanism." See Westerkamp, "Anne Hutchinson, Sectarian Mysticism, and the Puritan Order," *Church History* 59 (Dec. 1990): 484-5.

44 Winthrop, *History*, 1: 210.

45 See, for example, *History*, 1: 280; 2: 47, 72.

46 John Winthrop, "A Short Story of the Rise, reign, and ruine of the Antinomians, Familists, & Libertines, that infected the Churches of New-England" (1644), in *The Antinomian Controversy, 1636-1638: A Documentary History*, ed. David D. Hall (Middletown, Conn.: Wesleyan University Press, 1968), 201-2, 209.

47 See Thompson, Ellis, and Wildavsky, *Cultural Theory*, 34. For a discussion of how a similar movement occurred in church organization, see Dean Hammer, "Cultural Theory and Historical Change: The Development of Town and Church in Puritan New England," in *Politics, Policy & Culture*, eds. Dennis J. Coyle and Richard J. Ellis (Boulder: Westview, 1994).

48 Stephen Foster, "English Puritanism and the Progress of New England Institutions, 1630-1660," *Saints and Revolutionaries: Essays on Early American History*, eds. David D. Hall, John M. Murrin, and Thad W. Tate (New York: W. W. Norton, 1984), 32-3.

49 Winthrop, *History*, 1: 178-79, 214.

50 Konig, *Law and Society*, 26.

51 Winthrop, *History*, 1: 160.

52 Ibid., 2: 204, 209.

53 Ibid., 2: 226.

54 See Bozeman, *To Live Ancient Lives*.

55 Winthrop, *History*, 2: 229-30.

56 Delbanco, *Puritan Ordeal*, 74.

57 See, for example, Sacvan Bercovitch, *The American Jeremiad* (Madison: University of Wisconsin Press, 1978), 22.

58 David Hackett Fischer, *Albion's Seed: Four British Folkways in America* (New York: Oxford University Press, 1989), 166-7.

59 Stephen Foster, *Their Solitary Way: The Puritan Social Ethic in the First Century of Settlement in New England* (New Haven: Yale University Press, 1971), 28. See also Fischer, *Albion's Seed*, 177-80; and Daniels, *Puritans at Play*, 76-7.

60   Wall, *Massachusetts Bay*, 24.

61   Foster, *Their Solitary Way*, 35.

62   Cited in footnote in Winthrop, *History*, 2: 174-7.

63   Stephen Foster, "English Puritanism and the Progress of New England Institutions, 1630-1660," in *Saints and Revolutionaries: Essays on Early American History*, eds. David D. Hall, John M. Murrin, and Thad W. Tate (New York: W. W. Norton, 1984), 33-4.

64   For a discussion of the voluntary basis of Puritan society, see Perry Miller, "Errand into the Wilderness," in *Errand into the Wilderness* (Cambridge: Belknap Press, 1956), 147-8; Peter N. Carroll, *Puritanism and the Wilderness* (New York: Columbia University Press, 1969), 132; and Fischer, *Albion's Seed*, 78. For a discussion of the relationship between voluntarism and egalitarianism, see Wildavsky, "Choosing Preferences," 7. For a linking of this voluntary aspect of Puritanism with egalitarianism, see Richard J. Ellis, *American Political Cultures* (New York: Oxford University Press, 1993).

65   Strout sees at least part of this tension as having its origin in the Bay Colony's attempt to link Luther, with his emphasis on the "inner experience of second birth as an individual reality," with Calvin and his stress on the "social destiny of saints bound together in covenant." I think too much can be made of this distinction for two important reasons. First, this tension between individual and community resides in both theologians; the difference Strout points to develops fully only as Luther and Calvin were interpreted by others in subsequent years. Second, their similarities were recognized by Calvin when he insisted that his work was but a commentary on Luther. See Cushing Strout, *The New Heavens and New Earth: Political Religion in America* (New York: Harper Torchbooks, 1975), 18.

66   Quoted in Larzer Ziff, "The Social Bond of Church Covenant," *American Quarterly* 10 (1958): 457.

67   Miller, *The New England Mind: From Colony to Province* (Cambridge: Harvard University Press, 1953), 68.

68   Quoted in Foster, "English Puritanism," 19-20. See also Edmund S. Morgan's seminal work in which he traces the rise of the practice of the test of faith, *Visible Saints: The History of a Puritan Idea* (New York: New York University Press, 1963), 113. Supportive of the argument made earlier in the chapter about the transformation in the form of Puritan organization, Michael Ditmore has recently argued for a revision to Morgan's dating of the institutionalization of confessional narratives. Ditmore suggests that "the requirement was a conservative response to the Antinomian scandal and that it was specifically created at that time as a means of testing for and weeding out potentially radical elements." Ditmore further suggests that the likely creator of

this requirement was not John Cotton but Thomas Shepard. See Ditmore, "Preparation and Confession: Reconsidering Edmund S. Morgan's *Visible Saints*," *New England Quarterly* 67 (June 1994): 317-8.

69   We can find further evidence of this relationship between individual and communal redemption and damnation in the Puritan notion of communal culpability. Community vigilance as well as self-examination were necessary for individual growth and, as importantly, to protect the community from God's wrath. Just as the community was in some sense redeemed through the grace of its members, so the community was seen as culpable for individual sin. For the community not to punish individual disobedience would be to invite the wrath of God. See Edmund Morgan, *The Puritan Family: Religion and Domestic Relations in Seventeenth-Century New England* (New York: Harper & Row, 1966), 101.

70   Stoddard, for example, saw the church not as "a confused body of people; but they that are brought into order, and each must observe his proper station: it is compared to a natural body, wherein there are diverse organs appointed to their peculiar services" (*The Way for a People to Live Long in the Land that God Hath Given Them* [Boston, 1705], qtd. in Fischer, *Albion's Seed*, 190). Consistent with the concern for order, Stoddard wrote of the unfitness of the community to "judge & rule in the Church" and called, instead, for control by the ministers and elders (Perry Miller, *The New England Mind: From Colony to Province* [Cambridge: Belknap Press, 1953], 234, 258-9).

71   Harry S. Stout, *The New England Soul: Preaching and Religious Culture in Colonial New England* (New York: Oxford University Press, 1986), 100.

72   On a related note, Seligman, in *Innerworldly Individualism*, sees the practice of covenant renewals, which began later in the seventeenth-century, as a new dimension in "Puritan culture" (172-3). "With the practice of mass renewals," the affirmation of a "voluntary commitment to prepare for full communion" was transformed from "an individual practice" to "a communal rite" (174). I do not for a moment want to suggest that Puritan practices had not changed, but what is striking is how the legitimacy of both the individual salvatory experience and the church as a community of the faithful continued to be tied to each other.

73   John Winthrop, "A Short Story," in *Antinomian Controversy*, ed. Hall, 269.

74   Battis, *Saints and Sectaries*, 122.

75   See Winthrop, "Short Story," 267, 272-3, and "The Examination of Mrs. Anne Hutchinson at the Court at Newton," in *Antinomian Controversy*, ed. Hall, 336-9.

76   Winthrop, "Short Story," 253, 265, 274.

77   "Examination of Mrs. Anne Hutchinson," 312. See also Winthrop, "Short Story," 266-7.

78   Winthrop, *History*, 1: 239-240 .

79   Margaret E. Newell, "Robert Child and the Entrepreneurial Vision: Economy and Ideology in Early New England," *New England Quarterly* 68 (June 1995), 239-40. The success of Boston in attracting trade in commerce is discussed by Rutman, *Winthrop's Boston*, chapt. 7.

80   Thomas Shepard, "A Defence of the Answer made unto the Nine Questions or Positions sent from New-England against the reply thereto by Mr. John Ball" (London, 1648), in *The American Puritans: Their Prose and Poetry*, ed. Perry Miller (Garden City, New York: Doubleday, 1956), 27.

81   Edward Johnson, *Wonder-working Providence of Sions Saviour, in New England*, in *Collections of the Massachusetts History Society*, second series (Boston: John Eliot, 1814-1826), 3: 2. See Knight, *Orthodoxies*, for a discussion of how "preparationist rhetoric" was compatible with, and could be transformed into, the "way to wealth" of "emergent capitalism" (104).

82   Cotton Mather, *The Present State of New-England . . .* (Boston: Samuel Green, 1690), 44.

83   Quoted in Miller, *New England Mind: Colony to Province*, 4. It is in this regard that Michael Walzer suggests that "The anxiety of the Puritans led to a fearful demand for economic restrictions (and political control) rather than to entrepreneurial activity as Weber has described it" ("Puritanism as a Revolutionary Ideology," *History and Theory*, 3 [1963]: 66-7). For a helpful discussion of the controversy surrounding Weber's thesis on the spirit of capitalism, see David Little, *Religion, Order, and Law: A Study in Pre-Revolutionary England* (New York: Harper and Row, 1969).

84   See Newell, "Robert Child," 227 and Richard S. Dunn, *Puritans and Yankees: The Winthrop Dynasty of New England 1630-1717* (New York: Norton, 1962), chapt. 4.

85   Quoted in Newell, "Robert Child," 244.

86   "A Remonstrance and Petition of Robert Child, and others," from Ohio State University History Department web page.

87   Quoted in Samuel Eliot Morison, *Builders of the Bay Colony* (Boston: Houghton Mifflin, 1958), 257.

88   For a discussion of Child, see Morison, *Builders*, chapt. 8; and Newell, "Robert Child," 251. Newell provides an important addition to our

understanding of the Remonstrance by placing it in the context of contending economic concerns.

89 John Danforth, *Vile Prophanations*, 4.

90 John Whiting, *The Way of Israels Welfare* (Boston: Samuel Green, 1686), 16-7.

91 Danforth, *Vile Prophanations*, 39.

92 Quoted in Miller, *From Colony to Province*, 381.

93 Cotton Mather, "Magnalia Christi Americana," in *Selections*, ed. Kenneth B. Murdock (New York: Hafner, 1960), 170-1.

94 Cotton Mather, "Magnalia," 141-2.

95 Rutman, *Winthrop's Boston*, 190, 195.

96 In highlighting differences between the "preparationist" rhetoric of Thomas Shepard and Peter Bulkeley and the "spiritist" rhetoric of such ministers as John Cotton, Knight understates the ambivalence within the preparationist rhetoric toward the implications of the "language of labor" (*Orthodoxies*, 107).

97 John Higginson, *The Cause of God and His People in New England*, 1663, qtd. in Everett Emerson, *Puritanism in America, 1620-1750* (Boston: Twayne Publishers, 1977), 141.

98 Danforth, *Vile Prophanations*, 35, 39-40.

99 Samuel Wigglesworth, *An Essay for Reviving Religion* (Boston, 1733), 25-6, reprinted in *Puritan Sermons*, ed. Bosco, vol. 3.

100 Cotton Mather, *Present State*, 18, 27, 22-3.

101 Hambrick-Stowe insufficiently emphasizes this ambiguity in Puritanism when he argues that what "basically underlay the movement" was "the devotional impulse to separate from the world" (*Practice of Piety*, 42). The problem, I think, arises from one's perspective. If we approach Puritanism as a devotional movement then the statement is probably correct; but if we see Puritanism as a broader cultural movement (involved in issues of political authority) then there was a persistent ambiguity in its relationship to the world. Hambrick-Stowe seems to be getting at this later when he writes that the Puritans "temporarily separated from the world" but "denied the validity of monastic separation" (46-7).

102 Hooker, *Redemption*, 153-4.

103 Qtd. in John Adair, *Founding Fathers: The Puritans in England and America* (London: J.M. Dent & Sons Ltd, 1982), 135.

104 See Miller, *New England Mind: Colony to Province*, chapt. 26.

105 John Winthrop to Margaret, Sept. 9, 1630, in *Some Old Puritan Love-Letters–John and Margaret Winthrop–1618-1638*, ed. Joseph Hopkins Twichell (New York: Dodd, Mead, and Company, 1894), 169.

106 John Winthrop to John Winthrop, Jr., May 14, 1647, in *Winthrop Papers*, 5 vols. (Boston: The Massachusetts Historical Society, 1947), 5: 161.

107 Charles Cohen, *God's Caress: The Psychology of Puritan Religious Experience* (London: Oxford University Press, 1986), 18. See also Middlekauff, *The Mathers: Three Generations of Puritan Intellectuals, 1596-1728* (London: Oxford University Press, 1971), 312; and Hambrick-Stowe, *Practice of Piety*, 22.

108 The principal architects of our current understanding of the jeremiad are Perry Miller, "Errand," who sees the jeremiad as a tool of adaptation; Robert Middlekauff, *Mathers*, in which he describes the jeremiads of the second generation as expressions of a sense of abject despair and failure; and Bercovitch, *American Jeremiad*, who sees the essence of the jeremiad as one of "unshakable optimism" that provided "prophetic assurance" of progress "impervious to the reversals of history" (6-7, 16-17). Each of these interpretations seems to suggest more resolution to the Puritan sense of their place in creation than is warranted. Whether we look at the jeremiads as a whole, particular passages, or individual sentences, what is revealed is a conflict at the heart of Puritan identity between the sense of damnation and the hope of grace. Knight argues, for example, that "Bercovitch projects consensus onto first-generation Puritan culture when it did not exist, erasing significant differences and converting volatile events into inevitable outcomes" (*Orthodoxies*, 8).

109 Increase Mather, *The Day of Trouble is Near* (Cambridge: Marmaduke Johnson, 1674), 30.

110 Cohen, *God's Caress*, 13.

111 George Selement and Bruce C. Woolley, eds., *Thomas Shepard's Confessions* (Boston: Colonial Society of Massachusetts, 1981), 100.

112 Selement and Woolley, *Confessions*, 112-3.

113 Ibid., *Confessions*, 63, 64.

114 Patricia Caldwell, *The Puritan Conversion Narrative: The Beginnings of American Expression* (Cambridge: Cambridge University Press, 1983), 33-4.

115 George Fox, *The Journal of George Fox*, ed. Rufus Jones (New York: Capricorn Books, 1963), 97.

116 *Journal*, in *Quaker Spirituality: Selected Writings*, ed. Douglas V. Steere (New York: Paulist Press, The Classics of Western Spirituality, 1984), 165.

117 Samuel Sewall, *The Diary of Samuel Sewall*, 2 vols., ed. M. Halsey Thomas (New York: Farrar, Straus and Giroux, 1973), 1: 39-40.

118 Woolman, *Journal*, 167-8, 166.

119 Fox, *Journal*, 82.

120 *The Inheritance of Jacob*, in *Early Quaker Writings, 1650-1700*, eds. Hugh Barbour and Arthur O. Roberts (Grand Rapids, Michigan: William B. Eerdmans, 1973), 169.

Chapter 2

Crafting A Puritan Inheritance

Recent historiography has strongly refuted the thesis that the New England mind was at the core of American culture, with regional differences but a variation on a Puritan theme. There is no denying the strength of other regions and religions.[1] By the eighteenth-century, the Anglicans were thriving in Virginia and had made some inroads into Massachusetts and Connecticut. This was depicted most dramatically in the decision in 1722 by the Rector of Yale College, the Reverend Timothy Cutler, and several Tutors not to accept the Presbyterian ordination and to conform to the Church of England. The president of King's College (Columbia), Samuel Johnson, and his successor, Myles Cooper, provided opportunities for the Anglican view to be heard. And at the College of Philadelphia, Provost Smith and the Reverend Richard Peters were able to move the College toward Anglicanism. According to Ezra Stiles, Episcopalians had grown from an insignificant number in 1690 to 12,600 in 47 churches in 1760.[2] The Catholics had developed a model of toleration in Maryland. The Baptists had emerged from the Great Awakening with strength. The Quakers, under the guidance of William Penn, had been at the center of the development of Pennsylvania. And the Dutch and German Reformed Churches had reached some prominence in New York.

Yet, by the eve of the American Revolution, a Puritan tradition had become a part of a broader national vocabulary. At the core of this tradition was not a particular theology. What we see crafted, instead, was a legacy of a Puritan founding—a myth of origins that gave sustenance to an early American search for identity. The following three chapters will examine how this myth of origins was interpreted by revolutionary leaders, the Federalists, and the Whigs. The focus of this chapter is on how this Puritan past would become a prominent part of an American cultural vocabulary. What we discover is an inheritance that was crafted in accounts beginning with the first generation of Puritan settlers and extending through the historiographies written in the decades preceding the American Revolution. What gave prominence to this legacy was the Puritan's initial dominance and continued importance in those cultural institutions critical in shaping and transmitting this Puritan past.

The Origins of a Puritan Origin

The crafting of a Puritan founding legend would begin early. Already in the middle of the seventeenth-century, the Puritans would glance backward to exalt the founding generation—which was often themselves—for their piety. What seemed to capture the imagination, not only for these early interpretations but for later ones, as well, was the notion of a migration across the sea to an inhospitable wilderness. As a recent historian has noted, "New Englanders were the only colonists in British America self-conscious enough to locate the origins of their society in a 'Great Migration,'" a migration not significant in its size but one that would provide a "symbolic" basis of identity.[3]

Interpretations of a Puritan founding would begin with the first generation. William Bradford's recollections of the settling of Plymouth, perhaps the most notable of such chronicles, told of the toils and dangers that faced the first settlers. The uncertainties, in Bradford's telling, were not simply the hazards of the voyage and the want of material sustenance (though these were prominent enough). There was the greater task of constructing a community, a task made clear in a letter written by Robert Cushman as the ship was docked for repairs in Dartmouth, a letter written before Cushman turned back to London, unable to make the voyage. "How much more in the raising of commonwealths," wrote Cushman, "when the mortar is yet scarce tempered that should bind the walls!" Cushman expressed a concern that was Bradford's, as well, that violence might well break out as the members of the community became "ununited against ourselves." What was needed were "good tutors and regiment," or leaders and order. Cushman continued on this note of concern: "Where is the meek and humble spirit of Moses? and of Nehemiah who re-edified the walls of Jerusalem, and the state of Israel? Is not the sound of Rehoboam's brags daily here amongst us? Have not the philosophers and all wise men observed that, even in settled commonwealths, violent governors bring either themselves or people or both to ruin?"[4]

In this light, Bradford's chronicles served as an historical response to this problem. Bradford presents images of the afflictions and trials that these first settlers faced as they crossed a "vast and furious ocean" to a "desert wilderness," images that would become a staple of American rhetorical consumption. But amidst this struggle, Bradford shows how carefully "the first foundation of their government," the Mayflower Compact, was laid and provides portraits of the different wise men instrumental in the success of this early venture. Five years later, with the plantation now at "peace and health and contented minds," Bradford could finally write to Cushman that they "never felt the sweetness of the country till this year; and not only we but all planters in the land begin to do it."[5] There was for Bradford a moral lesson in this recounting, a tale told to a new generation of how the founding generation, tested by the sea, the wilderness, and divisions within, had constructed a pious commonwealth. It was a moral lesson that would also appear in his *Dialogue, or the Sum of a Conference between Some Young Men Born in New England and Sundry Ancient Men That Came out of Holland and Old England* (1648).[6] Still alive, Bradford made himself into an ancient.[7]

John Winthrop's self-titled *History of New England*, which would have its most measurable influence as it was used later by historians, gave narrative context to this founding era.[8] Though Winthrop did not make himself into an ancient, as did Bradford, he was able to see "himself as a character in the history he was writing," demonstrating in his writing a "self-conscious literary sensibility" that gave shape to the founding experience.[9] Winthrop did not just chronicle the toils of the early colony but gave narrative expression to the founding in the expanding context of New England. We see this contextualization, for example, in the preface to early "articles of confederation" agreed upon in 1643 by Massachusetts, Plymouth, Connecticut, and New Haven to coordinate military defense against hostilities (from a French rivalry in the North and from Indian attacks) and to coordinate commercial relations to compete with the Dutch. Writes Winthrop, "Whereas we all came into these parts of America with one and the same end and aim, namely, to advance the kingdom of our Lord Jesus Christ, and to enjoy the liberties of the gospel in purity with peace: and whereas by our settling, by the wise providence of God, we are further dispersed upon the seacoasts and rivers than was at first intended, so that we cannot, according to our desire, with convenience communicate in one government and jurisdiction: and whereas we live encompassed with people of several nations and strange languages, which hereafter may prove injurious to us or our posterity; and for as much as the natives have formerly committed sundry insolences and outrages upon several plantations of the English, and have of late combined themselves against us," then, Winthrop continues, "we therefore do conceive it our bounden duty, without delay, to enter into a present consociation amongst ourselves for mutual help and strength in all future concernment, that, as in nation and religion, so in other respects, we be and continue one. . . ."[10] History, for Winthrop, was a way of bearing witness to the "ongoing story" of the "continuing reformation of the present into the future": a working out of God's plan in this world.[11]

Edward Johnson's *Wonder-Working Providence*, the first published history of the Massachusetts Bay Colony, would make great use of the image of the Puritan's migration across the ocean. In the opening of his history, Johnson invokes this voyage simultaneously as a description of the ocean crossing for the "planting" of New England and as a metaphor for salvation in which "the Lord will create a new Heaven, and a new Earth in, new Churches, and a new Commonwealth together." Thus are gathered together in this first generation of founders "such Worthies who are hunted after as David was by Saul and his Courtiers" to brave the "tempestuous Seas" and build a community of "living stones as outwardly appear Saints by calling."[12]

Cotton Mather, in his widely read *Magnalia Christi Americana*, introduces his work by noting that he will discuss, first, "the *Actors,* that have, in a more exemplary manner served these *Colonies;* and give *Remarkable Occurrences,* in the exemplary LIVES of many *Magistrates,* and of more *Ministers,* who so *Lived,* as to leave unto Posterity, *Examples* worthy of *Everlasting Remembrance.*" Mather, like Johnson, would start with the voyage, seeing the first generation as "driven to seek a place for the Exercise of the *Protestant Religion,* according to the Light of their Consciences, in the Desarts of *America.*" Mather's task in recounting the lives of the founders was consciously historical: "But whether *New-England* may *Live* any where else or no, it must *Live* in our *History!*"[13] True to his desires, Mather's *Magnalia* would be read for the next century: by Benjamin Franklin, by the English historian Daniel Neal, and even later by such literary figures as Emerson, Harriet Beecher Stowe, and Nathaniel Hawthorne.[14]

As the Puritans found it advantageous to accommodate the new mood of the Enlightenment, a new version of the legend developed, one that synthesized piety and liberty.[15] With the publication of Daniel Neal's *The History of New England* in 1720 and *History of the Puritans* (1732-38), the Puritans of New England were provided with an important synthesis of Puritan tradition and enlightenment ideas, a view "rapidly absorbed into New England historical tradition."[16] In 1736 this legend reached official circles when the Reverend Thomas Prince, in his dedication to his *Chronological History of New England,* which drew upon these early chronicles, referred to Governor Jonathan Belcher, the House of Representatives, and the Council as descended from "the worthy fathers of these Plantations; whom yourselves and posterity cannot but have in everlasting honor, not only for their eminent selfdenial and piety, wherein they set examples for future ages to admire and imitate; but also for their great concern that the same vital and pure christianity and liberty both civil and ecclesiastical, might be continued to their successors; for which they left their own and their fathers houses, in the most pleasant places then on earth, with many of their dearest relatives, and came over the ocean into this then hideous Wilderness."[17] Prince continued this theme with an election sermon on the centennial celebration of the landing of the *Arbella* in which he looked back to "the beginning of this remarkable transaction" as the "afflicted" forefathers fled an oppressive England, "driven out of their churches" for "preserving their consciences pure." The present generation has inherited from these "pious ancestors" a "large land with commodious harbors and fruitful seas," "wise and religious laws, pious and learned magistrates and ministers, sober and virtuous educations," a system of schooling, and "free and pure churches," all of which create a "sober, civil, charitable, quiet, loyal people" who desire the preservation of their "constitution, laws, and liberties."[18]

The Institutional Transmission of a Puritan Inheritance

There was nothing natural or obvious about, and much to recommend against, the emergence of the Puritans as a cultural image. We have already begun accounting for this emergence by showing how early Puritan historiographers themselves created a founding legend that, as we will see, stood alone in early American writing in providing a usable past. What made this Puritan inheritance such a prominent part of an American cultural vocabulary was the dominance by the Puritans in the seventeenth-century of the primary institutions of cultural transmission and the diffusion of this Puritan past beyond its New England context through the Great Awakening and the French and Indian War.

Throughout the seventeenth-century, the Puritans in New England were the primary voice in the educational system and churches, largely determined the content of printed material, and were closely allied with the government. Because of this "unique social structure of interlocking institutions governed by a single nucleus of covenanted saints," congregations had "the coercive powers necessary to impose their brand of piety on society."[19] Central to this structure was a vast ministerial voice. By 1650 there were thirty-seven practicing ministers in Massachusetts, one for every 415 people.[20] Those ministers educated between 1676 and 1710 would "deliver roughly one-half million sermonic messages in the first four decades of the

eighteenth-century to a population totaling less than 150,000."[21]
The New England ministers all but monopolized communication and education in the seventeenth-century: they were de-
ferred to for their learning and godliness, and were found in
almost every town. They were "in effect the radio, television,
newspaper, magazine, schoolteacher, erudite professor, and
Fourth-of-July orator of that time and place."[22] There were "no
competing voices or rituals." The sermon, thus, was "as important for social meaning as for spiritual enlightenment. It
not only interpreted God's plan of redemption and told the
people how they must live as a church but also defined and
legitimated the meaning of their lives as citizen and magistrate, superior and inferior, soldier, parent, child and laborer."[23]
The New England ministers, by their sheer numbers, were able
to add to the "force of cultural inertia," thereby aiding Puritanism in finding its way "into traditional organization and
behavior."[24]

Church attendance was required, even for those who could
not demonstrate the requisite holiness to become members.
Competing churches or sects were not welcome in the community, as evidenced by the harsh measures taken against
Quakers and Baptists. And even dissent within the Puritan
community, as in the cases of Roger Williams and Anne
Hutchinson, was suppressed. The Puritan church, because of
the close ties between the magistrates and the religious community, maintained a monopoly on membership. Even after
other religious groups were "tolerated," if only because such
toleration was required as a condition of the new charter, taxes
were still collected for ministerial salaries, and a variety of
laws remained on the books (well into the eighteenth and even
into the nineteenth-century) prohibiting blasphemy, requiring
observance of the Sabbath, and prescribing official thanksgiving and fast days. It was not until 1727 that Episcopalians in
Massachusetts and Connecticut were relieved from having to
pay for the building of Congregational meetinghouses. In 1728
this same concession was granted to the Quakers and Baptists
in Massachusetts. These concessions were limited: any short-
fall in the salary of the Congregational pastors could be made
up by a second assessment in which other religious groups could
be included.

The control the Puritans held over education and the fierce struggles to maintain this influence were indicative of the importance they ascribed to proper learning, an importance the Federalists would later emphasize. Education was seen as necessary for the "religious welfare" of the children. The New England youth were taught to read so that they could experience the Bible first-hand, they were required to learn a catechism (which provided the children with the principles of their religion), and they were instructed in the capital laws, those laws supported by the Bible. The elementary school texts, which taught the children to read and write, also included Puritan doctrines and morality. The *New-England Primer*, which was used through the eighteenth-century, contained such verses as "In Adam's Fall, We Sinned All," to teach the alphabet.[25] Cotton Mather wrote *Good Lessons for Children*, a reader that was meant to improve the moral goodness of the child, as well.[26] Even the classics and other secular works that were read at Harvard were understood as supporting the lessons of the Bible.[27] Harvard served as an important source for promulgating a Puritan culture as graduates, inculcated with a common cultural identity, became leaders in congregations across New England.[28]

The predominant type of published material was Puritan in content and authorship. A review of a list of publications reveals a significant number of thanksgiving, election day, fast, and execution sermons, eulogies, books by noted Puritans, essays, literature, and poems. The only rival source of printed material was scientific, and even that was considered supportive of Puritan beliefs. What is more noteworthy is what was not published: criticisms of the Puritans, skeptical works, and tracts written by non-Puritans.[29] Puritan control of print diminished significantly by the end of the seventeenth-century, though, and by the beginning of the next century there were numerous published criticisms of the Puritans as well as writings that directly challenged Puritan authority.

The translation of Puritan ideals into institutional mechanisms was dealt a significant blow with the restoration of Connecticut's charter in 1690 and Massachusetts' in 1691. The colonial governor was determined by England, the franchise was extended to all who held property (regardless of church membership), and toleration of other religions was mandated. The new Massachusetts charter was seen as such a betrayal of Puritan ideals that Increase Mather, who had negotiated the charter with the government of William III, was lambasted for his failure upon his return home.

Yet, even with this setback Puritanism remained a significant cultural force. The sheer number of Congregationalists and Presbyterians all but guaranteed the transmission of a Puritan language for at least a couple of generations. The overwhelming majority of New England children continued to be raised in Puritan homes, educated by Puritans or those sympathetic to the Puritans, and indoctrinated at Puritan churches. New England residents existed in an environment dominated by a Puritan cosmology. Many Puritans physically moved beyond the New England boundaries, into Maryland, New York, New Jersey, Georgia, the Carolinas, Virginia, and into the frontier regions of Kentucky and Tennessee, carrying a Puritan outlook with them.[30] The Puritans of the seventeenth-century throughout the colonies left their progeny with legends of the founding generation, books and sermons, poems and stories, written histories, a system of public education, and a language to draw on to understand the world.

The number of Puritan ministers (preaching in churches as well as tutoring students for college) and writers (as well as the overwhelming numbers of Congregationalists, compared to other religious organizations) provided for the promulgation throughout New England of these accounts of the history and glory of the Puritan forefathers. Sermons were preached in rural communities rarely reached by books and papers.[31] By 1760, the Puritan writers, educators and clergy had been so successful in inculcating New England history into the public mind that the "appeal to history" could be made and "people could react to it without taking further thought."[32] Daniel Leonard, in his series of articles under the pseudonym "Massachusettensis," revealed his frustration in confronting just that fact. The alarm of the colonists against British actions was "conjured by the duty they owed themselves, their country, and their God, by the reverence due to the sacred memory of their ancestors, and all their toils and sufferings in this once inhospitable wilderness, and by their affections for unborn millions, to rouse and exert themselves in the common cause. This perpetual incantation kept the people in continual alarm." Leonard was only too aware of the powerful role of the church, and increasingly the press, as sociocultural agents of interpretation. "What effect must it have had upon the audience to hear the same sentiments and principles, which they had before read in a newspaper, delivered on Sundays from the sacred desk, with religious awe, and the most solemn appeals to heaven, from lips which they had been taught, from their cradles, to believe could utter nothing but eternal truths?"[33]

The Great Awakening

Critical to the diffusion of a Puritan legacy was the Great Awakening. Yet, scholarship on the Great Awakening reveals the almost intractable difficulties faced in defining and then tracing a Puritan legacy in American culture. After all, the Great Awakening was not a Puritan movement nor did it originate in New England. The catalyst for the movement, George Whitefield, was not a Puritan, let alone an American Puritan, but an Episcopal clergyman. The leading New England religious figure in the Awakening, Jonathan Edwards, is generally seen as repudiating one of the fundamental tenets of Puritanism, namely the notion of a national covenant.[34] And perhaps even more damaging, the Great Awakening had the long-term effect of both stimulating the emergence of dissident ("Separate") congregations within New England and of further weakening the ministerial hold over the religious "consciences" of the laity.[35] Not surprisingly, scholarship on the Awakening, and on Jonathan Edwards, has been guided by a search for "breaks" in the Puritan legacy: an Edwards who stands alone, breaking from Puritanism in the rejection of a covenant theology but understood by none of his contemporaries; an Edwards who extends a Puritan tradition but who is in turn betrayed by the moralism of the New Divinity;[36] an Edwards who creates a new egalitarian ethic of social harmony in American culture that would find its way into the Jeffersonian and Jacksonian mind;[37] or the Awakening as part of a more fundamental conceptual transformation which broke down "bounded, face-to-face, deferential communities" and "offered a new model of the church and its surrounding social world: a mobile, dynamic, expansive, potentially unbounded community held together by a common spirit among individual members of every locale."[38]

To be sure, there have been brave souls who have sought to place the Great Awakening in the context of a Puritan past. And there are plausible reasons for doing this. Most of the ministers involved in both promoting and reacting against the Awakening in New England shared a common education and upbringing steeped in the traditions of Puritanism. This is important, for these ministers, even as they were divided against themselves, still spoke in a language that drew from this Puritan past. This, suggests Harry Stout, applies even to Jonathan Edwards, who in his election day and fast day sermons "helped perpetuate that quintessentially Puritan notion of a righteous city set high upon a hill for all the world to see."[39]

Each of these seemingly divergent conclusions about the relationship of the Great Awakening to Puritanism appears defensible if the arguments are premised on identifying a thread that defines and unifies a tradition. Define the thread in a particular way—as a national covenant, as deferential authority relations, as premillennialism, or as a particular view of grace—and one can make a case for there being either continuity or discontinuity. Such an emphasis on tracing genealogies, though, risks miscasting the nature of tradition, which rests less on bloodlines and more on the appropriation of an interpreted past. Read in this way, the Great Awakening becomes important not as a Puritan movement, however defined, but as a movement that, even as it displaced a more rigid religious and moral structure, would draw upon and recast the language and the image of a Puritan past.[40] In developing this argument, I will focus on the New Lights, particularly the works of Jonathan Edwards. This is not because the Old Lights did not leave their legacy. On the contrary, the Old Lights' concern with order, their emphasis on the public rather than the private character of revelation, and their emphasis upon reason all found voice in the rhetoric of the Revolution and after. What makes Jonathan Edwards so important for us is that he broadened the language of Puritanism by lending intellectual legitimacy to its emotional component, by giving it popular legitimacy through a rhetoric that emphasized the apprehension of God's grace, and by extending the legend of a New England founding to make it a part of a larger American millennial promise.

Creation

Jonathan Edwards, in his narrative of conversions in Northampton, noted that the town was never "so full of love, nor so full of joy; and yet so full of distress, as it was then."[41] In making this statement, Edwards would make two fundamental claims about the nature of creation that drew upon his Puritan past: first, human depravity was inherent, universal, and destructive; and second, despite this depravity one was to exult in God's creation. Such exultation required the working of grace but, importantly, grace did not diminish (and in fact increased) the sense of one's own depravity.

Central to Edwards' writings was an understanding of human nature as originally and universally depraved. In Edwards' extended critique of John Taylor's defense of the Arminian position of human self-sufficiency, Edwards argued unequivocally that "all mankind come into the world in such a state, as without fail comes to this issue, namely, the universal commission of sin; or that every one who comes to act in the world as a moral agent, is, in a greater or lesser degree, guilty of sin." Sin was seen as a part of our natural state, which manifests itself as we become responsible for our choices (i.e., as we become moral agents). So powerful is this depraved nature that "none ever fail of *immediately* transgressing God's law, and so of bringing infinite guilt on themselves, and exposing themselves to eternal perdition, as soon as they are capable of it."[42]

This view of human depravity found its way into the rhetoric of Edwards and the other ministers of the Awakening. The sermons of the Great Awakening were often replete with images of the terror of God's wrath arising from human sin. Using imagery frequently heard by parishioners in the seventeenth-century, Edwards explained that "the axe is in an extraordinary manner laid at the root of the trees, that every tree which brings not forth good fruit, may be hewn down and cast into the fire." Edwards depicted the individual as hanging by a thread over hell's gaping mouth. What stood between eternal life and damnation was a wrathful God. "The God that holds you over the pit of hell, much as one holds a spider, or some loathsome insect over the fire, abhors you, and is dreadfully provoked: his wrath towards you burns like fire; he looks upon you as worthy of nothing else, but to be cast into the fire. . . ."[43] Rather than being at God's table and consumed by his grace, the sinners faced the ever present possibility of being devoured in the flames of hell. Edwards exclaimed in words reminiscent of Increase Mather's warnings, "And it would be a wonder, if some that are now present should not be in hell in a very short time, even before this year is out. And it would be a wonder if some persons, that now sit here, in some seats of this meeting-house, in health, quiet and secure, should be there before to-morrow morning."[44] The experience of sin was immediate.

These denunciations served an important purpose: they awakened the listener to one's truly miserable condition. Only by seeing the depravity of one's condition could one hope to apprehend God's beauty. "Persons are sometimes brought to the borders of despair," noted Edwards, in playing upon the familiar image of darkness before the dawn, "and it looks as black as midnight to them a little before the day dawns in their souls; some few instances there have been of persons who have had such a sense of God's wrath for sin, that they have been overborne and made to cry out under an astonishing sense of their guilt, wondering that God suffers such guilty wretches to live upon earth, and that he doth not immediately send them to hell; and sometimes their guilt does so glare them in the face, that they are in exceeding terror for fear that God will instantly do it," and most do not achieve this wretched state but begin to develop a heightened "sense of their own universal depravity and deadness in sin." Edwards portrayed those "under first awakenings" as reflecting on their own sins and seeking to "walk more strictly, and confess their sins, and perform many religious duties, with a secret hope of appeasing God's anger and making up for the sins they have committed." But as these efforts invariably fail to result in an apprehension of God's grace, the individual becomes more terrified of God's wrath, and redoubles this pursuit of grace. When told "they trust too much to their own strength and righteousness, they

go about to strive to bring themselves off from it, and it may
be, think they have done it, when they only do the same thing
under a new disguise, and still find no appearance of any good,
but all looks as dark as midnight to them." In this state "they
wander about from mountain to hill, seeking rest and finding
none: when they are beat out of one refuge they fly to another,
till they are as it were debilitated, broken, and subdued with
legal humblings; in which God gives them a conviction of their
own utter helplessness and insufficiency, and discovers the true
remedy."[45]

Pushed to the point of despair over one's condition, one
was thus prepared to receive God's grace, to partake in the joy
of creation. Conversion worked to both "[change] the heart
and [infuse] life into the dead soul." Grace often appeared as a
"glorious brightness" in which the converts' "minds [were]
wrapped up in delightful contemplation of the glory and won-
derful grace of God, and the excellency and dying love of Jesus
Christ."[46]

This new birth, while providing a moment of harmony and
security, also worked to increase one's sense of despair. Feeling their souls to be alive, notes Edwards, the converts are
"troubled" by "wandering thoughts" and "worldly dispositions."
Aware of their inability to sufficiently appreciate God's grace,
the converts "cry out of the hardness and wickedness of their
hearts; and say there is so much corruption, that it seems to
them impossible that there should be any goodness there."
Once awakened, people become more miserable as they now
"have a watchful eye upon their hearts, that they don't use to
have."[47] Edwards did not simply draw upon a Lockean empiri-
cism for explaining this new consciousness; rather, these new
perceptions of one's existence were communicated by the spirituality of God.[48] The experience of God's grace in turn made
individuals all the more miserable as it altered their perceptions of their condition. The saved, thus, came to see themselves as more wicked, more guilty, more undeserving of God's
love.

As in the jeremiad of the seventeenth-century, the sermons
of the Great Awakening and the thoughts of those listening to
the preaching revealed neither an abject pessimism nor an un-
abashed optimism, but an ongoing tension between despair
and joy. The two elements were related dynamically: without a

sense of sin, one could not exalt in God's grace; with grace the experience of sin became more vivid. There was hope in God, but He was a wrathful God, one who had grown impatient with His unregenerate flock. Godliness required this combination of fear and hope. The person not only trembled at God's word and His judgment but took hope in His promise of redemption. "Religious fear and hope are," noted Edwards, "once and again, joined together, as jointly constituting the character of the true saints."[49]

Self and Community

Like the Puritans of the previous century, Edwards stressed inward conversion. God imparted his grace directly to the individual, not through an intermediary (such as a priest or a bishop). The Great Awakening took this concept one step further: by calling into question traditional authority and the practices of the established elite and by using a rhetorical style that was accessible to all who wanted to listen, the New Lights brought forth a new individual, the layperson "who had been reborn in the Spirit and was living out the converted life." The "layman emerged as the central figure in the Christian community, prepared to judge all people and authority in terms of the presence of the Spirit."[50] The individual's relationship with God (internal authority), and not civil authority, structured the identity of the saints. This awareness by individuals of themselves as instruments of their own salvation served to increase the voice of the laity in church affairs as well as to provoke a questioning of the old ways.[51]

One of Edwards' greatest contributions to the interpretation of Puritanism in America was his attempt to provide a theological and psychological grounding for a principal component of the insular individual: the will. Like his ancestors, Edwards found himself fighting a two-flank war between the Arminians, who emphasized the role of the will in achieving salvation, and the Antinomians, who saw the will as irrelevant in the face of irresistible grace. Edwards performed an exquisite theological balancing act by placing responsibility, but not sovereignty, with the individual will.[52]

By the will, Edwards meant "that by which the mind chooses anything. The faculty of the will is that faculty or power or principle of mind by which it is capable of choosing: an act of the will is the same as an act of choosing or choice." What causes us to choose one thing over another are inclinations of the soul: we choose what we desire. Thus, in contradistinction to the Arminian notion of a self-determining will, for Edwards there was always something that preceded choice, that caused one to choose as one did. In the realm of morality, then, one chose to act in particular ways because of the "habits and dispositions of the heart, and moral motives and inducements." Through the exercise of this moral faculty one became a moral agent.[53]

Having returned agency to the individual, Edwards then argued that because of the "*total depravity and corruption of man's nature,* whereby his heart is wholly under the power of sin," the individual "is utterly unable, without the interposition of sovereign grace, savingly to love God, believe in Christ, or do anything that is truly good and acceptable in God's sight." Answering to the Arminian notion that the necessity of sinning undermined human freedom (and thus human agency), Edwards suggested that there was "*no other necessity* of sinning, than a moral necessity," which consisted of inclinations. That one exercised the will through the choice of what pleased one's depraved nature did not "excuse persons in the nonperformance of any good thing, or make 'em not to be the proper objects of commands, counsels and invitations."[54] Individuals were responsible for their depravity.

Though Edwards adamantly insisted upon the inability of individuals to will grace, there was still an emphasis on human agency regarding grace. The Puritan was not to wait for grace but was to seek it. Along these lines Edwards implored his listeners to in some way seize the opportunity God was offering them:

> And now you have an extraordinary opportunity, a day wherein Christ has thrown the door of mercy wide open, and stands in calling and crying with a loud voice to poor sinners; a day wherein many are flocking to him, and pressing into the kingdom of God. Many are daily coming from the east, west, north and south; many that were very lately in the same miserable condition that you are in, are now in a happy state, with their hearts filled with love to him who has loved them, and washed them from their sins in his own blood, and rejoicing in the hope of the glory of God. How awful is it to be left behind

at such a day! To see so many others feasting, while you are pining and perishing! To see so many rejoicing and singing for joy of heart, while you have cause to mourn for sorrow of heart, and howl for vexation of spirit![55]

This was not a statement of preparationism as much as a reminder to his audience that moral agency, and thus responsibility, rested with the individual.

The receipt of grace was tied to action. Once again, Edwards sought to argue against both the Antinomian attention to a "self-certifying moment of conversion" and the Arminian emphasis on works.[56] Edwards suggested that evidence of grace existed not in private revelation but in action, most notably the expression of love. "That which many call the witness of the Spirit, is no other than an immediate suggestion and impression of the fact, otherwise secret, that they are converted, or made the children of God, and as that their sins are pardoned, and that God has given 'em a title to heaven." Yet, such a witness may have "nothing in it spiritual and divine." Evidence of grace came not through "an inward suggestion of the Spirit of God, by a kind of secret voice speaking" which the devil could easily imitate but through "some work or effect of the Spirit, that is left as a divine mark upon the soul, to be an evidence, by which God's children might be known." This evidence was the act of love, both toward God and toward others.[57] God's grace was the communication of his love to us; evidence of our grace was our communication of that love to Him. Where the Antinomians insisted on the private authority of grace and the Arminians emphasized the public nature of grace through works, Edwards, like his Puritan predecessors, sought to locate grace at the conjuncture of the private and public. Grace was the experience of the insular individual in communion with God, yet was legitimated by public action.

God's power created a new "foundation" in the "nature of the soul, for a new kind of exercise of the same faculty of will." Edwards' argument was not that the individual could will grace or that grace came only to those who performed particular works. Rather, likeness to God required doing. Like the seventeenth-century Puritans who feared deadness to the world and to God, Edwards argued, "That religion which God requires, and will accept, does not consist in weak, dull, and lifeless wishes, raising us but a little above a state of indifference. . . . In nothing is vigor in the actings of our inclinations so requisite, as in religion; and in nothing is lukewarmness so odious." Godliness was a matter of both being and doing, for with grace came the will to act as required by God. Edwards revealed that

> every one that has the power of godliness in his heart, has his inclinations and heart exercised towards God and divine things, with such strength and vigor that these holy exercises do prevail in him above all carnal or natural affections, and are effectual to overcome them . . . From hence it follows, that wherever true religion is, there are vigorous exercises of the inclination and will towards divine objects: but by what was said before, the vigorous, lively, and sensible exercises of the will, are no other than the affections of the soul.[58]

Consistent with the precepts of experimental religion, one looked to experience to confirm belief. Assurance was to be obtained more through action than through self-examination. Ultimately, Edwards argued, pushing Puritanism beyond any statement made in the previous century, the individual would be judged by works. In his last sermon to his congregation, Edwards recalled, "I have often put you in mind, that whatever your pretences to experiences, discoveries, comforts, and joys, have been; at that day [of Judgment], every one will be judged according to his works. . . ."[59]

Having located responsibility in the individual, Edwards then sought to imbed this agency in a corporate mission characterized more by obedience than egalitarian volunteerism. In the controversy about whether authority rested with individual piety or corporate law, the Awakening ministers (like the Puritans before) chose both. While "Arminians wanted to justify sinners by a milder law" and the Antinomians wanted such justification to occur "without the law," the "Edwardians were beginning to believe that they alone preached the gospel *and* law." One of the signs of grace was precisely "a hearty approval of and cordial submission to the law."[60] This was a law that was Biblical in origin and ecclesiastical and political in impact.

The experience of individual grace did not in itself define the saint. People (and churches) could not simply retreat from the world, content with assurance of their own salvation that came from an emotional experience of grace. "It was against such a notion of sainthood—and such an interpretation of the meaning of Awakening—that Edwards and Gilbert Tennent and their colleagues were arguing when they rebuked the enthusiasm of the Moravians, Baptists, and Separates."[61] These Separates erred in abandoning the Puritan quest for community. Although the Separates shared their love for those within the "pure churches," that love did not extend to the rest of the community.[62]

Much of the message of the Great Awakening was that love for society was the essence of sainthood. The saint was to be totally committed to the creation of a harmonious society, for it was such harmony that the Puritans saw as the highest image of Divine beauty. A thing appears beautiful, according to Edwards, "when viewed most perfectly, comprehensively, and universally" with regard to "everything that it stands in connection with."[63] Unlike the Separates, who emphasized the moral excellences of the individual, Edwards argued that true Christians would be drawn to the harmonies among people, to a loving and universal communion. Edwards' definition of virtue as "benevolence to Being in general" made "heartfelt love of the beautiful society and active longing after its establishment the essence and test for Calvinists of the regenerate personality."[64] Individual rebirth meant averting one's eyes from oneself to a vision of community. Each person sought the general welfare, strove toward union, and loved others since redemption was social as much as it was individual. Edwards noted that the converted "remarkably appeared united in dear affection to one another, and many have expressed much of that spirit of love which they felt toward all mankind; and particularly to those that had been least friendly to them." Moreover, "Persons after their own conversion have commonly expressed an exceeding desire for the conversion of others: some have thought that they should be willing to die for the conversion of any soul. . . ."[65]

In speaking about the millennial promise of the true universality of religion, Edwards would extend the image of the Puritan founders. Though the millennium would likely begin in New England, suggested Edwards, the Puritan migration to a "wilderness, where nothing grows" could be read as foretelling the dawn of the millennium in America.[66] Accompanying the third edition of Edwards' *A Faithful Narrative* was a Preface, by four Boston ministers, that tied the founding image of "our forefathers," who transported "themselves over a vast ocean into this then howling wilderness," to a spiritual awakening that was spilling across town and region.[67] Notes Bercovitch, "The second- and third-generation clergy had extolled the immigrants as founding fathers, but they limited the legend perforce to the story of New England." Edwards, on the other hand, "rendered the legend of the founding fathers the common property of all New World evangelicals" by casting the founding as part of the fulfillment of a broader American millennialism.[68] It was a way of depicting American history that George Bancroft, a century later, would make note of and use in his acclaimed *History of the United States*.[69]

Edwards' talk of love and beauty and harmony that would arise from this spiritual awakening should not lead us to read a later egalitarian ethic into the Great Awakening.[70] Edwards' understanding of the community rested not on an egalitarian ethic based on voluntary association and a minimizing of authority through the equality of participants but on hierarchy. Both his theology and his political statements (the few there were) stressed harmony based on a recognition of one's place in a hierarchically ordered existence.

Underlying Edwards' theology and political theory was an aesthetic of a harmony of difference. For Edwards, what is virtuous is that which is beautiful, and what is beautiful is determined by the object of one's love. There is "primary beauty," which consists of the "beauty of spiritual and moral beings," and there is a "secondary beauty," which consists of "some image of this." Beauty is understood as a "mutual consent and agreement of different things in form, manner, quantity, and visible end or design." There is beauty, then, in the proportion of a triangle and the body, in benevolence, in the proportion of action and responsibility we associate with the exercise of justice, and in the proper ordering of society. "There is a beauty of order in society," suggested Edwards, "when the different members of society have all their appointed office, place and station, according to their several capacities and talents, and everyone keeps his place and continues in his proper business."[71] Edwards, in explaining this functional differentiation, drew upon the oft-used body metaphor. For the community to survive, like the body, each part must perform its function in service to the whole. "We see in the natural body, the hand is ready to serve the head, and all the members are ready to serve one another." The hand does not exist for itself, nor do the "ear, the eye, the feet." All of the parts are "employed not for themselves, as for their confined and partial welfare, but for the common good of the body." What is important in this respect, then, is a necessary (and enforceable) obedience to the dictates of the hierarchy, understood best as duty. "And if the head be dishonored, are not the members of the body immediately employed to remove that dishonor, and to put honor upon the head." The community had the right and responsibility to insure that the hierarchy was maintained.[72] And the individual had a duty to obey the dictates that were necessary to sustain a healthy community.[73]

The outpouring of love that characterized Edwards' vision of society resulted not in an egalitarian spiritual or secular community but in a recognition and acceptance of one's place in a hierarchy. "Love," wrote Edwards, "would dispose to those duties which [people] owe to one another in their several places and relations. It would dispose a people to all the duties which they owe their rulers, to give them all that honor and subjection which is their due." Such love would dispose one to proper deference to ministers and would "dispose to all suitable carriage between husbands and wives; and it would dispose children to obey their parents" and "servants to be obedient to their masters." The humility that results from this love "will tend to prevent a leveling behavior." Rather, those truly influenced by God's spirit "will be willing that their superiors should be known and acknowledged in their place, and it will not seem hard to them. They will not desire that all should be upon a level; for they know it is best that some should be above others and should be honored and submitted to as such, and therefore they are willing to comply with it agreeable to those precepts" of Romans, "'Render therefore to all their dues: tribute to whom tribute is due; custom to whom custom; fear to whom fear; honor to whom honor.'" The benevolence that binds a people does not have equality as its requisite. "Those who have a lower station in glory than others suffer no diminution of their own happiness by seeing others above them in glory. On the contrary they rejoice in it."[74]

The relationship between master and slave, magistrate and subject, minister and church member was not merely one of absolute obedience. Hierarchy was not a system of arbitrary authority but one based on a set of expectations on the part of both the ruler and the ruled. So, too, for Edwards love would dispose the subject to obedience and also "would dispose rulers to rule the people over whom they are set justly, sincerely seeking their good."[75] Importantly, this was not a system based on consent (as would be required in an egalitarian community) but one based on the fulfillment of roles for the good of the community. In drawing on, and in turn perpetuating, a language of authority that sought to balance the authority of the insular individual in claims of piety with the moral authority of the hierarchical community, Edwards gave to this language its fullest aesthetic expression.

The Years of War

The enthusiasm of the Great Awakening gave way to disappointment for many as the glorious millennial expectations went unfulfilled. Only a couple of years passed, though, before the sacred and secular were conjoined once again. This time the cause was a series of conflicts with the French, beginning with King George's War (1744-8) and extending through the French and Indian War (1754-63). These struggles were important because they helped harmonize some of the dissonance that arose from the Great Awakening. Most prominently, the Old Side and New Side Presbyterians reunited in 1758, the new alliance being dominated by the more evangelical New Side group.[76] Of critical importance, though, was how this new union responded to the hostility. What one discovers is a politicization of an elite, consisting of both the church clergy and the faculty of the major colonial colleges. Such men as Aaron Burr, Samuel Davies, and Samuel Finley of Princeton, Samuel Locke and Samuel Langdon of Harvard, and Naphtali Daggett of Yale were "awakened" during the Seven Years' War "to the wider significance of government and religion in British North America."[77] The result was a dramatic expansion of the rhetoric that began with reactions to the Andros regime in the previous century, a rhetoric that incorporated Whig themes of liberty and tyranny into a Puritan framework at the same time that the war was imbuing many with a growing sense of nation. The rather formal, legal meanings of liberty and tyranny took on a sacred cast as they blended with a Puritan vocabulary. Puritanism did not become Whig, nor did Whig become Puritan, but the vocabulary of both blended together to provide powerful emotional symbols capable of moving the colonists to act.[78]

The colonial roots of this nascent political vocabulary can be found in the years of the Andros regime in which, beginning with the revocation of the Massachusetts Bay charter in 1684, self-governing colonies came under increased royal control. With the end of Stuart-instituted dominion of New England in 1689, ministers sought to explain both their past (why had they come here) and their future (where were they going). They did this by identifying their purpose within the context of their rights as Englishmen. Thus, Increase Mather, in defending the charter he had negotiated with England, emphasized that "You have all English Liberties Restored to you" and some privileges not available to other English colonies, including elements of self-government and liberty of religious worship.[79] One sees not only an increased appearance of such words as "liberty" and "tyranny" from the pulpit but a changed meaning of these terms. The words acquired a Whig political meaning. Winthrop's liberty as consent to authority evolved into a liberty of active consent and protections from state encroachment into certain areas of life (particularly property ownership and religious practice). Yet, these English liberties were often placed within a Puritan context. Cotton Mather, for example, depicted the Andros tyranny as punishment for an iniquitous community, an unworthiness to God's purpose.[80]

The Anglo-French conflicts further advanced this merging of Whig and Puritan rhetoric by reading republican liberty into the Bible.[81] This "civil millennialism," the combination of "traditional Puritan apocalyptic rhetoric and eighteenth-century political discourse," provided a way for old forms to be made more plausible to a modern audience. The antichrist was seen in the forces of tyranny, and the millennium became an age of liberty. The conflict was depicted in cosmic categories: "Fighting the French became the cause of God; marching to battle hastened the destruction of antichrist; victory proclaimed a 'Salvation, a Deliverance, by far superior to any—nay to all that *New England* ever experienced.'"[82] Samuel Dunbar, for example, who had served as a chaplain during the French and Indian War, saw God's providence in guiding "his people in the wilderness" and saving "New-England from the powerful armament of their French enemies."[83] Even for those who warned against presuming "God's protection" or "signal advantages" over others, the war still appeared as a struggle to preserve the "inheritance" of "liberty, property, religion, [and] happiness" received from our "forefathers, and purchased by them at the expense of their ease, their treasure, their blood!"[84] With few exceptions "the clergy saw the war's end as unequivocal evidence that the kingdom of darkness could no longer restrain the latter-day glory."[85] The millennial promise, though, often appeared more as the unfolding of civil and religious liberty that had been endangered by the French than the spread of piety, as it had been in the Great Awakening. Puritanism had found a new expression: it could incorporate the new ideas of republicanism into a framework that would assume prominence in the rhetoric of the Revolution.

Crafting a Founding Legacy: Eighteenth-Century Historiography

This appeal of a Puritan legacy was not restricted to the New England audience. In 1732, Thomas Gordon, an Independent Whig, made the Puritan legend more palatable to a larger audience when he spoke of the Puritan founders, "who were many of them first driven thither by the Oppression and Barbarity of such courts here, especially in Archbishop Laud's Reign."[86] New England did "much more than the other regions toward articulating colonial experience within the providential dialectic." Because their presses were busier than those in the other colonies, "Boston imprints circulated down the coast," with the probable result "that the classic utterances of Massachusetts served as models for Presbyterians and Baptists as well as for 'low-church' Anglicans."[87] Religious issues received extensive coverage in the press, reaching their peak with the ecclesiastical dispute in 1766-1768. By the time of the Revolution everyone had become familiar with the religious arguments of the day. Tracts, newspaper articles, sermons, and books supporting the Puritan cause were present in the Middle and Southern Colonies.[88] These writings were not miraculously transmitted to these other regions but were promulgated by a Puritan denominational presence in the Middle and even Southern Colonies.[89]

New England was influential in the study and writing of American history as well, a history to which other colonies would often refer and to which students were exposed.[90] Only New England had a well-developed historiography before the American Revolution. Besides New England, only Virginia, New York, and New Jersey had published histories of any importance, and none compared in number or consequence with those of New England. The Reverend William Hubbard's first official history of Massachusetts, compiled from the journals of William Bradford and John Winthrop, served as an important original source for subsequent histories, including the monumental work of Thomas Hutchinson. Though Hutchinson's *History of Massachusetts* contained rather harsh criticisms of Puritan persecutions, the influence of the text on the public was through letters in the press which drew upon this history, although not the unflattering accounts of the Puritans, in their attacks on British actions.[91] It was not unimportant that Hutchinson noted in the preface that "The Massachusets (sic) colony may be considered as the parent of all the other colonies of New-England."[92] Even the widely read almanacs of the day recalled how "your pious Forefathers left their native Land, and planted an uncultivated Desart, which is now become a fruitful field."[93]

Testimony to the power of the Puritan legacy could be seen in how other colonies appropriated, as their own, images of the New England founding. New Netherland, in some early histories, got off to an inauspicious start. A 1649 document originally published in Dutch describes the condition of the settlements "in one word, (and none better presents itself), it is *bad government* . . . the true and only foundation stone of the decay and ruin of New Netherland."[94] The story told was one of mismanagement, greed, war, and neglect. Perhaps that is why William Livingston's description of the New York founding borrows so heavily from New England images when he wrote in 1755 to Sir Charles Hardy, the new governor,

> that the greatest number of our inhabitants, are descended from those, who with a brave and invincible spirit, repelled the spanish tyranny in the *Netherlands;* or from those, who for their ever-memorable opposition, to the arbitrary measures of King CHARLES Ist, were constrained to seek a refuge, from the relentless sword of persecution, in the then inhospitable wilds of AMERICA. From such ancestors, we inherit the highest relish for civil and religious LIBERTY.[95]

John Dickinson of Pennsylvania, as a member of the Stamp Act Congress, drafted a petition to George III in which Dickinson reminded the King that the colonies had been "originally planted" by English subjects who, "animated with the Spirit of Liberty," left England and "by their successful Perseverance in the Midst of innumerable Dangers and Difficulties, with a Profusion of their Blood and Treasure, have happily added these vast and valuable Dominions to the Empire of Great Britain." Dickinson, invoking a language associated with the New England founding, referred as well to these ancestors as having "converted" the "inhospitable Deserts of America" into "flourishing Countries." In his popular patriot song, Dickinson continued to ground his Whig rhetoric in a Puritan past:

> Our worthy *Forefathers*—let's give them a Cheer-
> To *Climates unknown* did courageously steer;
> Thro' *Oceans* to *Deserts* for *Freedom* they came,
> And dying bequeath'd us their *Freedom* and *Fame.*
>
> Their generous Bosoms all Dangers despis'd,
> So *highly,* so *wisely,* their Birth-Rights they priz'd,
> We'll keep what they gave, we will piously keep,
> Nor frustrate their Toils on the Land and the Deep.[96]

One study of the Middle Colonies notes how ministers, such as the Presbyterian William Foster, the Philadelphia revivalist George Duffield, and the New York Dutch minister John Henry Livingston, often "looked to the New England Puritan experience for the historical identity of [their] audience."[97]

Samuel Smith, a Quaker, in his history of New Jersey published in 1765, looked to New England history, as well. He wrote of the "religious and civil freedom" that motivated the New Jersey settlers, and rather than drawing contrasts between the persecution of the Puritans and the tolerance exhibited in New Jersey, suggested instead that the New England founders revealed "motives of like kind." Smith depicted the New Jersey founders as crossing the ocean "at their own expense" for an "unprov'd experiment."[98] Benjamin Franklin, despite his criticisms of the Puritan mind, called upon the Puritans when he wrote an anonymous letter to the press in 1768: "Boston man as I am, Sir, and inimical, as my country is represented to be, I hate neither England or Englishmen, driven (though my ancestors were) by mistaken oppression of former times, out of this happy country, to suffer all the hardships of an American wilderness."[99]

Virginians, too, found it convenient to invoke New England history at times. Richard Henry Lee, a leader in the early days of the Revolution, looked to New England as a model of a virtuous society.[100] Samuel Davies, a Presbyterian, dominated the literary scene not only in Virginia but in the entire South. His poetry, which "adhered to the religious view of the sublime that pervaded Calvinist oratory," was read from South Carolina to New Hampshire.[101] Even Thomas Jefferson, who estimated that "two-thirds of the people [in Virginia] had become dissenters at the commencement of the present revolution," recalled how the Puritan jeremiad was used as a model to incite people to action. With the implementation of the Boston Port Bill, wrote Jefferson, "We were under conviction of the necessity of arousing our people from the lethargy into which they had fallen, as to passing events; and thought that the appointment of a day of general fasting and prayer would be most likely to call up and alarm their attention." Looking to "revolutionary precedents and forms of the Puritans" during the French and Indian War, a "day of fasting, humiliation, and prayer" was established.[102]

In North Carolina the ancestors were depicted by Maurice Moore as coming over "to the deserts of America."[103] Kentucky newspapers contained speeches, poems, and songs that recalled the "poor Pilgrim" and repeated the opening scenes of the Puritans' settlement.[104] Robert Barnwell would speak in South

Carolina of how the Puritans were "transplanted into our con-
genial soil, a scion of that stalk of liberty" which began to un-
fold into "the germ of the American character."[105] And even in
Georgia the Provincial Congress listened to a sermon before
declaring their support for the Revolution. In this sermon, *The
Law of Liberty*, the Reverend John J. Zubly depicted America's
story as the unfolding of God's redemptive plan. Resistance to
England and to the depravity it represented was seen as the
only way to avert God's wrath.[106]

Though states were interested in retaining their own historical identity (and certainly their autonomy, as the Articles of
Confederation demonstrate), what is striking is how often the
colonists drew upon a New England legacy. Not until well after the American Revolution were many state histories, including that of the important state of Pennsylvania, published.[107]
In the meantime, New England continued to provide a ser-
viceable legend of America's ancestors, one propagated
through churches, newspapers, pamphlets, printed sermons,
word-of-mouth, schools and colleges, and books, including historical studies and school texts (which were written primarily
by New Englanders).[108]

Other religious groups would also have their impact, but
these groups, like other colonies, were not as successful at trans-
lating their religious legacy into a larger American political
context. Often the reason was intrinsic to the nature of the
particular religious movement. Many Quakers, because of their
concern with inward piety more than community development,
were unwilling to sustain the political endeavors of Penn. Such
issues as the Quakers' refusal to take an oath of office and
their refusal to serve in office during a time of war led to significant reductions in the number of Quakers holding public
office. More than half the Quaker officials in Pennsylvania,
for example, resigned rather than be involved in a war with
the Delaware and Shawnee Indians.[109] Judge Drayton of South
Carolina was only one of many to take issue with the Quakers'
refusal to "take up arms in defence of the confederacy," suggesting that they may be "the most inveterate enemies to the
independence of America."[110] Furthermore, Pennsylvania was
embroiled politically in a struggle between the Proprietary
party and the Quaker party, the latter led by Benjamin Franklin

and Joseph Galloway who were attempting to replace Penn's control with a royal charter. The power vacuum caused by this stalemate was filled by a group of radical republicans with a significant base of support in the Scotch-Irish Presbyterian community.[111]

The Baptists, too, were preoccupied with individual piety at the expense of political efficacy. To the extent that the Baptists did get involved in mobilizing the community of saints, it was largely due to the influence of Isaac Backus, a minister raised in Puritan New England, who sought in his famous *History of New-England* not to discredit the New England founding but to suggest that the Baptists were closer to the spirit of these founders.[112] George Tillinghast, for example, spoke at a Baptist meetinghouse of the spirit of the Puritans in opposing "ecclesiastical tyranny" which "was manifested a century afterwards, by their descendants, against the evils of political usurpation."[113] The Baptists, in their foray into eighteenth-century politics, devoted their energies to securing religious freedom for their worship. Often this meant playing off "colonial interests against those of the home government." The consequence was an inclination on the part of the Baptist clergy to "minimize or ignore the growing differences between the American colonies and the Mother Country," thus diminishing their ability to play a role in the secular controversy between England and her colonies.[114]

There was also the inability of many movements to develop a widespread membership. Given the intense dislike for "popery," Catholicism never had a chance of becoming widely accepted in the colonies. America was peopled, after all, by children of the Reformation who had regarded Catholicism as tyrannical and superstitious. The equation of Catholicism with the antichrist was pronounced by parents, schools, newspapers, and church sermons. The extent of distaste for Catholicism was seen in 1689 when the Catholic Proprietor of Maryland, Lord Baltimore, was overthrown by Protestants and all "Papists" were excluded from civil and military offices. In 1704 Catholics were required to hold their religious services in private houses.[115] Lord Baltimore, despite the institution of his statute of religious tolerance, faced "declining fortunes" as a national hero.[116]

For a variety of reasons the Episcopalians were unsuccessful in spreading their message. For one thing, Virginia lacked ministers with which to inculcate their own population and transmit their message to others. By 1649 there were only six ministers in Virginia, one for every 3,239 people.[117] This "lack of ministerial voice in Virginia in effect removed an impediment to straying from the traditional when other factors (initial settlement by individuals and tobacco-based agriculture) encouraged that straying."[118] Moreover, through numerous sermons and tracts, the Puritans were able to indoctrinate New England and influence other colonies to the extent that "the emerging Yankees were anti-Episcopal almost to a man."[119] The Anglicans (and, for that matter, other religious groups in the colonies) simply had no such manpower to influence colonial culture so widely.

Related to this was a corresponding inability to establish an intercolonial union. Whereas the Puritans had created an extensive network of communication among themselves and with supporters in England, including intercolonial meetings and committees of correspondence, the Anglicans had no such support.[120] The Episcopalian minister Henry Caner wrote in 1763, "We are a Rope of Sand; there is no union, no authority among us; we cannot even summon a Convention for united Counsell and advice, while the Dissenting Ministers have their Monthly, Quarterly, and Annual Associations, Conventions, &c., to advise, assist, and support each other in any Measures which they think proper to enter into."[121]

The Episcopalians had other problems in broadening their message, as well. Despite being the first European settlers in America, the Jamestown settlers were unable to create a legacy. Captain John Smith, who served as President of the Virginia settlement, began *The Proceedings and Accidents of the English Colony in Virginia* on a note of failure. His recounting, Smith wrote, would serve to explain "how it came to passe there was no better speed and successe in those proceedings." Smith's account is replete with tales of "crosses, trecheries, and dissentions," "maligners" within the community, squabbling, and "idleness and carelesnesse."[122] Smith's silences are as important as his statements. Absent are statements of principled motives (whether true or not) for creating the settlement, a sense of higher purpose or meaning to the endeavor. Thus, even as one reads of idleness in Puritan tracts, one gets the sense that these invocations, while sincere, served to rededicate the community to some higher purpose. But there is no call to rededicate oneself in Smith's account; only a finality in his explanation of unequivocal failure.

The factional strife was played out in an issuance by the General Assembly in Virginia, denouncing Smith. The report portrayed life under Smith's administration as "severe and Crewell," the alloted food as "mouldy, rotten, full of Cobwebs and Maggotts loathsome to man and not fytt for beasts." It even revealed that some settlers fed on the "Corps of dead men." How difficult it is to build a founding legend when, upon the killing of a horse by Indians, the settlers wished "whilst she was a boyling that Sr Tho: Smith were upon her backe in the kettle."[123]

Subsequent generations of Episcopalians did little to enhance the image of the Virginia Company. Robert Beverley, in his history of Virginia published in 1705, saw the Company as concerned only with material gain. He wrote, "the chief Design of all Parties concern'd was to fetch away the Treasure from thence, aiming more at sudden Gain, than to form any regular Colony, or establish a Settlement in such a Manner, as to make it a lasting Happiness to the Country."[124] William Byrd ridiculed the efforts of the Virginia founders: "As it happen'd some Ages before to be the fashion to Santer to the Holy Land, and go upon other Quixot adventures, as it was now grown the Humour to take a Trip to America." The settlers who preceeded the Jamestown settlement were "inflamed by the charming account given of Virginia" and thus were "idle and extravagant" as they "expected they might live without work in so plentiful a country." Their demise: "by some fatal disagreement, or laziness, [they] were either starved or cut to pieces by Indians." Byrd introduced his discussion of the Jamestown settlement by observing that "like true Englishmen, they built a church that cost no more than fifty pounds, and a tavern that cost five hundred." By contrast, Byrd portrayed New Plymouth inhabitants as "frugal and industrious, giving no scandal or bad example" whereas Virginians "thought their being members of the established church sufficient to sanctify very loose and profligate morals."[125]

Even had the Anglicans been widely accepted in the early eighteenth-century, they most likely would not have been able to retain that position. American attitudes changed dramatically over the course of this century, from a provincial mentality to a desire for an identity independent from England. As relations soured between England and her colonies, any group as closely associated with England, as were the Episcopalians, would have been endangered. Though it is impossible to test such a counterfactual hypothesis, we can find some validation in the decline of Anglicanism in America, beginning in the 1750s and accelerating through the next two decades as hostility to England increased.[126] The attempt by Anglicans to seize control of the development of Kings College and the inflammatory rhetoric that followed riveted public attention during the early 1750s. In the pamphlets and articles of the time the Anglicans were depicted as subverting civil and religious liberty.[127] In a sense, such disputes acted as a prelude to the controversies on the eve of the Revolution.

"In the long run," notes Lawrence Buell, "the legend of America's Pilgrim-Puritan pedigree won out over the claims of less conspicuous victims of persecution, such as the South Carolina Huguenots or the Pennsylvania Quakers, or less high-minded founds, such as the more avowedly opportunistic colonists of Virginia."[128] Puritanism survived because it had become a strong institutional force. And Puritanism became usable because it provided an adaptive discursive space for articulating the concerns of subsequent generations.

Notes

1   Most recently, see Ronald Hoffman and Peter J. Albert, eds., *Religion in a Revolutionary Age* (Charlottesville: University Press of Virginia, 1994); and Roger Finke and Rodney Stark, *The Churching of America, 1776-1990: Winners and Losers in Our Religious Economy* (New Brunswick, N.J.: Rutgers University Press, 1992).

2   Carl Bridenbaugh, *Mitre and Sceptre* (London: Oxford University Press, 1962), 76-7, 68-9, 182, 179. See also Richard Bushman, *From Puritan to Yankee* (New York: Norton & Co., 1967), 166.

3   Virginia DeJohn Anderson, *New England's generation: The Great Migration and the formation of society and culture in the seventeenth century* (New York: Cambridge University Press, 1991), 4. Anderson suggests that the symbolic importance of the Migration was "invented not by the founders of New England but by their descendants . . ." (16). Where Anderson's focus is on the second and third generation of Puritan descendants, I will be looking at how the legend gets reinterpreted in the next century.

4   William Bradford, *Of Plymouth Plantation*, ed. Samuel Eliot Morison (New York: Alfred A. Knopf, 1952), 56-7, 61.

5   Ibid., 63, 75, 178.

6   See Anderson, *New England's generation*, 202. Mark L. Sargent places this *Dialogue* and Bradford's later writings in the context of attempts by Bradford to "square Separatist tradition with the Congregational polity." Bradford's *Dialogue* becomes an act of interpretation to answer to not only contemporary concerns but an audience outside Plymouth. Notes Sargent, "What the ancients 'remember' is shaped largely by the ideological and life choices facing the young." "William Bradford's 'Dialogue' with History," *New England Quarterly* 65 (Sept. 1992): 421, 414.

7   Bradford's reference to his generation as ancients is striking in light of Jesper Rosenmeier's argument that Bradford saw in the ancients the most perfect image of the divine. "'With my owne eyes': William Bradford's *Of Plymouth Plantation*," *The American Puritan Imagination: Essays in Revaluation*, ed. Sacvan Bercovitch (Cambridge: Cambridge University Press, 1974), 78.

8   Two of the three volumes of Winthrop's notebooks were finally published in 1790. The remaining notebook, as well as new transcriptions of the other notebooks, was edited by James Savage and published in 1825-26. Before their publication, the notebooks were borrowed by William Hubbard, Cotton Mather, Thomas Prince, Ezra

Stiles, Jonathan Trumbull, and Jeremy Belknap. See Richard S. Dunn, "John Winthrop Writes His Journal," *William and Mary Quarterly*, 3d series, 41 (April 1984): 186.

9   James Moseley, *John Winthrop's World: History as a Story; The Story as History* (Madison: The University of Wisconsin Press, 1992), 63.

10 John Winthrop, *The History of New England from 1630 to 1649*, 2 vols., ed. James Savage (New York: Arno Press, 1972), 2: 101.

11 Mosely, *John Winthrop's World*, 137-8. See also Dunn, "John Winthrop," 196.

12 *Wonder-Working Providence*, in *Collections of the Massachusetts Historical Society*, 2nd series (Boston: John Eliot, 1814), 2: 52-3.

13 *Selections from Cotton Mather*, ed. Kenneth B. Murdock (New York: Hafner, 1926), 1-2, 5, 8. See also Sacvan Bercovitch's excellent discussion in *The Puritan Origins of the American Self* (New Haven: Yale University Press, 1975).

14 Murdock, "Introduction," in *Selections*, xxxix.

15 For a discussion of this accommodation in the Puritan's view of Providence from a supernaturalism to a view in which "nature and reason coincided nicely with self-interest, not just for ministers but for the entire province," see Michael Winship, *Seers of God: Puritan Providentialism in the Restoration and Early Enlightenment* (Baltimore: Johns Hopkins University Press, 1996), 144. Norman Fiering points out how the new moral philosophy of the enlightenment, which in other countries was being expressed as extreme naturalism, skepticism, nominalism, anticlericalism, materialism, or atheism, was incorporated at Harvard in the early eighteenth-century into the "inherited religious tradition." Even the Neoplatonists at Harvard at the end of the seventeenth-century "had a close historical and philosophical kinship to New England Puritans." See Norman Fiering, *Moral Philosophy at Seventeenth-Century Harvard: A Discipline in Transition* (Chapel Hill: University of North Carolina Press, 1981), 241, 247.

16 Bridenbaugh, *Mitre and Sceptre*, 175.

17 Thomas Prince, *Chronological History of New England in the Form of Annals* (Boston, 1736; Cumming, Hilliard, and Co., 1826), Dedication, 1: ii-iii.

18 Thomas Prince, "The People of New-England" (Boston, 1730), in *The Wall and the Garden: Selected Massachusetts Election Sermons 1670-1775*, ed. A. W. Plumstead (Minneapolis: University of Minnesota Press, 1968), 200-201, 203, 209.

19 Harry S. Stout, *The New England Soul: Preaching and Religious Culture in Colonial New England* (New York: Oxford University Press, 1986), 23.

20 Darrett Rutman, *American Puritanism: Faith and Practice* (New York: J. B. Lippincott, 1970), 51.

21 Stout, *New England Soul*, 149.

22 Rutman, *American Puritanism,* 87. See also Richard D. Brown, *Knowledge is Power: The Diffusion of Information in Early America, 1700-1865* (New York: Oxford University Press, 1989), chapt. 1, in which he describes the hierarchical transmission of this information.

23 Stout, *New England Soul*, 23.

24 Rutman, *American Puritanism*, 51.

25 "The New-England Primer" (Boston, 1727), in *The New-England Primer: A History of Its Origin and Development*, ed. Paul Leicester Ford (New York: Dodd, Mead, & Co., 1897).

26 Edmund S. Morgan, *The Puritan Family: Religion and Domestic Relations in Seventeenth-Century New England* (New York: Harper and Row, 1966), 88-90, 101. Cotton Mather also abridged John Cotton's "Spiritual Milk for Babes" and wrote on the importance of catechism. See "Cotton Mather's Views on Catechising," [1708], in Ford, *New-England Primer*.

27 See Samuel E. Morison, *The Founding of Harvard College* (Cambridge: Harvard University Press, 1935) and *Harvard College in the Seventeenth Century* (Cambridge: Harvard University Press, 1937).

28 Stout, *New England Soul*, 57.

29 See David D. Hall, "The World of Print and Collective Mentality in Seventeenth-Century New England," in *New Directions in American Intellectual History*, eds. John Higham and Paul K. Conkin (Baltimore: Johns Hopkins University Press, 1979), 174.

30 Morgan, *Puritan Family*, 12.

31 Bridenbaugh, *Mitre and Sceptre*, 176; Wesley Frank Craven, *The Legend of the Founding Fathers* (New York: Cornell University Press, 1956), 43. See Ezra Stiles, *Christian Union*, for his calculation of the sectarian population in New England. In 1760 he estimated Congregationalists to number 440,000 compared with 12,600 for Episcopalians, 16,000 for Friends, and 22,000 for Baptists.

32 Bridenbaugh, *Mitre and Sceptre*, 177; also 176, 178.

33 [Daniel Leonard], Massachusettensis, *Massachusetts Gazette and Boston Post-Boy* (Dec. 12, 1774-Apr. 3, 1775), Dec. 19, 1774, in *Tracts of the American Revolution: 1763-1776*, ed. Merrill Jensen (Indianapolis: Bobbs-Merrill, 1967), 284-5. See Paul K. Conkin, *Puritans & Pragmatists* (Bloomington: Indiana University Press, 1976), 114 and Stout, *New England Soul*, for a discussion of the role of the weekly sermon in New England. See Bridenbaugh, *The Spirit of '76* (New York: Oxford

University Press, 1975), 87, for the importance of the newspaper in forging unity in public opinion.

34   See Perry Miller, *Jonathan Edwards* (Westport: Greenwood Press, 1973); Miller, "The Marrow of Puritan Divinity," in *Errand Into the Wilderness* (Cambridge: Belknap Press, 1956); Conrad Cherry, "The Puritan Notion of the Covenant in Jonathan Edwards' Doctrine of Faith," *Church History* 34 (1965); and Adam Seligman, *Innerworldly Individualism: Charismatic Community and Its Institutionalization* (New Brunswick: Transaction, 1994), 181.

35   See Stout, *New England Soul*, 207-11.

36   For a critique of this dichotomy as well as a thorough bibliography, see William Breitenbach, "Piety and Moralism: Edwards and the New Divinity," in *Jonathan Edwards and the American Experience*, eds. Nathan O. Hatch and Harry S. Stout (New York: Oxford University Press, 1988), 177-204.

37   The most significant statement of this argument is Alan Heimert's *Religion and the American Mind from the Great Awakening to the Revolution* (Cambridge: Harvard University Press, 1966).

38   Timothy D. Hall, *Contested Boundaries: Itinerancy and the Reshaping of the Colonial American Religious World* (Durham: Duke University Press, 1994), 12, 6-7.

39   Stout, "The Puritans and Edwards," in *Jonathan Edwards and the American Experience*, eds. Nathan O. Hatch and Harry S. Stout (New York: Oxford University Press, 1988), 157. See also Stephen R. Yarbrough and John C. Adams, *Delightful Conviction: Jonathan Edwards and the Rhetoric of Conversion* (Westport: Greenwood Press, 1993), 23.

40   Emory Elliot, for example, notes that the Great Awakening and the French and Indian Wars revitalized Puritanism at a time when it "might have undergone severe deterioration" (*Revolutionary Writers: Literature and Authority in the New Republic* [New York: Oxford University Press, 1982], 28).

41   Jonathan Edwards, "A Faithful Narrative of the Surprising Work of God in the Conversion of Many Hundred Souls in Northampton, and the Neighboring Towns and Villages" (London, 1737), in *The Works of Jonathan Edwards*, 14 vols., ed. C. C. Goen (New Haven: Yale University Press, 1972), 4: 151.

42   Edwards, "The Great Christian Doctrine of Original Sin Defended" (Boston, 1758), in *The Works of Jonathan Edwards*, 14 vols., ed. Clyde A. Holbrook (New Haven: Yale University Press, 1970), 3: 114, 134.

43   Jonathan Edwards, "Sinners in the Hands of an Angry God," 1741, in *Jonathan Edwards*, eds. Clarence H. Faust and Thomas H. Johnson (New

York: Hill and Wang, 1935, 1962), 172, 165, 164. Edwards wrote that he attempted to use both persuasion and fear to awaken his audience. See his "Farewell Sermon," preached July 1, 1750, in *Jonathan Edwards*, ed. Faust and Johnson, 192.

44   Edwards, "Sinners," 170; Increase Mather, *The Wicked mans Portion* (Boston, 1675), 16, reprinted in *The Puritan Sermon in America, 1630-1750*, 4 vols., ed. Ronald Bosco (Delmar: Scholars' Facsimiles & Reprints, 1978), vol. 1.

45   Edwards, "Faithful Narrative," 4: 162-6.

46   Ibid., 4: 177, 181.

47   Ibid., 4: 186-7.

48   See Allen C. Guelzo, *Edwards on the Will: A Century of American Theological Debate* (Middletown: Wesleyan University Press, 1989), 28-35.

49   Edwards, "A Treatise Concerning Religious Affections" (Boston, 1746) in *The Works of Jonathan Edwards*, 14 vols., ed. John E. Smith (New Haven: Yale University Press, 1959), 2: 103.

50   Jerald C. Brauer, "Puritanism, Revivalism, and the Revolution," in *Religion and the American Revolution*, ed. Jerald C. Brauer (Philadelphia: Fortress Press, 1976), 26. See also Harry S. Stout, "Religion, Communications, and the Ideological Origins of the American Revolution," *The William and Mary Quarterly* 34 (Oct. 1977): 529-30.

51   Bushman, *Puritan to Yankee*, 195, 220. For a fascinating discussion that places the Great Awakening in a much larger perspective of a consumer revolution in which the revivals addressed a "new public—a mass audience that transcended denominational, national, and even continental boundaries" (7), see Frank Lambert, *'Pedlar in Divinity': George Whitefield and the Transatlantic Revivals, 1737-1770* (Princeton: Princeton University Press, 1994).

52   For an extended discussion of Edwards' notion of the will, see Guelzo, *Edwards on the Will*.

53   Jonathan Edwards, "A Careful and Strict Enquiry into the Modern Prevailing Notions of that Freedom of Will" (Boston, 1754), in *The Works of Jonathan Edwards*, 14 vols., ed. Paul Ramsey (New Haven: Yale University Press, 1957), 1: 137, 138-48, 156-7, 165.

54   Ibid., 1: 432-3.

55   Edwards, "Sinners," 170-1.

56   Breitenbach, "Piety," 182.

57   Edwards, "Religious Affections," 2: 229, 233, 232, 236.

58   Ibid., 2: 206, 213, 214.

59   Edwards, "Farewell Sermon," 191.

60   Breitenbach, "Piety," 187-8.

61   Alan Heimert and Perry Miller, eds., *The Great Awakening* (Indianapolis: Bobbs-Merrill, 1967), li-lii.

62   See Heimert, *Religion and the American Mind*, 127.

63   Edwards, "The Nature of True Virtue," in *Jonathan Edwards*, eds. Faust and Johnson, 540.

64   Edwards, "Nature of True Virtue," 540; Heimert, *Religion and the American Mind*, 112.

65   Edwards, "Faithful Narrative," 4: 184.

66   Jonathan Edwards, "Some Thoughts Concerning the Present Revival of Religion in New-England" (Boston, 1742), in *The Works of Jonathan Edwards*, 14 vols., ed. C.C. Goen (New Haven: Yale University Press, 1972), 4: 358, 356, 353.

67   Joseph Sewall, Thomas Prince, John Webb, and William Cooper, "Preface to the Third Edition (Boston, 1738)," Edwards, "Faithful Narrative," 4: 138.

68   Sacvan Bercovitch, *The Rites of Assent: Transformations in the Symbolic Construction of America* (New York: Routledge, 1993), 154.

69   George Bancroft, *History of the United States* (Boston: Little, Brown, and Co., 1860), 3: 399.

70   An argument for the egalitarianism of Edwards is made by Heimert, *Religion and the American Mind*, 307.

71   Edwards, "Nature of True Virtue," 561, 568.

72   Edwards, "Charity and Its Fruits," in *The Works of Jonathan Edwards*, 14 vols., ed. Paul Ramsey (New Haven: Yale University Press, 1989), 8: 271.

73   Edwards, "Nature of True Virtue," 569.

74   Edwards, "Charity," 8: 136, 242-3, 375.

75   Ibid., 8: 136.

76   Briefly, the Old Side Presbyterians, whose governing body was the Synod of Philadelphia and who were primarily ministers trained in Scotland, believed Presbyterianism should be tightly and centrally controlled. This included the requirement that ministers receive a formal education and subscribe to the Westminster Confession, articles of faith drawn up by the Presbyterians during the Puritan Revo-

lution in England. Ministers were to be licensed by the Philadelphia Synod. On the other side was a group of ministers mostly from New England who refused to subscribe to the Confession. A third group emerged within Presbyterianism composed of the Scotch-Irish immigrants. Tennent, the leader of this latter group, established the Log College in Pennsylvania and began to train and ordain his own graduates, much to the displeasure of the Philadelphia Synod. The experience of grace, not formal education, so Tennent argued, was all the qualifications necessary to be a minister. In 1741 Tennent was ejected from the Synod of Philadelphia, at which point he formed the Synod of New York with the New England clergy. Tennent's group and the New England ministers formed what became known as the New Side pro-revival party, and the Philadelphia group became known as the Old Side party. See Heimert and Miller, *The Great Awakening*, xxix-xxxv.

77 David Robson, *Educating Republicans: The College in the Era of the American Revolution, 1750-1800* (Westport, Conn.: Greenwood, 1985), 43. See also Charles Akers, *The Divine Politician: Samuel Cooper and the American Revolution in Boston* (Boston: Northeastern University Press, 1982), 31-39.

78 For an important discussion of the multivocal nature of symbols, see Victor W. Turner, *The Ritual Process: Structure and Anti-Structure* (New York: Aldine, 1969). For an application of Turner's anthropological work to an American context, see Donald Weber, *Rhetoric and History in Revolutionary New England* (New York: Oxford University Press, 1988).

79 *The Great Blessing of Primitive Counsellours Discoursed in a Sermon. . . .* (Boston, 1693), 21, reprinted in *Increase Mather: Jeremiads*, ed. Sacvan Bercovitch (New York: AMS Press, Inc., n.d.).

80 *Things for a Distres'd People to Think Upon* (Boston, 1696), 25, reprinted in *The Puritan Sermon in America, 1630-1750*, ed. Ronald Bosco (Delmar: Scholars' Facsimiles and Reprints, 1978), 3: 159. For a discussion of this new attention to English liberties, see Stout, *New England Soul*, 118-22 and Miller, *The New England Mind: From Colony to Province* (Cambridge: Harvard University Press, 1953), 149-72.

81 The most significant statement of this argument is in Nathan O. Hatch, *The Sacred Cause of Liberty: Republican Thought and the Millennium in Revolutionary New England* (New Haven: Yale University Press, 1976) and "The Origins of Civil Millennialism in America: New England Clergymen, War with France, and the Revolution," *William and Mary Quarterly*, 3d Series, 31 (July 1974): 407-30. Hatch is arguing most directly against Heimert's assertion of the irrelevance of the Seven Years' War on the "mainstream of history." See also Heimert, *Religion*, 86, and John Berens, *Providence & Patriotism in Early America, 1640-1815* (Charlottesville: University Press of Virginia, 1978), chapt. 2.

82   Hatch, "Civil Millennialism," 408, 422. See also Ruth Bloch, *Visionary Republic: Millennial Themes in American Thought, 1756-1800* (Cambridge: Cambridge University Press, 1985), 36-7, although she does not place these millennial themes within the context of a nascent political vocabulary.

83   Samuel Dunbar, "The Presence of God with his People, their only Safety and Happiness" (Boston, 1760), in *Political Sermons of the American Founding Era, 1730-1805*, ed. Ellis Sandoz (Indianapolis: Liberty Press, 1991), 217-8.

84   Jonathan Mayhew, "A Sermon Preach'd in the Audience of His Excellency William Shirley" (Boston, 1754), in *The Wall and the Garden*, ed. A. W. Plumstead (Minneapolis: University of Minnesota Press, 1968), 311-12.

85   Hatch, "Civil Millennialism," 422.

86   [Thomas Gordon], *A Sermon Preached before the Learned Society of Lincoln's Inn, on January 30, 1732. By a Layman* (London, 1733), quoted in Bridenbaugh, *Mitre and Sceptre*, 175.

87   Perry Miller, "From the Covenant to the Revival," in *The Shaping of American Religion*, eds. James Ward Smith and A. Leland Jamison (Princeton: Princeton University Press, 1961), 1: 325.

88   Bridenbaugh, *Mitre and Sceptre*, 190-3.

89   I think it is easy to understate the infiltration of Puritanism, not as a set of unified religious practices and beliefs, but as it provides a discursive space from which other sects would emerge. The relationship of the Congregationalists in New England to Puritanism is well established, but so too there is a relationship to the Presbyterians in the Middle Colonies and even some of the Baptist and Presbyterian groups in the South. Recent evidence indicates a substantial presence of these groups (in proportion to other religions) in the Middle and Southern colonies. See Finke and Stark, *Churching of America*, 29.

90   Notes Robson, *Educating Republicans*, "The notebook of Harvard sophomore Benjamin Wadsworth for 1766-67 gives an insight into undergraduate reading. Among his notes history predominated, including William Douglass' *A Summary. . . of the British Settlements in North America* (Boston, 1755), Thomas Hutchinson's *A History of the Province of Massachusetts Bay* (2 vols., Boston, 1764, 1767), Daniel Neal's *History of the Puritans*, Charles Rollin's *Ancient History*, and David Hume's *History of England* (88).

91   Craven, *Legend of the Founding Fathers*, 11, 43.

92   Thomas Hutchinson, *The History of the Colony and Province of Massachusetts-Bay*, 3 vols., ed. Lawrence Shaw Mayo (Cambridge: Harvard University Press, 1936; New York: Kraus Reprint, 1970), 1: xxix.

93 Nathaniel Low, *An Astronomical Diary, or Almanack For. . . 1769* (Boston, 1768), in Raymond R. Allan, "'To Reach Men's Minds': Almanacs and the American Revolution, 1760-1777," *The New England Quarterly* 51 (Sept. 1978): 379.

94 "The Representation of New Netherland, 1650," in *Original Narratives of Early American History: Narratives of New Netherland, 1609-1664*, ed. J. Franklin Jameson (New York: Charles Scribner's Sons, 1909), 15: 320.

95 "The Watch-Tower," No. 42, *N.Y. Mercury*, September 8, October 6, Sup., 1755, qtd. in Bridenbaugh, *Mitre and Sceptre*, 176-7.

96 *The Writings of John Dickinson*, ed. Paul Leicester Ford, *Political Writings, 1764-1774* (Philadelphia: The Historical Society of Pennsylvania, 1895), 1: 193-4, 431.

97 Keith Griffin, *Revolution and Religion: American Revolutionary War and the Reformed Clergy* (New York: Paragon, 1994), 75. See also 45, 73-4, 79, 81.

98 Samuel Smith, *The History of The Colony of Nova-Caesaria, or New-Jersey: Containing an Account of Its First Settlement, Progressive Improvements, The Original and Present Constitution, and Other Events, to the year 1721. With Some Particulars Since; And A Short View of Its Present State* (Burlington, N.J.: James Parker, 1765), xi-xii.

99 Anonymous letter to *The Pennsylvania Chronicle*, Dec. 5-12, 1768, in *The Papers of Benjamin Franklin*, ed. William B. Willcox (New Haven: Yale University Press, 1972), 15: 67.

100 Pauline Maier, *The Old Revolutionaries: Political Lives in the Age of Samuel Adams* (New York: Vintage Books, 1980), 199.

101 Emory Elliot, *Revolutionary Writers*, 24-5. See, for example, Davies' *Miscellaneous Poems, Chiefly on Divine Subjects* (Williamsburg: Hunter, 1752).

102 Thomas Jefferson, "Notes on Virginia," in *The Life and Selected Writings of Thomas Jefferson*, eds. Adrienne Koch and William Peden (New York: Modern Library, 1972), 273; Jefferson, "Autobiography," in *Writings*, eds. Koch and Pedan, 8-9.

103 Maurice Moore, "Justice and Policy of Taxing the American Colonies in England" (1765), in *Some Eighteenth Century Tracts Concerning North Carolina*, ed. William K. Boyd (South Carolina: The Reprint Company, 1973), 171.

104 *Argus of Western America*, Frankfort (Ky.), August 30, 1826 and the *Patriot*, Georgetown (Ky.), July 13, 1816, cited in Robert P. Hay, "Providence and the American Past," *Indiana Magazine of History* 65 (June 1969): 84, 81-2.

105   Robert Barnwell, *An Oration, delivered before The Philomathean Society and Inhabitants of Beaufort, South-Carolina, on Monday, July 4, 1803, In Commemoration of American Independence* (Charleston, 1803), 9.

106   Miller, "From the Covenant to the Revival," 331-2.

107   There were a number of descriptions and histories of other colonies printed in England, often in an attempt to encourage migration to the colonies. These histories were not published in America until much later, often in the nineteenth-century. Many of the early histories, such as those of New Netherland, were written in the original language of the immigrants.

108   Craven, *Legend of the Founding Fathers*, 11; Bridenbaugh, *Mitre and Sceptre*, 184-5.

109   See Cushing Strout, *The New Heavens and New Earth: Political Religion in America* (New York: Harper Torchbooks, 1975), 24, and Daniel J. Boorstin, *The Americans: The Colonial Experience* (New York: Vintage Books, 1958).

110   "Speech in the general assembly," Jan. 20, 1778, in *Republication of the Principles and Acts of the Revolution in America*, ed. Hezekiah Niles (New York: A. S. Barnes & Co., 1876), 370-1.

111   See Eric Foner, *Tom Paine and Revolutionary America* (London: Oxford University Press, 1976), 58-61.

112   Lawrence Buell, *New England Literary Culture: From Revolution Through Renaissance* (Cambridge: Cambridge University Press, 1986), 228.

113   George Tillinghast, *An Oration, Commemorative of the Nineteenth Anniversary of American Independence, Delivered at the Baptist Meeting-House in Providence, on the Fourth Day of July, A. D. 1794* (Providence, [1794]), 5.

114   John M. Bumsted and Charles E. Clark, "New England's Tom Paine: John Allen and the Spirit of Liberty," *The William and Mary Quarterly* 3d Series, 21 (1964): 555-6; Hatch, *Sacred Cause*, 19. See also Clark, *Language*, 372-81.

115   Pauline Maier, *Old Revolutionaries*, 206.

116   Craven, *Legend of the Founding Fathers*, 89.

117   Darrett Rutman, *American Puritanism: Faith and Practice* (New York: J. B. Lippincott, Comp., 1970), 59, 51. Similar shortages of established Anglican congregations and permanent ministers existed in East and West Jersey. See Patricia U. Bonomi, "Religious Dissent and the Case for American Exceptionalism," in *Religion in a Revolutionary Age*, eds. Ronald Hoffman and Peter J. Albert (Charlottesville: University Press of Virginia, 1994), 37.

118　Rutman, *American Puritanism*, 51.

119　Bridenbaugh, *Mitre and Sceptre*, 58.

120　See Maier, *Old Revolutionaries*, 78-81; Pauline Maier, *From Resistance to Revolution: Colonial Radicals and the Development of American Opposition to Britain, 1765-1776* (New York: Vintage Books, 1972), 222; Bridenbaugh, *Mitre and Sceptre*, 189.

121　Quoted in Bridenbaugh, *Mitre and Sceptre*, 184. See also 179, 187-8.

122　Smith, "The Proceedings and Accidents of the English Colony in Virginia," in *Travels and Works of Captain John Smith*, eds. Edward Arber and A. G. Bradley (Edinburgh: John Grant, 1910), 2: 385, 477, 498, 395, 615.

123　"The Tragical Relation of the Virginia Assembly, 1624," in *Original Narratives of Early American History*, vol. 9, *Narratives of Early Virginia, 1606-1625*, ed. Lyon Gardiner Tyler (New York: Charles Scribner's Sons, 1930), 422-3.

124　Robert Beverley, *The History and Present State of Virginia*, ed. Louis B. Wright (London, 1705; Chapel Hill: University of North Carolina Press, 1947), 55.

125　*William Byrd's Histories of the Dividing Line betwixt Virginia and North Carolina*, in *A Journey to the Land of Eden and Other Papers* (Vanguard Press, 1928), 11-13, 16.

126　Bridenbaugh, *Mitre and Sceptre*, 111.

127　Ibid., chapt. 6.

128　*New England Literary Culture: From Revolution Through Renaissance* (Cambridge: Cambridge University Press, 1986), 197.

Chapter 3

The Puritans in Revolutionary Discourse

On July 4, 1776, John Hancock, president of the Continental Congress stated, "We are now a nation, and I am ready to hear you vote on the question, 'Resolved, That Dr. Franklin, Mr. Thomas Jefferson and Mr. John Adams be a committee to prepare a device for a seal of the United States of North America.' " In August 1776 the committee, which also included the French artist, Du Simitiere, presented its work. Benjamin Franklin put forth his proposal to the Congress:

> Moses ~~in the Dress of a High Priest~~ standing on the Shore, and extending his Hand over the Sea, thereby causing the same to overwhelm Pharoah who is sitting in an open Chariot, a Crown on his Head & a Sword in his Hand. Rays from a Pillar of Fire in the Clouds reaching to Moses, ~~expressing~~ to express that he acts by ~~the~~ Command of the Deity
> Motto, *Rebellion to Tyrants is Obedience to God.*[1]

The event Franklin chose to portray was that of the Israelite's flight from Egyptian slavery, a clear allusion to the current crisis. The Egyptian army caught up with the Jews at the Red Sea, and there it was determined to force God's people to return to bondage. But in this dire time, the Lord caused the Sea to part, allowing safe passage of His people. When the Egyptians followed, they were engulfed in the sea as God closed the channel. As for the motto, although there was some dispute about its origin, the meaning was clear: rebellion and not obedience to secular authority was the signature of divinity, an idea given religious sanction in Jonathan Mayhew's famous sermon, *A Discourse Concerning Unlimited Submission and Non-Resistance to the Higher Powers.*[2]

Thomas Jefferson then presented his idea for a seal. Although Franklin and Jefferson had not consulted each other, one side of Jefferson's seal picked up where Franklin's ended. Jefferson suggested an emblem depicting the Israelites in the wilderness, led by a cloud by day and a pillar of fire by night. God's favored people, having escaped the Egyptians, were on the way to the promised land, the land of Canaan. According to the book of Exodus, having wandered for three days with only bitter water from a stream to drink, the travelers became disgruntled. In answer to the prayers of Moses, the Lord not only sweetened the water but brought forth a stream of fresh and abundant water. God then delivered manna to the grumbling Israelites after they had wandered for three more days in the wilderness. God, in the image of the cloud and pillar of fire, had stayed with his people, providing them with safety and abundance.

So impressed was Jefferson with Franklin's motto and design that Jefferson's second proposal, the conjoint design of the committee, closely resembled Franklin's.[3] His description of this second seal was as follows:

> Pharaoh sitting in an open chariot, a crown on his head & a sword in his hand passing thro' the divided waters of the Red sea in pursuit of the Israelites: rays from a pillar of fire in the cloud, expressive of the divine presence, reachi & command, reaching to Moses who stands on the shore &, extending his hand over the sea, causes it to overwhelm Pharaoh. Motto. Rebellion to tyrants is obed[ce] to god.[4]

It would have been one thing for a Congregational minister from Boston, or even John Adams, a Puritan in upbringing and temperament, to propose such a design. But it should excite our attention when Franklin, who had supposedly consigned God to the status of watchmaker, and Jefferson, the eighteenth-century rationalist, did so.

What Franklin's and Jefferson's comments alert us to is how easily religious and political images were joined in the public realm as the colonists sought to legitimate their break with England and articulate their vision of the future. Though this blending is often recognized,[5] there nevertheless appears to be an implicit division of labor when it comes to inquiring into the framework for the formation of the American nation. To understand the intellectual currents that served to legitimate not only the break with England but the consolidation of the nation, scholars scour the political and legal tracts of the time for clues about the arguments that framed the debate. If one wants to understand the fervor, particularly of the revolutionary period, however, one then reads the sermons. Perry Miller early on spelled out the dimensions of this approach to early American scholarship:

> To understand the Revolutionary mind from the side of its religious emotion is to gain a perspective that cannot be acquired from the ordinary study of the papers of the Congresses, the letters of Washington, the writings of Dickinson, Paine, Freneau, or John Adams. The "decent respect" that these Founders entertained for the opinion of mankind caused them to put their case before the civilized world in the restricted language of the rational century.

One has to turn, then, to the "patriotic clergy."[6] The most influential works on this revolutionary period have followed Miller's lead. Scholars like Alan Heimert, Donald Weber, Harry S. Stout, and Barry Shain, who have sought to demonstrate the role of religion in early American thought, rely primarily on political sermons.[7] Nathan O. Hatch looks predominantly at sermons, examining how republican ideas influenced the religious message of the time.[8] And Sacvan Bercovitch's primary sources consist of sermons and literature.[9] Not surprisingly, those who have sought to downplay the influence of religion on political ideology have concentrated, as has Bernard Bailyn, on pamphlets of the time.[10] Gordon Wood, in his most recent work, even goes so far as to suggest that "At the time of the Revolution most of the founding fathers had not put much emotional stock in religion, even when they were regular churchgoers." They saw themselves, in words quite reminiscent of Miller, as "enlightened gentlemen," but ones (and this departs from Miller) who equated ministerial words with superstition.[11]

How are we to understand Franklin's and Jefferson's conjoining of religion and politics in their proposed seals? To a certain extent, the sermons of the period are an important source for understanding colonial religious culture. As Harry Stout has argued, "Collectively over the entire span of the colonial period, sermons totaled over five million separate messages in a society whose population never exceeded one-half million and whose principal city never grew beyond seventeen thousand. The average weekly churchgoer in New England (and there were far more churchgoers than church members) listened to something like seven thousand sermons in a lifetime, totaling somewhere around fifteen thousand hours of concentrated listening." Of particular significance, these sermons were heard at a time when "there were at the local level few, if any, competing public speakers offering alternative messages. For all intents and purposes, the sermon was the only regular voice of authority."[12]

These sermons are important, but incomplete, as they do not tell us how these religious messages were translated into a language outside the church. To understand how these religious messages played themselves out politically, we need to supplement discussions of sermons by paying attention to the rhetoric of the political and community leaders of the day, particularly as they spoke or wrote about ostensibly secular issues. Such rhetoric appears in political pamphlets and newspapers of the time. But it also shows up in a newly emerging form of public address: the political oration. The reason this form of rhetoric should attract our attention, at least initially, is because of its increasing popularity at this time, from its beginnings in 1771 as the Boston political elite used the March 5, 1770, "Boston Massacre" to express their outrage at British actions. The commemoration became an annual event until 1783 when, with the conclusion of hostilities, it was replaced with an official Fourth of July celebration. Other occasions, including commemorations of the Pilgrim landing, would further promote this spread of political oratory.

These speeches increasingly became "events": widely publicized, well attended by an increasingly diverse and politically active crowd,[13] and widely distributed in print, reaching the most remote of areas.[14] The orations appear to us now as cultural artifacts in which orators, as they attempted to speak in a publicly accessible language, drew upon (and in the process modified) popular images of the time. In this way, we are likely to see a blending of different images as orators were constrained neither by the religious message of sermons nor the formal prose of legal treatise. As we look at one such recurring image, that of the Puritans and Pilgrims, we see the crafting of this legacy into a part of a much broader political, legal, and ideological discourse that served to legitimate the premises and promises of the American Revolution.

Considerable effort has been expended in identifying these premises, with much of that energy directed toward arguing for the predominance of one idiom over another in the structuring of revolutionary discourse. So a whole scholarship has developed around showing how a "peculiar inheritance of thought" provided an ideological guise through which the colonists viewed the world.[15] Perhaps the most sophisticated methodological statement of this approach comes from J. G. A. Pocock, who, in his influential study of the "Atlantic republican tradition," describes a republican language that unites Florentine, English, and American thought and, to a large extent, structures it as "threads in the pattern."[16] Though at various times arguing against a "binary reading of the debate" between liberal and civic republican scholarship and suggesting that his real desire is to understand the "plurality of languages interacting in a giving society," Pocock's approach seems, at critical times, to undercut this claim.[17] He writes, for example, in assessing the liberal argument, that "The interpretation put forward by Bailyn and Wood altogether replaces that of Boorstin and Hartz, who seem to have held that there was no ideology in America, because ideology could be produced only by Old World social tensions which had not been transplanted."[18] This statement seems as ungenerous to Boorstin and Hartz as others have been to Pocock, for if there is one argument that Hartz does make, it is that liberalism becomes "fixed" and "dogmatic" and that liberalism, as it posits a particular set of values and orientations, "shapes the outcome" of different struggles, specifically the struggles between old Whig and new democrat.[19] Such claims would seem to arise from Pocock's notion of idioms as necessarily agonistic. He suggests, for example, that by "imputing 'paradigm' status to "Machiavellian discourse,'" he was not foreclosing the possibility of other paradigms; only that "any alternative 'paradigm' would find it difficult to grow up, would have to compete for paradigm status by means of an intensively contested dialogue with the pre-existing discourse. . . ."[20]

We can agree with Pocock that "patterns of language and thought" both constrain "thinkers as agents in the world of speech" and are, in turn, modified "by the speech-acts they perform."[21] But to assume that these patterns must thereby be in conflict is to anticipate how the colonial mind structured the world. We can provide some test of Pocock's hypothesis, not by burrowing another historical tunnel, but by exploring the meanings and associations that become embedded in the image of the Puritans. What we should discover, following Pocock, is either a fairly consistent ideological framework or a hotly contested one. What we in fact discover, as we look at invocations of the Puritans, is neither a consistent perceptual model that structured the thinking of individuals nor contested paradigms but a complex association of words and meanings, of both a Lockean and a republican language, combined in a discursive space.[22]

This should not surprise us completely, as the colonists were exposed to a plurality of views, and colonial writings themselves were littered with references to Locke, Sidney, Burgh, Bolingbroke, Trenchard and Gordon, Harrington, Blackstone, Hoadly, and Hutchinson, to name only the most prominent figures. To examine more fully the nature of this revolutionary discursive space, I will look at how the Puritans were used to provide a Lockean justification for rebellion, one founded on a "right of soil." But alongside these Lockean expressions was a republican language of civic virtue and corruption that was also read into a Puritan past. The result, as we look at the language that surrounds this invocation of the Puritans, is neither a grand synthesis nor the predominance of one idiom, but a mingling of a Lockean notion that gave civic meaning to the Puritan insular self with a republican notion of organic community, a mingling that resulted in an ambivalence in revolutionary rhetoric toward the nature of authority.

Liberalism

The sense that American political thought rested on a Lockean foundation had been the consensus of scholarship for at least a century.[23] Critical to this conception was the idea that legitimate authority was grounded in the consent of individuals and that government existed primarily to secure private rights, including (or, perhaps, particularly) those of property. Though Locke's emphasis on individual rights and the liberty of conscience seems far afield from the repressiveness of seventeenth-century American Puritanism, the overthrow of the Andros regime and, later, the Great Awakening provided a foundation of popular assertiveness that made a synthesis of Lockean ideas with Puritan images much more of a possibility, if not a necessity, for the Puritan ministers.[24]

Lockean ideas did not come to American shores in isolation but were read alongside traditional Puritan tracts and were often placed in the context of a prior experience of tyranny under the Andros regime.[25] In one of the first examples of the intermingling of Lockean individualism and Puritanism, the Congregationalist minister John Wise, who in 1687 had led Ipswich in a protest against the tax policy of Governor Andros, wrote in 1717 of reason as making the individual the authority for his own actions. The "Dictate of Right Reason" is "founded in the Soul of Man." So Wise reasoned, "That which is to be drawn from Mans Reason, flowing from the true Current of that Faculty, when unperverted, may be said to be the Law of Nature; on which account, the Holy Scriptures declare it written on Mens hearts. For being indowed with a Soul, you may know from your self, how, and what you ought to act." Every person "must be conceived to be perfectly in his own Power and disposal, and not to be countrouled by the Authority of any other." This being the case, Wise drew the Lockean conclusion that "every Man has a Prerogative to Judge for himself, *viz.* What shall be most for his Behoof, Happiness and Well-being."[26] There were two important implications of Wise's arguments. First, the individual (subject to the dictates of God) was assumed to have authority over and responsibility for his or her own actions. Second, and perhaps more importantly, the end to which people could legitimately use this reason was in pursuit of their own happiness, one that was spiritual in origins as it depended on the proper ordering of the soul. It was a powerful idea that was to gain increased voice over the years, culminating in the Declaration of Independence.

Jonathan Mayhew, who declared the most important teachers of liberty to be "Sidney and Milton, Locke and Hoadly," provided an early statement of the Lockean basis of authority.[27] In his influential sermon on civil resistance on the anniversary of the execution of Charles I, Mayhew recited words reminiscent of Winthrop's speech before the General Court. Quoting from the apostle Peter, Mayhew suggested, "Since, therefore, magistracy is the ordinance of God, and since rulers are by their office benefactors to society, by discouraging what is bad and encouraging what is good, and so preserving peace and order amongst men, it is evident that ye ought to pay a willing subjection to them; not to obey merely for fear of exposing yourselves to their wrath and displeasure, but also in point of reason, duty, and conscience. Ye are under an indispensable obligation, as Christians, to honor their office, and to submit to them in the execution of it." The happiness of society required obedience to authority; disobedience was "political sin" and "a heinous offence against God and religion."[28]

Although Mayhew argued for submission to authority as both a political and religious necessity, it was an authority that had a Lockean foundation. Citing Biblical authority and drawing from the Puritan assertion that all societies are founded on covenant, Mayhew claimed that though all civil magistrates "are appointed and ordained of God," the "apostle plainly intimates that rulers derive their authority immediately not from God but from men."[29] It was an argument made by the Puritan John Wise earlier in the century and by Winthrop in his defense before the General Court in 1637.[30] Unlike Winthrop and Wise, though, who suggested that once the community had covenanted to form a government they agreed to submit to rulers for their own good, Mayhew argued that "the people" are the "proper judges" of when the ruler has properly executed the "trust" that exists between the government and the governed. Referring to Romans 13:8, traditionally used in defense of absolute secular authority, Mayhew suggested, instead, that "what these dues are, and to whom they are to be rendered, the Apostle saith not but leaves to the reason and consciences of men to determine." In Mayhew's most radical statement, he asserted that not only can one legitimately resist a tyrant, but it is one's "duty" to do so.[31] The individual, imbued with reason and bound to authority, was heralded as the most powerful check on tyranny.

As Locke gained wider circulation in the colonies, his thoughts (and often his exact words) were found in a growing number of sermons and speeches. The orthodox Congregationalist Elisha Williams, writing in response to a Connecticut law banning itinerant preachers, argued that "every Christian has *a Right of judging for himself* what he is to believe and practice in Religion" according to the rule of Scripture. (It should be noted that Williams believed that the right should extend only to Protestants.) As was common in those days, Williams extracted major portions of Locke's *Second Treatise* in advancing his argument. Like Wise, Williams suggested that "the *Freedom* of *Man* and *Liberty* of *acting* according to his own *Will* (without being subject to the Will of another) is grounded on his having *Reason*. . . ." Paraphrasing Locke, Williams wrote, "So that we are *born Free* as we are *born Rational*."[32] Williams, in an argument that would be drawn on extensively by the patriot preachers, took his argument still further by tying a Lockean notion of the inalienability of property to the purpose of government as providing protections to this property. Since "*every Man* having a *Property* in his own *Person*, the *Labour of his Body* and *the Work of His Hands* are properly his own, to which no one has Right but himself," so "*The great End of civil Government, is the Preservation of their Persons, their Liberties and Estates, or their Property.*"[33] Moses Mather would be one of many revolutionary ministers to make this sovereignty of the individual the basis for an attack on British actions. As "By nature, every man (under God) is his own legislator, judge, and avenger, and absolute lord of his property," so, according to Mather, he retains this voice in civil society.[34]

Locke did not simply enter the sermons of the Puritan ministers, though; Lockean liberalism would come to be associated by many with a Puritan past. It was no small interpretive feat to refashion the Puritans in Lockean garb. We have already seen the basis for this reinterpretation with such prerevolutionary historiographies as Daniel Neal's *The History of New England* and the *History of the Puritans*, but what we find in the political rhetoric of the revolutionary era is the elaboration of a Puritan inheritance, one that saw in the Puritan flight from Europe both a Lockean love of liberty and a government founded by compact.[35]

The image of the Puritans as a Lockean force of liberty would play a prominent role in the Boston Massacre orations of the revolutionary period. In the first commemoration of the massacre in 1771, James Lovell, the usher of the public Latin school in Boston, drawing upon the historiographic language of the period, recalled how the Puritan "fathers left their native land, risqued all the dangers of the sea, and came to this then savage desert" in pursuit of liberty. While the "brave spirit" of these founders "still exists in vigor," Lovell would add to this the notion that the Puritans served to provide a legal basis for colonial claims against England. Speaking to the issue of who has legal rights over the colonies, Lovell recalled how the Puritans, by entering into "mutual, sacred compact" with England, secured colonial legislative authority.[36] Now England threatened the colonists' birthright as Englishmen and as heirs of the Puritans.

Governor Hutchinson, who would remain a Loyalist, would take issue with this claim of a Puritan compact, a claim made not only by Lovell but by others. Hutchinson argued, instead, that the "charter, as well as the patent to the Council of Plymouth, constitutes a corporation in England, with powers to create a subordinate government or governments within the plantation, so that there would always be subjects of taxes and impositions both in the kingdom and in the plantation."[37] In response, the House of Representatives of Massachusetts not only reaffirmed the notion that the Puritans entered into "compact" with the king, but extended the argument made by Jeremiah Dummer in *A Defence of the New-England Charters* (London, 1721): "Mr. Dummer says, 'it seems reasonable enough to think that the crown,' and, he might have added, our ancestors, 'intended by this injunction to provide for all its subjects, they should be protected by the same mild laws, and enjoy the same happy government, as if they continued within the realm."[38]

In 1772, Joseph Warren, a Boston physician, would again draw upon the memory of the Puritans, this time placing them alongside ancient Rome in their attachment to a free constitution. For Warren, who is seen by scholars as typical of the revolutionary republican ideal,[39] the Puritans left England because they realized the impossibility of restoring "the free constitution of their native land" to "its pristine purity." But there is a Lockean sense that follows from this republican vocabulary.

Warren exalted the Puritans because they "fairly purchased" the Indian lands and "cultivated the then barren soil, by their incessant labor, and defended their dear-bought possessions with the fortitude of the christian, and the bravery of the hero." It was for this liberty, which rested first and foremost on freedom from arbitrary control over one's property, that the Puritans passed over the "rough ocean" to this "dreary wilderness" and "patiently bore the severest hardships" and "rugged toils." "Certainly," suggested Warren, "it never entered the hearts of our ancestors that, after so many dangers in this then desolate wilderness, their hard-earned property should be at the disposal of the British parliament." Calling on this inheritance, Warren implored the audience to never part with this sacred dedication to liberty: "Stain not the glory of your worthy ancestors." Warren concluded his oration by pointing to their inheritance as God's favored people, a covenant that Perry Miller has identified as operating in the colonial mind.[40] If "with united zeal and fortitude" the colonists would "oppose the torrent of oppression," then "the same Almighty Being who protected your pious and venerable forefathers—who enabled them to turn a barren wilderness into a fruitful field, who so often made bare his arm for their salvation, will still be mindful of you, their offspring."[41] In 1775 Warren issued a more militant call for action: "Our fathers having resolved never to wear the yoke of despotism, and seeing the European world, at that time, through indolence and cowardice, falling a prey to tyranny, bravely threw themselves upon the bosom of the ocean, determined to find a place in which to enjoy their freedom, or perish in the glorious attempt."[42]

Samuel Adams, too, in a popular revolutionary pamphlet would recount "our Ancestors" who "came over to this Country" so that they "might not only enjoy their civil but their religious rights." The immediate issue was attempts by England, as Adams and other colonists saw it, to "establish an American Episcopate."[43] What Adams was referring to was the creation of the Society for the Propagation of the Gospel, an Anglican organization ostensibly designed to spread the gospel to Indians. Such attempts were passionately denounced in the colonial press, as in one cartoon that appeared in 1769, entitled "An Attempt to Land a Bishop in America." The cartoon, which reminds us again of how Puritan and Lockean tracts were read side-by-side, shows bishops retreating to England by ship, with a crowd yelling "Calvin's Works," "liberty and freedom of conscience," and "Locke."[44]

Adams, who at other times would sound like a republican, would also invoke these same ancestors, as did Warren, as having established a *"right of Soil"* by earlier grants, purchases, and labors in cultivating the land.[45] In fact, this notion of an inheritance of Lockean rights and property became a refrain of a number of pamphlets. James Otis would talk of the "sufferings" of "Our fore-fathers" who toiled "on their little plantations," thinking that they "were earning a sure inheritance for the posterity."[46] So, too, in a pamphlet published from New York to South Carolina, William Hicks appropriated the image of the Puritans as landing in "the deserts of America" so that they may "dispose of their acquired property" by their, rather than English, purposes.[47] And a resolution by the Continental Congress to take up arms explained the "justice of our cause" by describing how "Our forefathers, inhabitants of the island of Great Britain, left their native land, to seek on these shores a residence for civil and religious freedom. At the expence of their blood, at the hazard of their fortunes, without the least charge to the country from which they removed, by unceasing labor, and an unconquerable spirit, they effected settlements in the distant and inhospitable wilds of America, then filled with numerous and warlike nations of barbarians."[48]

In a later oration, Silas Downer, a Providence lawyer, noted how "Our forefathers" had "endured all sorts of miseries and hardships" to escape the "unnatural oppressions" of England. It was in this new world that the Puritans "hoped and expected that the blessing of freedom would be the inheritance of their posterity, which they preferred to every other temporal consideration." Speaking for the nonimportation of British goods, Downer noted, "Should these our noble ancestors arise from the dead, and find their posterity trucking away that liberty, which they purchased at so dear a rate, for the mean trifles and frivolous merchandize of *Great Britain*, they would return to the grave with a holy indignation against us." Downer called for all to take every action to preserve their inheritance. "We cannot, we will not, betray the trust reposed in us by our ancestors, by giving up the least of our liberties."[49]

Trust, indeed. The Lockean founding allowed the colonists to frame the struggle as a recovery of an original compact, a compact to which the Puritans were the original parties and the colonists, as inheritors of the trust, were the aggrieved party. This Lockean founding served as a hortatory device as well, a call in a time in which filial piety was still persuasive, to live up to the pious struggle for liberty won with such difficulty by the Puritans. In declaring their independence, the colonists would create a Lockean past.

Republicanism

A substantial body of contemporary scholarship has sought to minimize the influence of Lockeanism in America and has argued, instead, for the primacy of civic humanism or radical Whig thought in the colonial mind.[50] Stated in its simplest form, this republican tradition emphasized the cultivation of civic virtue and the maintenance of liberty through the corporate pursuit of the public good.[51] In speaking this language, the colonists would draw on the classical language of Cicero who wrote of "service to the state" as "the most glorious function of the wise and the chief mark or duty of the good."[52] Or they could find in Machiavelli that "it is not individual prosperity, but the general good, that makes cities great," a general good achievable only with a willingness by the people to sacrifice and dedicate themselves to "the life and liberty of the country."[53] But what the colonists read most widely, and what is seen as most influential in shaping colonial thought, are the writings of the radical Whigs, critics of the English "Court" and ministerial corruption. Figuring most prominently were the works of Lord Bolingbroke, John Trenchard and Thomas Gordon, and the more contemporaneous works of James Burgh, Richard Price, and Joseph Priestly.[54]

What united these writers, argues Bailyn, was "their obsessive concern" with ministerial corruption as the "Court," through bribery, venality, and manipulation, was seen as wresting control of government from the hands of Parliament. "Everywhere, they agreed, there was corruption—corruption technically, in the adroit manipulation of Parliament by a power-hungry ministry, and corruption generally, in the self-indulgence, effeminizing luxury, and gluttonous wealth." This preoccupation with corruption underlies what Bailyn suggests was a colonial "theory of politics" in which power, as it inherently seduces those who hold it, stood opposed to liberty. Power corrupted as it stirred within individuals a natural lust for domination. This theory, it is suggested, would provide a "framework" for a colonial sense of themselves as "independent, uncorrupted, landowning yeoman farmers" who were threatened by the "venal surrogates" of a corrupt British ministry.[55]

Less clear is what defines the contours of this framework. Republicanism, as a revolutionary ideology, appears to stand for anything and mesh with everything: a notion of human nature as sinful,[56] as having "selfish proclivities,"[57] as being "malleable";[58] a notion of authority that is at once hierarchical,[59] egalitarian (at least latently),[60] and easily blended with "a libertarian context";[61] and a hope for the future premised on both religious regeneration[62] and an enlightened sensibility in which humans rationally order their community life.[63] One can see the looseness of this vocabulary, for example, in Pocock's identification of a republican discourse with the dialectic of "virtue" and "corruption" as the terms of this dialectic are continually redefined to keep the tradition "alive." It becomes difficult to envision what would not be included in this republican dialectic, an envisioning which Pocock himself states would be "hard to imagine." Some indication of the all-encompassing nature of this dialectic can be seen when he casts the "post-behavioral revolution" as still fitting within the republican "language of jeremiad."[64]

In tracing a particular idiom, by engaging in "tunnel history,"[65] there is a tendency to try to fit historical statements into particular idiomatic categories, creating an artificial sense of discursive continuity. What I want to do is locate this republican language not in isolation from, but as it interacts with, other idioms. To draw on a metaphor used by Pocock, rather than tracing a "thread" in the web of discourse, I am attempting to identify the space of that discourse by examining the connections and contours that comprise that web. What I want to suggest is that around the specific image of the Puritans, and the more general concern with corruption, we see not a theory of politics but an association of seemingly contending notions of authority united more by an effort to legitimate the American Revolution than by any theoretical or ideological consistency.[66] My efforts to depict the irresolute nature of this colonial discursive space will proceed as follows: First, I will look at the writings of the radical Whigs and suggest that we cannot distill from their writings a unified theory of politics about the nature of authority. The reason for this is that they did not posit a neat dichotomy between ministerial corruption and yeoman innocence. Instead, as corruption was seen as imminent in all individuals, we see recourse to either the hierarchical impulse of Bolingbroke or the strict, moralistic individualism of Burgh.[67] Second, I will return to colonial rhetoric and show how this ambivalence was reflected in invocations of a Puritan past. A significant aspect of the colonists' rhetoric consisted of concerns with their own corruption, not as something potential that becomes expressed in instances of power but as something that is imminent in human action. This concern with corruption was often expressed in a language of patriotism but was illustrated as a backsliding from the civic virtues of a Puritan past. In the final section, I will look at specific examples of colonial rhetoric and show how, by way of a Puritan past, a republican language of civic community was placed alongside a Lockean language of rights.

The Radical Whigs and the Rhetoric of Corruption

When James Burgh, in the preface to his *Political Disquisitions*, specifically rejected any suggestion that it was his "design to form a *system* of politics," we should take such warnings seriously.[68] *Disquisitions*, indeed, reads more as a compilation of Opposition writings, including those of Bolingbroke and Trenchard and Gordon, than as a theory of politics. Distilling a political theory from radical Whig thought becomes a somewhat elusive project, for although the Whigs were united in their criticisms of English ministerial power, they disagreed in fundamental ways about the proper structuring of authority relations. We get some sense of this as we look at the works of Trenchard and Gordon, Bolingbroke, and Burgh, Opposition writers who were among the most widely read and quoted by colonists.

John Trenchard and Thomas Gordon, authors of the popular *Cato's Letters*, perhaps come the closest to capturing an egalitarian spirit as they rested political authority on a faith in the natural simplicity of the people. Trenchard and Gordon, like other radical Whigs, traced a general decline in morals to ministerial corruption. The ministers, as they "promote Luxury, Idleness, and Expence, and a general Depravation of Manners, by their own Example, as well as by Connivance and publick Encouragement," will free an otherwise virtuous people "from all the Restraints of private and publick Virtue. From Immorality and Excesses they will fall into Necessity; and from thence into a servile Dependence upon Power."[69] Virtue was upheld through the proper construction of laws, the protection of liberty, and the promotion of equality. "Where Liberty is thoroughly established, and its Laws equally executed, every Man will find his Account in doing as he would be done unto, and no Man will take from another what he would not part with himself: Honour and Advantage will follow the Upright, Punishment overtake the Oppressor." What had to be guaranteed was liberty that would allow the individual to develop habits of industry, frugality, and simplicity. Just as corruption could be traced to tyranny, so "all Civil Virtue and Happiness, every moral Excellency, all Politeness, all good Arts and Sciences, are produced by Liberty. . . ."[70] There is in this solution a notion that people, but for the allurement of power, are naturally virtuous. "Let People alone, and they will take Care of themselves, and do it best," wrote Gordon. Statesmen were no more capable of administering the state than the commonfolk, as suggested by Cincinnatus who "was taken from the Plough to save and defend the *Roman* state; an Office which he executed honestly and successfully, without the Grimace and Gains of a Statesman." The "People" were seen to have "natural Qualifications equal to those of their Superiors; and there is oftener found a great Genius carrying a Pitch-fork, than carrying a White Staff."[71]

Lord Bolingbroke, too, spoke of the "degeneracy of our age," which he viewed as arising out of ministerial corruption and the rise of commercial interests.[72] Unlike Trenchard and Gordon, though, Bolingbroke saw the masses as passionate and easily corrupted. Government itself, notes Bolingbroke, arose out of the "depravity of multitudes" who are "designed to obey" the "few designed to govern."[73] Thus, Bolingbroke would argue for a more nostalgic, hierarchical conception of authority in which virtue rested with the "landed men," whom he saw as the "true owners of our political vessel."[74]

James Burgh would invoke neither the "country" nostalgia of Bolingbroke nor the egalitarian spirit of Trenchard and Gordon but, instead, as Isaac Kramnick has persuasively argued, would express a "self-consciously more urban, more middle-class, more definitively individualistic Protestant orientation."[75] In the opening of *The Dignity of Human Nature* (1754), Burgh portrayed the activities of a corrupt luxury class: "While a continual round of idle and expensive amusements fill up the bulk of our time, and is looked upon as the very Dignity of High Life; while the rage of gaming is carried to an excess beyond example, so that even the sacred day of rest brings no rest from that endless drudgery, and children in their non-age are, to the disgrace of common sense, initiated by matters hired for the purpose, and furnished with printed systems of the liberal science of card-playing; while the grand study of people of rank is, How to drown thought. . . ."[76] The problem for Burgh was that such luxury was corrosive: "Where riot and luxuries are not discountenanced, the inferior rank of men become presently infected, and grow lazy, effeminate, impatient of labour, and expensive, and, consequently, cannot thrive by trade and tillage. . . ."[77]

But Burgh was less than gracious in his depiction of human nature, as well. He opened his *Political Disquisitions* by suggesting that "man, whom we dignify with the honourable title of *Rational*," is "much more frequently influenced, in his proceedings, by supposed interest, by passion, by sensual appetite, by caprice, or by anything, by nothing, than by reason." For that reason, we see not a libertarian impulse but a claim that "in all civilized ages and countries" it has "been found proper to frame laws and statutes fortified by sanctions, and to establish orders of men invested with authority to execute those laws, and inflict the deserved punishments upon the violators of them."[78] Such laws should include severe taxation on "whatever tends to the increase of luxury and extravagance" while allowing "industry and frugality [to] escape free." And there was also a call for personal reform of one's character: the paying of debts, keeping of promises and trusts, and the necessity of those in "high stations" who were in a position to serve the public interest to perform their duties with patriotism.[79] On both these scores, the American Puritans even get mentioned by Burgh as promoting the "education of their planters; which, if not entirely virtuous, has a show of virtue."[80]

Read on their own terms, the radical Whigs did not provide anything like a theory of politics or a consistent paradigm for understanding political authority. Certainly, radical Whig writings were read as justifying an opposition to a corrupt English rule. But alongside republicanism, whatever its variants, was read a Puritan past that gave to the revolutionary promise the anxiety of sin.[81] We see the rhetorical invocation of a Puritan past used to make communally culpable a revolutionary generation that had become corrupt.

A Republican Inheritance
To the Puritans the colonists would credit not only their apprehensiveness "and aversion to lordships, temporal and spiritual"[82] but republican virtues of simplicity and frugality that were besieged by a corrupt and corrupting force. Perhaps the most extended discussion of this connection came from John Adams in his "Dissertation on the Canon and Feudal Law," an essay that first appeared in the *Boston Gazette* in response to the Stamp Act. After demonstrating how the Puritans embodied Enlightenment ideals, Adams went on to show how they undertook a moral struggle against tyranny. On one side was evil: the "age of darkness," the "dark ribaldry of hereditary, indefeasible right" in which "the priesthood had enveloped the feudal monarch in clouds and mysteries." Against this corruption, this confusion and darkness, were the forces of enlightened virtue. Contrary to the reign of popery and monarchy, the Puritans established a system of government that was "a plain, simple, intelligible thing, founded in nature and reason, and quite comprehensible by common sense." Although Adams did not discuss in any detail the particular form of government established by the Puritans, he did point out that

popular power (by this, Adams meant power for property hold-
ers, not mass democracy) served under the Puritans as "a
guard, a control, a balance, to the powers of the monarch and
the priest," and that the clergy were made independent of the
civil powers, left to their own "industry, virtue, and piety."[83]

The "ardor for liberty and thirst for knowledge" underlay
this Puritan inheritance. Adams depicted the Puritans as the
transmitters of courage and glory, and the colonists as the re-
cipients of a proud inheritance. In so doing, Adams elevated
the Puritans and, in particular, the Puritan passage across the
ocean to a new land, to almost mythic proportions: noble goals,
success against almost insurmountable odds, heroic. Adams
began the legend:

> Let us read and recollect and impress our souls the views and ends of
> our own more immediate forefathers, in exchanging their native coun-
> try for a dreary, inhospitable wilderness. Let us examine into the na-
> ture of that power, and the cruelty of that oppression, which drove
> them from their homes. Recollect their amazing fortitude, their bit-
> ter sufferings,—the hunger, the nakedness, the cold, which they pa-
> tiently endured,—the severe labors of clearing their grounds, build-
> ing their houses, raising their provisions, amidst dangers from wild
> beasts and savage men, before they had time or money or materials
> for commerce. Recollect the civil and religious principles and hopes
> and expectations which constantly supported and carried them
> through all hardships with patience and resignation. Let us recollect
> it was liberty, the hope of liberty for themselves and us and ours,
> which conquered all discouragements, dangers and trial.[84]

Adams was not simply telling a story. He was speaking the language of tradition as he implored his listeners to recall the
meaning of their ancestry, even as he created it, so that they
might act as inheritors of the tradition. Just as the Puritan
ancestors were imbued with a sense of liberty, so the colonists
must cultivate that same spirit. Just as the founders braved
great odds in their fight for liberty, so the task facing the
Americans more than a century later would require courage.

Like their Puritan ancestors, Adams suggested, the colonists
were currently besieged by evil. Adams saw in British actions
"a direct and formal design on foot, to enslave America." By
imposing the Stamp Act, England was seeking to establish the
canon and feudal law in America, to "strip us in a great mea-

sure of the means of knowledge, by loading the press, the colleges, and even an almanack and a newspaper, with restraints and duties; and to introduce the inequalities and dependencies of the feudal system, by taking from the poorer sort of people all their little subsistence, and conferring it on a set of stamp officers, distributors, and their deputies."[85] England was placed on the side of Roman Catholicism, tyranny, ignorance, and cruelty, and against the side of the Puritans, Reformation, the Enlightenment, liberty, learning, and humaneness. To lose to England was to sacrifice virtue, liberty, and dignity.

Other orators would give to America's Puritan past not just a republican, but a Roman hue. Thomas Dawes, for example, suggested that "Like the gods, our first fathers had but few desires, and those to be satisfied by the works of virtue." The image Dawes drew upon was that of Marcus Aurelius who, "in imitating the gods," strove to "have as few wants as possible."[86] Joseph Warren, whom we have already encountered depicting the Puritans as Lockeans, also recast Winthrop's warning aboard the *Arbella* that if their venture fails they will "be made a story and a by-word through the world" into a republican concern with corruption.[87] Recalling the decline of Rome, but echoing the concerns of Winthrop, Warren noted how Rome "stands to this day, the scorn and derision of nations." What Rome demonstrated was that "public happiness depends on virtuous and unshaken attachment to a free constitution," this same attachment "founded on free and benevolent principles, which inspired the first settlers of this country."[88]

Although American statesmen and ministers assumed the mantle of innocence under attack from a corrupt England, such claims of innocence should be read as exoneration from punishment by England and not as a guiltlessness before God. In fact, such claims of innocence were often tempered by a sense of pervasive sin.[89] Notes Shain, in his discussion of the "Calvinist" foundation of revolutionary thought, only a "handful" of the American elite were willing to concede that "humans might have had more of an inner light" than suggested by reformed doctrine, "but no prominent American has been shown to have thought that people were born free of the deformed and selfish nature so aptly described by the dogma of original sin."[90] Indeed, notions of sin would assume prominence in a colonial vocabulary, as suggested by the thousands of sermons spoken and published for a wide readership[91] and by the intermingling of religion and education. This intermingling is attested to by the practice of appointing ministers as presidents of colleges,[92] by the literature,[93] newspaper correspondence and diaries,[94] and by the political pronouncements, such as days of thanksgiving and humiliation.[95] My interest here is not to recount these pronouncements but to show how a Puritan past was invoked to articulate a sense of sin.

After justifying rightful possession of the colonial lands based on Puritan deeds, thus providing what we have already seen as a Lockean response to a long-running legal argument, Samuel Webster, in a typical denunciation of America's sins, decried the wickedness of a chosen people. Despite God's favoring of America, "we have been, and still are, an evil and unthankful people. And I fear we grow worse after all our mercies. Wickedness of almost every kind, I fear, prevail'd more than ordinarily." Webster, like his Puritan predecessors as well as his contemporaries, recited the litany of sins:

> What filthiness & uncleanness among our youth, till many are become a derision!—What intemperance—What injustice & oppression! What lying and backbiting! What unchristian strife & contention in towns and churches! What thefts and burglaries—Yea, what murders are found among us! 'Tis endless to reckon them up—it cannot be done![96]

Individual sin translated into communal culpability. In a popular sermon of the time, the president of Harvard College, Samuel Langdon, declared, "But, alas! have not the sins of America, and of New England in particular, had a hand in bringing down upon us the righteous judgments of Heaven?" As men and women were held accountable for their actions, any punishments by a righteous God for dereliction were thereby just. "However unjustly and cruelly we have been treated by man," Langdon continued, "we certainly deserve, at the hand of God, all the calamities in which we are now involved."[97] In a sermon delivered a few weeks after the closing of the Boston port, Nathaniel Niles, an eastern Connecticut minister and future legislator, spoke of how "we have reason to fear some almost unparalleled calamity" because of the backsliding of the colonists. "Let us learn to live in the plain manner of our fore-fathers," declared Niles, invoking the memory of the Puritans. The "rich inheritance" left by our predecessors had been "wasted" in "riotous living. Let us soon return to our father's house, least we be reduced to the want, even of husks to eat."[98]

This language of sin would find its way into governmental and personal correspondence, as well. As the colonies entered into hostilities with the British, the political rhetoric turned both more militant (calling for separation from rather than conciliation with England) and self-condemning. The Council of Watertown's Proclamation of a day of Thanksgiving, in keeping with the Puritan tradition, recited the litany of God's "judgments," including the burning of towns, the closing of seaports, and the spread of sickness, and pleaded for mercy from "an ungrateful people."[99] Similarly, in reenacting the Puritan practice of a day of humiliation, the Continental Congress called for "a day of public humiliation, fasting, and prayer; that we may, with united hearts and voices, unfeignedly confess and deplore our many sins" and "humbly" beseech God to "forgive our iniquities, to remove our present calamities, [and] to avert those desolating judgments, with which we are threatned. . . ."[100] John Adams' wife, Abigail, used this Puritan voice in her private correspondence. The difficulties facing Boston following the closing of the port, according to Abigail, reflected God's punishment of a sinful people. "I greatly fear that the arm of treachery and violence is lifted over us, as a scourge and heavy punishment from Heaven for our numerous offenses, and for the misimprovement of our great advantages." In this time of crisis, Mrs. Adams invoked the Puritans as a model of purity. If the colonies were to "inherit the blessings of our fathers," they will need to return to the Puritans' "primitive simplicity of manner."[101]

The orations of the day also drew frequently on this notion of human depravity. Jonathan Mason, a prominent lawyer, speaking on the anniversary of the Boston massacre, decried "the want of patriotism" that has led us "to weep over the wanton massacre of innocent men."[102] Sounding a similar theme, the New York legislature warned that "internal discord," "pusillanimous impatience under unavoidable burthens," an "immoderate attachment to perishable property," and "intemperate jealousy" of government officials risked undermining all that "our hardy ancestors traversed the trackless ocean to seek in the wilds of the new world"; namely, "a refuge from the oppressions of the old."[103] Faced with setbacks in the battlefield, as well as problems of recruitment and supply for the militia, Thomas Dawes warned of "that langour which, like a low hung cloud, overshadows a great part of the thirteen states." The moment was a "crisis pregnant with fate and ready to burst with calamity."[104]

By first locating the image of the Puritans in revolutionary discourse, we have been able to gain a sense of the contours of the space that surround it. What we see are not only a number of different associations made to the Puritan past, but intimations that colonial discourse drew upon, and mixed together, the languages and assumptions of both Lockeanism and civic republicanism. It is around the idea of corruption that we will see in the next section not a unified theory of power that structured this revolutionary space but an ambivalence about the nature of authority.[105] In justifying their resistance, colonists could point to a corrupt and tyrannical English ministry. Authority to resist this corruption, as we saw in Mayhew's famous sermon, was vested in the individual. But when the question arose as to what constituted good government, we will see articulated a different notion of authority in which individuals were incorporated into a corporate body. As corruption was seen as an inherent aspect of the human character, this body appears more hierarchical and regulatory of human behavior. We see this ambivalence about the nature of colonial innocence played out in Franklin's and Jefferson's proposed seals, as the Israelites were both righteous in their fleeing from Egyptian bondage and wary of their sinfulness in their efforts to establish a new community. And we see this ambivalence in revolutionary rhetoric as a Puritan past provided a rhetorical space in which a Lockean language of rights was placed alongside a republican language of a civic body.

Liberalism and Republicanism: The Space of Authority

Though it is recognized, by proponents of liberal and republican interpretations alike, that one can identify a number of different "sources and traditions" in colonial thought, these different traditions are often treated as either mutually incompatible strands or are subsumed into one or another dominant strand.[106] Thus, Bailyn sees radical Whig thought as bringing "these disparate strands of thought together" and shaping them "into a coherent whole."[107] In a discussion of Congregational political thought, Kuehne recognizes in his introduction the diverse philosophic strands that informed revolutionary discourse. Yet, he sees the Congregationalists as recasting their political theory, which had rested on a faith in the English Constitution, into a "state-of-nature theory."[108] And Shain, though defining discrete strands that informed colonial thought, seeks to identify which strand "was preeminent and provided the foundation for American political thought."[109]

Located around the invocation of a Puritan past, though, is neither the incorporation of these separate strands into a coherent whole nor a recognition of the incompatibility of the strands, but a merging of a Lockean and republican language that spoke to a colonial ambivalence toward authority. It is, perhaps not coincidentally, a similar ambivalence that we saw emerge in the early Puritan communities as they sought to reconcile the claims of the insular individual with those of the hierarchic community.

Abraham Williams, a Congregational minister, provided an early and what would later become a quite conventional appropriation of the language of liberalism and republicanism in an election sermon on the eve of the Stamp Act. Government arose from the needs of self-preservation as individuals in the "State of Nature" came together to protect themselves and their property against the encroachments of others. As individuals "surrender" to the community their right to judge "in their own case," it becomes the "End and Design of civil Society and Government" to protect the "Rights and Properties" of its members secured through the "Fruits of [their] own Labour." The relationship, then, of the rulers to the ruled is that of a "Trust" in which the rulers assume the obligation to protect the rights of the community and individuals are "obliged in their private Stations and Occupations, to mind their own Business, with Industry, Frugality and Uprightness."[110]

But to these Lockean origins was appended a notion of the civic body. Though society originated in the state of nature, individuals "were formed for Society" and their "various Affections, Propensities and Passions" can be developed only through "social Intercourse." There is, thus, an interdependence posited by Williams that goes beyond the mutual protection of rights. "To a Man detached from all Society, many essential Parts of his Frame are useless—are troublesome," including not only material assistance but our "temporal Happiness." Moreover, Williams extended this image of the body to civil society. The end of civil society is not simply the protection of our rights but the maintenance of harmony, "*that the Members have the Care one for another, and there be no Schism in the Body.*" Though we are born equal, notes Williams in his Lockean moment, the harmony of society rests upon a functional inequality of its parts. "Every Person has his proper Sphere, and is of Importance to the whole; and the public Peace and Welfare is best secured and promoted, by every Member attending to the proper Business of his particular Station." Extending this notion of inequality again to the body, Williams writes: "A Society without different Orders and Offices, like a Body without Eyes, Hands, and other Members, would be uncapable of acting, either to secure its internal Order and Well-being, or defend itself from external Injuries."[111]

Underlying both this Lockean language of "trusts" and the more classical image of the "natural Body" is a notion of corruption. Civil society and government, argued Williams, were made necessary by "the *Depraved* Nature of Man, since the *Apostacy.*" Not only do people come together for mutual protection against the "*Envy, Ambition, Covetousness,* and *Sensuality*"of others, but it becomes the purpose of government "that the Unjust and Rapacious may be restrained, the ill Effects of their Wickedness be prevented, the secular Welfare of all be secured and promoted." The maintenance of such order rests ultimately on the incorporation of the individual into a hierarchical civic body, an incorporation, much like we saw in earlier Puritan political theory, to which the individual submits as a part of society.[112]

Samuel Sherwood's famous sermon on the eve of the Revolution pointed, as well, to these conflicting images of the Lockean individual and the hierarchical community. Sherwood argued, on the one hand, that societies "have their beginning and origin in voluntary compact and agreement" arising out of a "state of nature." Yet, in joining society, individuals become a part of "the body politic" which is "like the natural body." The potential implications of this Lockean appropriation seemed even to have struck the author, who in his introduction to the published sermon reaffirmed that he is a "firm friend to good order and regularity; that all ranks of men move in strait lines, and within their own proper spheres."[113]

Nathaniel Niles imagined a republican community in which all would "unite in the same grand pursuit, the highest good of the whole." In this dedication to the public body, "there would be no room for the emotions of any of the angry painful passions; but, on the contrary, every soft and pleasing affection of every soul, would be called forth into vigorous and harmonious exercise." Sounding more like Edwards than Trenchard at this juncture, Niles explained how each person "would choose to move in his proper sphere, and that all others should move in theirs. This would at once constitute pure felicity and exalted beauty. How *good* and how *pleasant* it is for brethren to dwell together in unity." But such a state "has never taken place, in perfection, in this world, nor will it hereafter." The reason for this, Niles continued, was because of "the perverseness of our selfish hearts, which prevents our pursuit and enjoyments of the delights of perfect liberty." There was, thus, a focus by Niles on the role of the legislature and executive in making and administering laws that "produce the highest good of the community," for good government "is essential to the very being of liberty."[114]

We can see this ambivalence between a liberty that derives from the authority of the insular self and a liberty born of submission to a corporate order in the 1780 Constitution of Massachusetts. One can get some sense of the backdrop to these constitutional discussions from an earlier proclamation by the General Court of Massachusetts that "Piety and Virtue . . . alone can Secure the Freedom of any People" and, thereby, called for both civil and religious leaders to punish "every Person" who commits "Debauchery, Prophaneness, Corruption, Venality, all riotous and tumultuous Proceedings" or who "shall be guilty of any Immoralities whatsoever."[115] In the 1780 Constitution and the accompanying address, there is a republican language of the "*whole Body* of the People" formed through

"social compact" and guided by "social affection." Such a social affection would bring "a greater Stability to any Constitution, and, in its operation, a greater Degree of Happiness to
the Society."[116] Yet, what comprises this body are "men" who
"are born free and equal, and have certain natural, essential,
and unalienable rights; among which may be reckoned the right
of enjoying and defending their lives and liberties; that of acquiring, possessing, and protecting property; in fine, that of
seeking and obtaining their safety and happiness."[117] This notion of pre-social rights that reside with the individual is reinforced by the prominence given to the constitutional provi-
sion guaranteeing the "free exercise of *the Rights of Conscience.*"
This must be read carefully, for what is suggested here is not a
notion of autonomy but of insularity. The public worship of
God remained "important to the happiness of Society" as it
"has a tendency to inculcate the Principles thereof, as well as
to preserve a People from forsaking Civilization, and falling
into a state of Savage barbarity." Excluded from holding office, though, were Catholics, precisely because "Spiritual Jurisdiction" resided with a Pope and not with the insular self
and, thus, was viewed as "subversive of a free Government established by the People."[118]

Samuel Cooper, minister of the Brattle Street Church and
one of the most prominent leaders of the revolutionary cause,[119]
speaking on the day of the implementation of the new Massachusetts constitution in 1780, brought together "the immortal
writings of Sidney and Locke." In exploring "this passage of
sacred writ," Cooper turned to another sacred government,
that of the Israelites. What he found, and this had become
quite common by this time, was "a free republic" in which "sovereignty resided in the people." Born of consent, the Massachusetts constitution was to be praised because it continued
to recognize that authority rested with the individual, that
"'These fields and these fruits are my own: The regulations
under which I live are my own; I am not only a proprietor in
the soil, but I am part of the sovereignty of my country.'"[120]

Although these Lockean fields may be his own, they were
not his to be tilled as he wished. For the liberty that Cooper
spoke of (and at this point he is true to Locke) was a godly life,
not a life of "licentiousness." Moreover, this community of sov-

ereign individuals was to be understood as a "political body" in which "the very vitals of the community" had to be protected from corruption within. What was needed, continuing this shift to a more republican language, was public virtue, "the true spirit of a commonwealth, centering all hearts, and all hands in the common interest." It is this spirit that will give the constitution "life and vigour to all its limbs" and "freshness and beauty to its whole complexion."[121] When asking about the legitimate exercise of power, Cooper returned to the Lockean foundations of the individual; when inquiring into the nature of good government, he drew upon republican notions of virtue and the political body. And in this merging of a Lockean and republican vocabulary, Cooper articulated what we saw earlier as a Puritan ambivalence toward the nature of authority, made more modern but no more resolute.

There is a messiness here that arises as orators and ministers drew not from discrete philosophic and theological strands—whether that be Lockeanism, republicanism, or Puritanism—but from a much more fluid discursive space. In this space, diverse images, symbols, questions, and ideas were combined with an ease that belies the difficulty of tracing their origins at this time. Thus, Warren and Adams invoked republican notions of civic responsibility and a Lockean concept of liberty, all cloaked within the inheritance of Puritanism. Benjamin Rush and Christopher Marshall, both evangelicals, opposed each other on the question of the regulation of prices for the good of the community. Whereas Rush spoke in a language of individual rights, Marshall envisioned communal responsibility as overriding self-interest.[122] Even a soldier, upon his decision to enlist, justified the war according to a vision of purity as well as an appeal to self interest.[123]

Interestingly, in tracing the revolutionary invocations of the Puritans, what figures much less prominently than is often assumed by scholars is the appearance of a providential language specifically associated with this Puritan past. Such language certainly existed, most obviously when Winthrop's words aboard the *Arbella*, "that wee shall be as a Citty upon a Hill, the eeies of all people are uppon us," were placed in service to the Revolution.[124] So the Massachusetts legislature would declare that "The eyes, not only of North America and the whole

British empire, but of all Europe, are upon you."[125] Announced Richard Henry Lee of Virginia in support of declaring independence, "the other nations of the globe, whose eyes are intent upon this great spectacle. . . anticipate from our success more freedom for themselves, or from our defeat apprehend heavier chains and a severer bondage."[126] "The eyes of Europe, nay of the world," stated John Rutledge of South Carolina, "are on America."[127] Jonathan Austin concurred when he remarked that "the eyes of the good and great, in every clime, are upon the present contest."[128] And David Ramsay declared, "The tyrants and landlords of the Old World, who hold a great part of their fellow men in bondage because of their dependence for land, will be obliged to relax of their arbitrary treatment, when they find that America is an asylum for free-men from all quarters of the globe."[129]

Liberty may, indeed, have been a sacred cause, but its explicit connection to a Puritan past is tenuous. As we look at specific invocations of the Puritans, we find not just this providential rhetoric of a chosen people, but a much richer set of associations. Incorporated into a Puritan legacy were Roman virtues, Lockean origins that gave a legal basis for colonial claims, and an ambivalence toward authority that would continue to find expression in the ensuing decades of American political discourse.

Notes

1 Richard Patterson and Richardson Dougall, *The Eagle and the Shield: A History of the Great Seal of the United States* (Washington, D.C.: Department of State, 1976), 14.

2 The source of this motto has been variously attributed to Cassius, John Bradshaw (President of the commission that sentenced Charles I), and Benjamin Franklin. Patterson and Dougall, *Eagle and the Shield*, 14 and B. J. Cigrand, *Story of the Great Seal of the United States or History of American Emblems* (Chicago: Camerson, Amberg & Co., 1892), 113. Jonathan Mayhew, "A Discourse Concerning Unlimited Submission and Non-Resistance to the Higher Powers" (Boston, 1750), in *The Pulpit of the American Revolution*, ed. John Wingate Thornton (Boston: Gould and Lincoln, 1860).

3 Du Simitiere proposed a seal consisting of an eye of Providence, the Goddess of Liberty, a Norman shield with a coat of arms of different nations that peopled America, and a liberty pole topped with a cap depicting the ancient symbol of liberty. The obverse side of Jefferson's first seal paid homage to the Saxons through the depiction of Hengist and Horsa, two warriors who had established the Saxons in England. John Adams chose Hercules for his seal. The final proposed seal was rejected. Five subsequent committees failed to please Congress, as well. Only in 1782 was a seal finally adopted.

4 Patterson and Dougall, *Eagle and the Shield*, 16.

5 See, for example, Jerald C. Brauer, who suggests that the language articulated by the Puritans was "merged with parallel, similar, and, at times, even dissimilar values and beliefs from other sources to produce a new ideology which formed and shaped the resistance of the American colonies against Crown and Parliament." "Puritanism, Revivalism, and the Revolution," in *Religion and the American Revolution*, ed. Jerald C. Brauer (Philadelphia: Fortress Press, 1976), 18. Nathan Hatch spends considerable time arguing against what he sees as a contemporary intellectual separation of the historical themes of religion and politics, "two conceptual worlds that for Revolutionary clergymen were never separate." See *The Sacred Cause of Liberty: Republican Thought and the Millennium in Revolutionary New England* (New Haven: Yale University Press, 1976), 58. As I will suggest, these two worlds were not completely separate for political leaders, either. For a recent exploration of law and religion as the two "dominant idioms of discourse, daily reiterated, practically applied and prominent partly by reason of being lastingly contested," see J. C. D. Clark, *The Language of Liberty 1660-1832: Political Discourse and Social Dynamics in the*

Anglo-American World (Cambridge: Cambridge University Press, 1994), 11. For a recent attempt to trace the role of reformed-Protestant thought in colonial political theory, see Barry Shain, *The Myth of American Individualism: The Protestant Origins of American Political Thought* (Princeton: Princeton University Press, 1994).

6   Perry Miller, "From the Covenant to the Revival," *The Shaping of American Religion*, eds. James Ward Smith and A. Leland Jamison (Princeton: Princeton University Press, 1961), 1: 341-2. Richard Brown, in his exploration of the communication networks of the clergy during this time, seems to modify this thesis by suggesting that, in general, the political concerns among rural clergy were generally subordinated to religious ones. Brown does point to exceptional figures, such as Reverend Jonas Clark, who, it is said, "led the community into Revolution." *Knowledge is Power: The Diffusion of Information in Early America, 1700-1865* (New York: Oxford University Press, 1989), 74.

7   Alan Heimert, *Religion and the American Mind from the Great Awakening to the Revolution* (Cambridge: Harvard University Press, 1966); Donald Weber, *Rhetoric and History in Revolutionary New England* (New York: Oxford University Press, 1988); Harry S. Stout, *The New England Soul: Preaching and Religious Culture in Colonial New England* (New York: Oxford University Press, 1986); and Shain, *Myth of American Individualism*. Stout devotes less than three pages to lay orations.

8   Hatch, *Sacred Cause*.

9   Sacvan Bercovitch, *The American Jeremiad* (Madison: University of Wisconsin Press, 1978).

10 Bernard Bailyn, *The Ideological Origins of the American Revolution* (Cambridge: The Belknap Press, 1967).

11 Gordon S. Wood, *The Radicalism of the American Revolution* (New York: Vintage, 1991), 330. This stands in contrast to an earlier statement of his: "To most of the Revolutionaries there was no sense of incompatibility in their blending of history, rationalism, and scripture; all were mutually reinforcing ways of arriving at precepts about human and social behavior. . . ." *The Creation of the American Republic, 1776-1787* (New York: Norton, 1969), 8. See also Oscar and Mary Handlin, "Introduction," *The Popular Sources of Political Authority: Documents on the Massachusetts Constitution of 1780* (Cambridge: Belknap Press, 1966), 53, when they write that the "rhetoric in the 1770's," apparently even of the ministers since this statement is a comment on a sermon, "no longer corresponds to the traditional contents [of Puritan theology]; instead it is used to express purely secular and rationalistic concepts."

12 Stout, *New England Soul*, 3-4.

13 See Robert Middlekauff, *The Glorious Cause* (New York: Oxford University Press, 1982), for a discussion of the development of a "more

varied participation in public life, and a more popular politics" (188). See also Gerd Hurm, "The Rhetoric of Continuity in Early Boston Orations," in *The Fourth of July: Political Oratory and Literary Reactions, 1776-1876*, eds. Paul Goetsch and Gerd Hurm (Tübingen: Narr, 1992), 64.

14   Fred Somkin, *Unquiet Eagle* (Ithaca: Cornell University Press, 1967), 9.

15   The phrase is from Bailyn, *Ideological Origins*, 95. Bailyn later writes that "these ideas" of "civic humanism" or "classical republicanism" were not felt by the colonists "to be incompatible with what would later be described as 'liberalism'" (*Faces of Revolution: Personalities and Themes in the Struggle for American Independence* [New York: Alfred A. Knopf, 1990], 206). Everyone engaged in this debate seems to recognize, at various moments, that "The major novelty and most important contribution of revisionary work has not been to deny that Revolutionary Americans and Jeffersonian Republicans were Lockean and liberal, but to demonstrate that liberal ideas were only part of their inheritance. . . ." See Lance Banning, "Jeffersonian Ideology Revisited: Liberal and Classical Ideas in the New American Republic," *The William and Mary Quarterly*, 3d series, 43 (January 1986), 12. But little concerted effort has been made to actually examine the relation of liberal and republican ideas in American rhetoric and thought. Some exceptions include Banning, "Jeffersonian Ideology"; James T. Kloppenberg, "The Virtues of Liberalism: Christianity, Republicanism, and Ethics in Early American Political Discourse," *The Journal of American History* 74 (June 1987): 9-33, and John L. Brooke, *The Heart of the Commonwealth: Society and Political Culture in Worcester County, Massachusetts 1713-1861* (Cambridge: Cambridge University Press, 1989).

16   J. G. A. Pocock, "*The Machiavellian Moment* Revisited: A Study in History and Ideology," *Journal of Modern History* 53 (March 1981), 52. In a less elegant form, two historians in their discussion of Federalism note that "ideas are simply *there*" and that individuals in the 1790s had to "choose one abstraction or the other," a Country or Court ideology. See Stanley Elkins and Eric McKitrick, *The Age of Federalism* (New York: Oxford University Press, 1993), 13, 24.

17   J. G. A. Pocock, "Between Gog and Magog: The Republican Thesis and the *Ideologia Americana,*" *Journal of the History of Ideas* (1987), 344-5.

18   J. G. A. Pocock, *The Machiavellian Moment: Florentine Political Thought and the Atlantic Republican Tradition* (Princeton: Princeton University Press, 1975), 509.

19   Louis Hartz, *The Liberal Tradition in America* (New York: Harcourt, Brace & World, 1955), 9, 18.

20   Pocock, "Between Gog and Magog," 345.

21   Pocock, "*Machiavellian Moment* Revisited," 50.

22   See also Joyce Appleby, "Republicanism and Ideology," *American Quarterly* 37 (Fall 1985): 461-73, for a critique of the methodological assumptions of republican revisionist scholarship.

23   For the two classic works on Locke's influence on early American thought, see Carl Becker, *The Declaration of Independence: A Study in the History of Political Ideas* (New York: Vintage, 1922) and Louis Hartz, *Liberal Tradition*. For more recent discussions of Locke's influence, see Joyce Appleby, *Liberalism and Republicanism in the Historical Imagination* (Cambridge: Harvard University Press, 1992); John P. Diggins, *The Lost Soul of American Politics: Virtue, Self-Interest, and the Foundations of Liberalism* (Chicago: University of Chicago Press, 1984); Jay Fliegelman, *Prodigals & Pilgrims: The American Revolution against Patriarchal Authority, 1750-1800* (Cambridge: Cambridge University Press, 1982); and Isaac Kramnick, *Republicanism and Bourgeois Radicalism: Political Ideology in Late Eighteenth-Century England and America* (Ithaca: Cornell University Press, 1990).

24   Cotton Mather, for example, in his biography of William Phips, provides an early justification for the overthrow of the "*Arbitrary Government*" of Andros. See "Magnalia Christi Americana," in *Selections From Cotton Mather*, ed. Kenneth Murdock (New York: Hafner, 1965), 175. For a weakening of deference in New England, see Stout, *New England Soul*; Perry Miller, *The New England Mind: From Colony to Province* (Cambridge: Harvard University Press, 1953), chapt. 22; and David D. Hall, *The Faithful Shepherd: A History of the New England Ministry in the Seventeenth-Century* (Chapel Hill: University of North Carolina Press, 1972). For a discussion of a similar transformation in "popular assertion" in a non-Puritan context, see Rhys Isaac, *The Transformation of Virginia, 1740-1790* (Chapel Hill: University of North Carolina Press, 1982), chaps. 9, 11-13.

25   Stout, *New England Soul*, 260.

26   John Wise, *A Vindication of the Government of New-England Churches* (Boston: J. Allen, for N. Boone, 1717), 34-5, 39.

27   Quoted in Bernard Bailyn, ed., *Pamphlets of the American Revolution, 1750-1776* (Cambridge: Belknap Press, 1965), 209. Mayhew serves as a good example of what I will later argue, namely, that the languages of Lockeanism and republicanism appear side-by-side in revolutionary discourse. Bailyn sees Mayhew as part of the republican tradition because he borrows from Hoadly (*Ideological Origins*, 52); Diggins sees him as drawing, at least in part, from a Lockean tradition because he borrows from Locke (*Lost Soul*, 33); and Appleby depicts him as part of the movement toward liberalism (*Liberalism and Republicanism*, 156-7).

28   Jonathan Mayhew, "Discourse," 58-9, 60.

29   Ibid., 56, 67. See Bernard Bailyn's discussion of Jonathan Mayhew in "Religion and Revolution: Three Biographical Studies," *Perspectives in American History* 4 (1970), 111-24.

30   See Wise, *Vindication*; John Winthrop, "A Defence of an Order of Court Made in the Year 1637," in *The Puritans: A Sourcebook of Their Writings*, eds. Perry Miller and Thomas Johnson (New York: Harper & Row, 1963), 199.

31   Mayhew, "Discourse," 87, 83, 79. See also [Stephen Case?], "Defensive Arms Vindicated" ([New-Marlborough], 1783), in *Political Sermons of the American Founding Era 1730-1805*, ed. Ellis Sandoz (Indianapolis: Liberty Press, 1991), 741.

32   Elisha Williams, "The essential Rights and Liberties of Protestants. A Seasonable Plea for The Liberty of Conscience, and The Right of private Judgment, in Matters of Religion. Without any Controul from human Authority. Being a Letter, from a Gentleman in the Massachusetts-Bay to his Friends in Connecticut" (Boston: S. Kneeland and T. Green, 1744), in *Puritan Political Ideas: 1558-1794*, ed. Edmund Morgan (Indianapolis: Bobbs-Merrill, 1965), 268, 270.

33   Williams, "Essential Rights," 271-2. See also Moses Mather, "America's Appeal to the Impartial World" (Hartford, 1775), in *Political Sermons*, ed. Sandoz, 444.

34   Moses Mather, "America's Appeal," 446. See also Samuel West, "On the Right to Rebel Against Governors . . . May 29, 1776" (Boston, 1776), in *Pulpit of the American Revolution*, ed. Thornton.

35   This answers to one criticism made by Pocock of current historiographic attempts to construct an American founding myth. There may have been "no scribes of the covenant," as Pocock suggests, but attempts to create them did not originate with modern historians. See "Between Gog and Magog," 337, 342.

36   James Lovell, "Oration, Delivered at Boston, April 2, 1771," in *Republication of the Principles and Acts of the Revolution in America*, ed. Hezekiah Niles (New York: A. S. Barnes, 1876), 17, 19.

37   "Speech to the Council and House of Representatives," Feb. 16, 1773, in *Republication of the Principles*, ed. Niles, 83.

38   See "Answer of the House of Representatives," March 2, 1773, in *Republication of the Principles*, ed. Niles, 88, 91. Samuel Adams, too, would invoke "Our Ancestors" as having secured the charter after the fall of the Andros regime that would protect colonial rights from unconstitutional taxation. See "A State of the Rights of the Colonists" (1772), in *Tracts of the American Revolution, 1763-1776*, ed. Merrill Jensen (In-

dianapolis: Bobbs-Merrill, 1967), 245. See also Stephen Hopkins, "The Rights of Colonies Examined," in *Tracts*, ed. Jensen, 43; and [William Goddard?], "The Constitutional Courant: Containing Matters Interesting to Liberty, and No Wise Repugnant to Loyalty," in *Tracts*, ed. Jensen, 81, in which the image of the ancestors as arriving in "uncultivated desarts" is invoked in developing this argument.

39 See, for example, Wood, *Creation of the American Republic*, 105.

40 See Perry Miller, "From the Covenant to the Revival."

41 Joseph Warren, "Oration, Delivered at Boston, March 5, 1772," in *Republication of the Principles*, ed. Niles, 20-4. See also Samuel Cooke, "A Sermon" (Boston, 1770), in *The Wall and the Garden: Selected Massachusetts Election Sermons 1670-1775*, ed. A. W. Plumstead (Minneapolis: University of Minnesota Press, 1968), 339. This same notion of the Puritans as proprietors of the land also appears in Warren's Boston massacre commemoration in 1775 and in a March 19, 1766, letter to Rev. Edmund Dann, Rector of Wroxeter, Salop, in England. See James Spear Loring, *The Hundred Boston Orators* (Boston: John P. Jewett and Co., 1854), 51. Warren would also employ a more republican notion of self-sacrifice in the name of the Puritans.

42 Warren, "Oration," 1775, in *Republication of the Principles*, ed. Niles, 25. See also Samuel West, "On the Right to Rebel," 310-1. Samuel Sherwood, too, in a famous Revolutionary War sermon, uses the Lockean assumption that "Property is prior to all human laws, constitutions and charters" to demonstrate that "Our fathers acquired property in this land, and were rightfully possessed of it." England, in this Lockean guise, appears as the breaker of a compact protecting this property. See "Scriptural Instructions to Civil Rulers" (New-Haven, 1774), in *Political Sermons*, ed. Sandoz, 398. The Lockean language of "trust," which proceeds on these same premises, would be used by many orators to justify resistance to Britain. See [Stephen Case?], "Defensive Arms Vindicated," 737. See also Samuel Cooke's famous election sermon following the Boston Massacre in which he states that "The people, the collective body only, have a right under God to determine who shall exercise this trust for the common interest, and to fix the bounds of their authority" ("A Sermon" [Boston, 1770], in *Wall and the Garden*, ed. Plumstead, 328).

43 Adams, "State of the Rights of the Colonists," 250.

44 See Kramnick, *Republicanism*, 181.

45 Adams, "State of the Rights of the Colonists," 251.

46 James Otis, "The Rights of the British Colonies Asserted and Proved," in *Tracts*, ed. Jensen, 23-4.

47   William Hicks, "The Nature and Extent of Parliamentary Power Considered" (1768), in *Tracts*, ed. Jensen, 169-70.

48   Continental Congress, "Declaration on Taking up Arms (July 6, 1775)," in *Journals of the Continental Congress, 1774-1789*, 34 vols. (Washington: Government Printing Office, 1905), 2: 142. See also 2: 156. This is remarkably similar to the language in a resolution entered into the Sept. 17, 1774, record of the Continental Congress by delegates of Suffolk in Massachusetts in reaction to what became known as the Intolerable Acts. See *Journals of the Continental Congress*, 1: 32: "And whereas, this, then savage and uncultivated desart, was purchased by the toil and treasure, or acquired by the blood and valor of those our venerable progenitors; to us they bequeathed the dearbought inheritance, to our care and protection they consigned it, and the most sacred obligations are upon us to transmit the glorious purchase, unfettered by power, unclogged with shackles, to our innocent and beloved offspring." See also, "The Petition Remonstrance and Address of the Town of Pittsfield to the . . . General Assembly," Dec. 26, 1775, in *Popular Sources of Political Authority*, eds. Handlin and Handlin, 61.

49   [Silas Downer], "A Discourse at the Dedication of the Tree of Liberty" [Providence, 1768], in *American Political Writings during the Founding Era: 1760-1805*, 2 vols., eds. Charles S. Hyneman and Donald S. Lutz (Indianapolis: Liberty Press, 1983), 1: 98, 107. Liberty is also associated with the "genuine spirit of our ancestors" in "The Constitutional Courant: Containing Matters Interesting to Liberty, and No Wise Repugnant to Loyalty," in *Tracts*, ed. Jensen, 85. The notion of the Puritans as providing an "asylum against despotism" that had been inherited by the colonists was often repeated. See "An Address by the State of Massachusetts Bay," Jan. 26, 1777, in *Republication of the Principles*, ed. Niles, 134-5; recollections of revolutionary war veterans in "Gathering of Connecticut Pensioners at Hartford," Aug. 7, 1820, in *Republication of the Principles*, ed. Niles, 151; "An Address from the Legislature of the State of New York, to their Constituents," March 13, 1781, in *Republication of the Principles*, ed. Niles, 186; and "Charge" by Judge Drayton to the Grand Jury, Oct. 21, 1777, Charleston, South Carolina, in *Republication of the Principles*, ed. Niles, 347, in which he speaks of the common basis of American religion in establishing "an asylum against despotism."

50   The classic statements of this argument are Caroline Robbins, *The Eighteenth-Century Commonwealthman: Studies in the Transmission, Development and Circumstance of English Liberal Thought from the Restoration of Charles II until the War with the Thirteen Colonies* (Cambridge: Harvard University Press, 1961); Bailyn, *Ideological Origins*; Wood, *Creation of the American Republic*; Pocock, *Machiavellian Moment* and his later article, *"The Machiavellian Moment* Revisited." See also Frank I. Michelman, "The Supreme Court 1985 Term," *Harvard Law Review* 100 (1986): 4-77, and Paul Rahe, *Republics Ancient and Modern: Classi-*

cal Republicanism and the American Revolution (Chapel Hill: University of North Carolina Press, 1992). For a review of this republican scholarship, see Robert E. Shalhope, "Republicanism and Early American Historiography," *William and Mary Quarterly*, 3d series, 39 (1982): 334-359; and *The Roots of Democracy: American Thought and Culture, 1760-1800* (Boston: Twayne, 1990). Shain, *Myth of American Individualism*, has argued, as well, against a notion of "individualism" in colonial thought, but has argued for reformed-Protestant thought, rather than republicanism, as forming the basis for a revolutionary language of community.

51   See Shain, *Myth of American Individualism*, 268-76.

52   Marcus Tullius Cicero, *On the Commonwealth*, trans. George H. Sabine and Stanley B. Smith (Indianapolis: Bobbs-Merrill, 1976), 126.

53   Niccolò Machiavelli, *The Prince and The Discourses* (New York: The Modern Library, 1950), 282, 528.

54   For the importance of these opposition writers, see Bailyn, *Ideological Origins*, 35-54; Kramnick, *Republican*, 201; and Lance Banning, *The Jeffersonian Persuasion: Evolution of a Party Ideology* (Ithaca: Cornell University Press, 1978), 62.

55   Bailyn, *Ideological Origins*, 48, 51-2, 54, 70, chapt. 3.

56   Wood, *Creation of the American Republic*, 114-18.

57   Shalhope, *Roots of Democracy*, 46.

58   Ibid., 45.

59   Wood, *Creation of the American Republic*, 67, 71, 479-80.

60   Wood, *Radicalism of the American Revolution*, 234.

61   Bailyn, *Ideological Origins*, 40.

62   Wood, *Creation of the American Republic*, 118-24; Shalhope, *Roots of Democracy*, 45-6.

63   Wood, *Radicalism of the American Revolution*, 330.

64   Pocock, *Machiavellian Moment*, 526, 507-8, 545.

65   Pocock, "*The Machiavellian Moment* Revisited," 53.

66   This notion of a distinct, synthesizing framework that structured colonial thought has come under increasing criticism as scholars have begun noting "ambivalence, inconsistencies, and ironic incongruities" in colonial attitudes. See Robert E. Shalhope, "Republicanism, Liberalism, and Democracy: Political Culture in the Early Republic," in *The Republican Synthesis Revisited: Essays in Honor of George Athan Billias*, eds. Milton M. Klein, Richard D. Brown, and John B. Hench (Worces-

ter: American Antiquarian Society, 1992), 56. See also Kloppenberg, "Virtues"; Michael Lienesch, *New Order of the Ages: Time, the Constitution, and the Making of Modern American Political Thought* (Princeton: Princeton University Press, 1988); and Lance Banning, *The Sacred Fire of Liberty: James Madison and the Founding of the Federal Republic* (Ithaca: Cornell University Press, 1995), 215.

67   Isaak Kramnick has suggested, as well, that part of the appeal of James Burgh, as of republicanism itself, was that he was able to speak in the languages of republican virtue, the individualistic politics of Locke, and the Protestant moralism of "frugality, thrift, and self-denial." Kramnick's interest in this essay is in examining how Burgh "moved the significant center of opposition ideology" in English writing and, thus, Kramnick asserts more than demonstrates the association of republican and Protestant themes on American soil. My argument picks up on this suggestion and examines how republicanism becomes associated with a Puritan past. See Kramnick, *Republican*, 255, 196, 247, 257-8.

68   James Burgh, *Political Disquisitions*, 3 vols. (Philadelphia: Bell and Woodhouse, 1775), 1: xxi.

69   John Trenchard and Thomas Gordon, *Cato's Letters*, in *The English Libertarian Heritage*, ed. David L. Jacobson (New York: Bobbs-Merrill, 1965), 54-5.

70   *Cato's Letters*, 137-8.

71   *Cato's Letters*, 130, 95-6, 61.

72   Lord Bolingbroke, "Reflections on the State of the Nation," *The Works of Lord Bolingbroke*, 4 vols. (Philadelphia: Carey and Hart, 1841), 2: 458. See also Bolingbroke, "Reflections," in *Works*, 2: 455, and Bolingbroke, "A Dissertation on Parties," in *Works*, 2: 9-10. Bolingbroke was famous for coining the phrase "Robinocracy" to describe the ministry of Robert Walpole. See Bailyn, *Ideological Origins*, 49-50.

73   Bolingbroke, "Dissertation," 2: 90.

74   Bolingbroke, "Reflections," 2: 457-8; "Dissertation," 2: 11.

75   Kramnick, *Republicanism*, 205.

76   James Burgh, *The Dignity of Human Nature* (London: C. Dilly, 1794, first printed 1754), iv.

77   Burgh, *Political Disquisitions*, 3: 31.

78   Burgh, *Political Disquisitions*, 1: 1-2.

79   Burgh, *Dignity of Human Nature*, 331-3, 342-4.

80   Burgh, *Political Disquisitions*, 3: 31.

81 In assessing the nature of political authority as it intersected with religious concepts, Patricia Bonomi, for example, does not talk about the notion of depravity. This is striking since she is arguing for how easily "the dissenting mentality," including that of the New England Congregationalists, "flowed in with the emergent republican understanding of the political radicals." See Bonomi, "Religious Dissent and the Case for American Exceptionalism, in *Religion in a Revolutionary Age*," eds. Ronald Hoffman and Peter J. Albert (Charlottesville: University Press of Virginia, 1994), 50.

82 "Novanglus," February 13, 1775, in *Tracts*, ed. Jensen, 327.

83 Adams, "A Dissertation on the Canon and Feudal Law," in *The Works of John Adams*, 10 vols., ed. Charles Francis Adams (Boston: Little, Brown & Co., 1865), 3: 454, 452-3.

84 Ibid., 3: 455, 462.

85 Ibid., 3: 464.

86 Thomas Dawes, Jr., "Oration Delivered at Boston, March 5, 1781," in *Republication of the Principles*, ed. Niles, 67.

87 John Winthrop, "A Modell of Christian Charity," in *Puritans*, eds. Miller and Johnson, 199.

88 Warren, "Oration (1772)," 21.

89 See Benjamin Hichborn, "Oration Delivered at Boston, March 5, 1777," in *Republication of the Principles*, ed. Niles, 50; "Speech of an Honest, Sensible, and Spirited Farmer of Philadelphia County, Addressed to an Assembly of His Neighbors on His Engaging in the Continental Service, May, 1776," in *Republication of the Principles*, ed. Niles, 222; *Rules and Regulations for the Massachusetts Army* (Salem, 1775), footnote in Samuel West, "On the Right to Rebel," in *Pulpit of the American Revolution*, ed. Thornton, 308; Nathan Fiske, *An Oration Delivered at Brookfield, No. 14, 1781. In Celebration of the Capture of Lord Cornwallis and his whole Army at York-Town and Gloucester, in Virginia, By the combined Army under the Command of His Excellency General Washington, On the 19th of October, 1781* (Boston, [1781]), 7. We even see this in Thomas Paine, "Crisis No. VIII," in *Common Sense and The Crisis* (Garden City: Dolphin, n.d.), 188-9.

90 Shain, *Myth of American Individualism*, xv, 225.

91 See Stout, *New England Soul*, intro., chapt. 14; Edmund Morgan, "The American Revolution Considered as an Intellectual Movement," in *Paths of American Thought*, eds. Arthur M. Schlesinger, Jr. and Morton White (Boston: Houghton Mifflin, 1963), 11-33; and John Berens, *Providence & Patriotism in Early America, 1640-1815* (Charlottesville: University Press of Virginia, 1978), chapt. 3.

92 See David Robson, *Educating Republicans: The College in the Era of the American Revolution, 1750-1800* (Westport, Conn.: Greenwood Press, 1985), chapt. 2.

93 See Bercovitch, *American Jeremiad*; Ruth Bloch, *Visionary Republic: Millennial Themes in American Thought, 1756-1800* (Cambridge: Cambridge University Press, 1985).

94 See Charles Royster, *A Revolutionary People at War: The Continental Army and American Character, 1775-1783* (New York: W. W. Norton, 1979).

95 See Shain, *Myth of American Individualism*, 197-8.

96 Samuel Webster, *The Misery and Duty of an Oppress'd and Enslav'd People* (Boston, 1774), 29.

97 Samuel Langdon, "Government corrupted by Vice, and recovered by Righteousness . . . May 31, 1775" (Watertown, 1775), in *Pulpit of the American Revolution*, ed. Thornton, 247. Langdon would combine both a republican sense of a corrupt ministry with a Lockean view of civil society and justification for rebellion (243-5, 250).

98 Nathaniel Niles, "Two Discourses on Liberty" (Newburyport, Mass, 1774), in *American Political Writings*, eds. Hyneman and Lutz, 1: 273-6.

99 "Proclamation of Thanksgiving," by the Council of Watertown, Massachusetts, Nov. 4, 1775, in *Republication of the Principles*, ed. Niles, 124.

100 *Journals of the Continental Congress*, June 12, 1775, 2: 87.

101 Abigail Adams to John Adams, Oct. 16, 1774, in *Familiar Letters of John Adams and His Wife Abigail Adams, During the Revolution*, ed. Charles Francis Adams (New York: Hurd and Houghton, 1876), 48.

102 Jonathan Mason, "Oration," in *Republication of the Principles*, ed. Niles, 65.

103 "Address of the New York legislature to their Inhabitants, March 13, 1781," in *Republication of the Principles*, ed. Niles, 186.

104 Dawes, "Oration," 72.

105 For a discussion of this "ambivalence" as it related to the establishment of a Constitution, see Lance Banning, "The Problem of Power: Parties, Aristocracy, and Democracy in Revolutionary Thought," in *The American Revolution: Its Character and Limits*, ed. Jack P. Greene (New York: New York University Press, 1987).

106 The phrase is from Bailyn, *Ideological Origins*, chapt. 2.

107 Bailyn, *Ideological Origins*, 34.

108 Dale Kuehne, *Massachusetts Congregational Political Thought, 1760-1790: The Design of Heaven* (Columbia: University of Missouri Press, 1996), 123.

109 Shain, *Myth of American Individualism*, 124.

110 Abraham Williams, "A Sermon Preach'd at Boston, Before the Great and General Court or Assembly Of the Province of the Massachusetts-Bay in New England, May 26, 1762" (Boston: S. Kneeland, 1762), in *Political Writing*, eds. Hyneman and Lutz, 1: 6-7, 12. In justifying resistance to Britain, one sees in the *Journals of the Continental Congress* numerous assertions of the "immutable laws of nature" and the right to "life, liberty, & property" that can be "ceded" to a sovereign power only with one's "full and free consent, when they in their judgment deem it just and necessary to give them for public service, and precisely direct the easiest, cheapest, and most equal methods, in which they shall be collected" ("Non-importation Agreement," in *Journals of the Continental Congress*, Oct. 14, 1774, 1: 67; "Address To the Inhabitants of the Province of Quebec," in *Journals of the Continental Congress*, Oct. 26, 1774, 1: 107; see also "To the oppressed Inhabitants of Canada," in *Journals of the Continental Congress*, May 29, 1775, 2: 69).

111 Williams, "Sermon," 1: 5. Brooke, too, points to this combination of a Lockean defense of natural rights and a more Harringtonian corporate vision of society. See *Heart of the Commonwealth*, 158-9.

112 Williams, "Sermon," 1: 6-7.

113 Sherwood, "Scriptural Instructions to Civil Rulers," 383, 388, 386, 378.

114 Nathaniel Niles, "Two Discourses," 1: 269-70.

115 "A Proclamation, By the Great and General Court of the Colony of Massachusetts-Bay," Jan. 23, 1776, in *Popular Sources of Political Authority*, eds. Handlin and Handlin, 68.

116 "An Address of the Convention, for Framing a New Constitution of Government, for the State of Massachusetts-Bay, to Their Constituents (1780)," in *Popular Sources of Political Authority*, eds. Handlin and Handlin, 434-5, and "A Constitution or Frame of Government," in *Popular Sources of Political Authority*, eds. Handlin and Handlin, 441.

117 "A Constitution or Frame of Government," in *Popular Sources of Political Authority*, eds. Handlin and Handlin, 441-2.

118 "An Address of the Convention," 434-6, 440.

119 See Charles Akers, *The Divine Politician: Samuel Cooper and the American Revolution in Boston* (Boston: Northeastern University Press, 1982).

120 Samuel Cooper, "A Sermon Preached Before His Excellency John Hancock. . .October 25, 1780" in *Political Sermons of the American Found-*

ing Era, 1730-1805, ed. Ellis Sandoz (Indianapolis: Liberty Press, 1991), 639, 631, 635, 643.

121   Ibid., 647-8, 653.

122   Eric Foner, *Tom Paine and Revolutionary America* (London: Oxford University Press), 114.

123   "Speech of an Honest, Sensible, and Spirited Farmer . . . May, 1776," in *Republication of the Principles*, ed. Niles, 221-2.

124   John Winthrop, "Modell," 199.

125   "Address of the Provincial Congress to the Inhabitants of the Towns and Districts of Massachusetts-Bay, Dec. 4, 1774," in *Republication of the Principles*, ed. Niles, 109.

126   Richard Henry Lee, "Patriotic Speech of Richard Henry Lee of Virginia, Delivered June 8th, 1776, Urging an Immediate Declaration of Independence," in *Principles*, ed. Niles, 397. See also George Washington, "Circular," June 18, 1783, in *The Documentary History of the Ratification of the Constitution*, 18 vols. (Madison: State Historical Society of Wisconsin, 1981), 13: 64.

127   "Speech of John Rutledge, President, to the General Assembly, April 11, 1776," in *Republication of the Principles*, ed. Niles, 327.

128   Jonathan W. Austin, "An Oration Delivered at Boston, March 5, 1778," in *Republication of the Principles*, ed. Niles, 56.

129   David Ramsay, *An Oration on the Advantages of American Independence: Spoken Before a Public Assembly of the Inhabitants of Charlestown in South-Carolina, on the Second Anniversary of the Glorious Aera* (Charlestown, 1778), 16.

Chapter 4

The Federalists and the Moderation of Passion

The Americans emerged from the Revolutionary War with political and military victory as well as a favorable peace treaty. Poems, newspapers, treatise, speeches, and letters all attested to the overwhelming sense of optimism that swept America after the Revolution. David Humphreys provided a typical accolade to America's future. America, the "favor'd land," was "A paradise new-risen from the wild" with "Delightful prospects."

> While thus the nation boasts its pow'rful state,
> Endow'd with all which constitutes it great,
> In calm security the land shall rest,
> 'Her people blessing, by her people blest.[1]

Combining empirics with prophecy, Ezra Stiles, the president of Yale College, noted how American population growth fulfilled "the prophecy of Noah," making the "American Israel high above all nations which he [God] had made, in numbers, and in praise, and in name, and in honor!"[2]

The unbounded enthusiasm that marked these few years immediately following the victory at Yorktown and Britain's surrender was evidenced in the activities of the time. The culmination of the war had ended the years of hardship and shortages: goods from France, Holland, Russia, Germany, and especially England poured into the new states. Foreign countries extended credit to American merchants, both parties certain of the bright prospects of America's economic condition. Merchants, in turn, sold their goods on credit to a population demanding lace, silk, velvet, new clothing, furniture, saddles, blankets, linens, and almost every other luxury imaginable. Merchants explored new avenues of trade, including expeditions to China. Internal improvement projects sprang up across the country. And organizations for the betterment of humanity were created: societies for the freeing of slaves, for temperance, the arts and sciences, philanthropy, and philosophy.[3]

For some, perhaps even for most, the forces of interest and egalitarianism unleashed by the revolutionary overturning of hierarchical patterns of deference were celebrated.[4] But for a growing number of people who had once expressed hope in the Revolution, a group who would be instrumental in calling for the reform of the Articles of Confederation and would later coalesce around the Federalist label, there was disillusionment. The energy and spirit of the Revolution had given way in Federalist eyes to selfishness, luxury, and folly.[5] "From our primaeval simplicity of manners," remarked David Daggett, a Connecticut lawyer, in recalling the Puritan ancestors, "we soon degenerated into that licentiousness which is ever to be found among the more polished parts of the world, and at the commencement of the late war, tho' not as yet hackneyed in the ways of vice, we were by no means signalized for that sacred veneration for religion and social virtues, which was so conspicuous a century or two before."[6] An "almost impenetrable gloom" had descended across the new nation: "Patriotism is fled," our citizens could no longer be inspired by "that disinterested love of their country," we had adopted "the luxury, the follies, the fashions" of the country we once detested, and we had "prostitute[d]" ourselves "to the vile purposes of licentiousness."[7] For Alexander Hamilton, writing in defense of the new Constitution, the nation was teetering perilously on the brink of disaster, ready to "plunge . . . into the abyss that awaits us below."[8] America had emerged from the Revolution as a glorious example to the world; yet, spoke one orator at the time, "our political affairs wear a gloomy aspect."[9] A weak government threatened to destroy American commerce, throw the nation further into debt, and lead to "licentiousness and anarchy" through its inability to enforce order.[10]

The depravity that threatened the new nation could be seen in many different forms. For some, the "triumph of folly" was not just extravagance but the attempt by the lower classes to emulate the styles of the upper class. So "ridiculous" it was to see "even our country-girls in their market-carts, and upon their panniered horses," riding "through our streets with their heads deformed with the plumes of the ostrich, and the feathers of other exotick birds." To counter such opulence, John Gardiner looked to the model of Puritan Massachusetts in its adoption of *"sumptuary laws."* Just as the Massachusetts Colony taxed "persons wearing ribbons, or great boots (leather being so scarce a commodity in this country), lace, points, &c. silk hoods, or scarfes," so "every article of needless dress, and shew, and vain expense" should be assessed.[11]

The concern with extravagant dress, though in part a reaction to the breakdown of patterns of deference, was often a manifestation of a much larger worry: the public debt. The flurry of purchasing that followed the cessation of hostilities had plunged the nation deep in debt. "Our valuable exports have been wantonly sacrificed for European trifles, which, far from enriching, have served to impoverish our country," announced Jonathan Austin.[12] Many orators had to look no further than the "rapid degeneracy of our manners" and "a sudden depravity" for the source of the debt.[13]

Discord within the country was also seen as an indication of the degeneracy of the citizenry. Where once people were united in "common interest" against Britain, now that "the impulse of foreign force was removed, the little politicks of each state engrossed the publick attention—federal ideas were obscured, and the national character has been falling a victim to local prejudice."[14] Myriad factional conflicts arose during this period of confederation: nationalists, who desired a strong central government, fought those who wanted to secure state sovereignty; small farmers decried the scarcity of specie to pay their debts, arguing instead for paper money; merchants requested that states and the federal Congress regulate shipping in favor of American commerce; and manufacturers and artisans successfully demanded tariffs to limit foreign imports. People appeared to have lost their "patriotic sentiments" and submitted, instead, to their base self-interest. "Thus have arisen contentions and civil discord in almost every state in the union." Massachusetts "has long been torn with intestine factions, and

[its] government almost prostrated by a despicable banditti,"
the participants in the Shays' Rebellion. New York "is rioting
on thousands, annually drained from our coffers" while
"Rhode-Island has acted a part, which would cause the savages
of the wilderness to blush."[15]

Discord, dissension, dissatisfaction, and even insurrection
had clouded the Revolutionary hopes. One can almost hear
the confusion in the voice of Timothy Dwight, the president of
Yale College, as he cast about in search of a satisfactory vision
of the future: "In such a period as the present, when the state
of society is so disturbed, when the minds of men are so generally set afloat, and when so many ancient landmarks, so many
standards of opinion and practice, are thrown down; when
ambition, avarice, and sensuality, deliberate and decree, and
violence and cruelty are charged with the execution, throughout a great part of the civilized world; a contemplative and
serious mind cannot but ask, *What shall the end of these things
be?*"[16] Dwight was not alone in this feeling.

This falling away was all the more to be feared because, for
many, the citizens of this New Israel risked squandering their
status as God's favored people. "The people of America," wrote
John Adams, "have now the best opportunity and the greatest
trust in their hands that Providence ever committed to so small
a number since the transgression of the first pair; if they betray their trust, their guilt will merit even greater punishment
than other nations have suffered, and the indignation of
Heaven."[17] The eyes of Europe were still upon America, but
where once Europeans "extolled our success, and predicted
our future greatness," they "now laugh at our folly . . . bur-
lesque our policy, and contemn [sic] our dishonesty."[18]

Although America was blessed to be "separated by nature
from every other power of importance in the world," and thus
"must always be secure while she has harmony at home," such
harmony was not yet assured; the Revolution had not been
completed.[19] Benjamin Rush, for example, an outspoken Pennsylvania Federalist, drew a distinction between the "*American
Revolution*" and "*the late American war.*" "The American war is
over: but this is far from being the case with the American
revolution." What remained to be done was "to establish and
perfect our new forms of government" and "to prepare the
principles, morals, and manners of our citizens, for these forms

of government, after they are established and brought to perfection."[20] Joel Barlow, who had been raised in the conservative environment of Federalist Connecticut and tutored at Yale College by the Puritan Timothy Dwight, expressed the concerns of the nation quite succinctly:

> The present is justly considered an alarming crisis; perhaps the most alarming that America ever saw. We have contended with the most powerful nation and subdued the bravest and best appointed armies; but now we have to contend with *ourselves*, and encounter passions and prejudices more powerful than armies and more dangerous to our peace. It is not for glory, it is for existence that we contend.[21]

There was "no enemy to fear but from ourself," pronounced Benjamin Hichborn.[22] Rush's and Barlow's words spoke to a shift in the self-perceived task of a large segment of the colonial elite: from a concern with winning a war to the establishment of durable political and social institutions. The aim of the struggle exhibited a corresponding shift from independence to who would define the emergent institutions and cultural patterns. The political rhetoric prevalent in New England and even in the Middle Colonies and South during the two decades following the end of the Revolution reflected the pervasive fear that the new institutions were to be constructed and secured in an environment that was perceived to be unredeemed.[23]

Again and again this theme of the tentativeness of Revolutionary gains was enunciated. "Now, if ever, is the time to keep a more than ordinary watch over our manners" to "check that subtle secret poison, which lurks under the pomp of luxury, and the charms of pleasure!"[24] The Puritan jeremiad gave form to this anxiety, lending to political rhetoric a sense of the new nation as teetering perilously on the precipice, with damnation or salvation depending on the actions of the current generation. "On the present crisis depends your fate," observed one anonymous writer. "If you make use of your opportunity, you secure the good of many generations: But, if you neglect it, you may be doomed to drudge in your own fertile fields, and, what would be otherwise a blessing, will be a snare and a misfortune to you."[25] The road to redemption would not be an easy one. "Much remains to be done," warned Levi Frisbie, to keep the nation from sinking "into carelessness and indolence, pride and luxury, folly and dissipation," as well as "envy, self-ishness, avarice and ambition." If the nation were unable to maintain the proper vigilance, then these vices would "mis-guide our councils, corrupt our government, enervate our strength, destroy our order and security, dissolve our union, blast all our glory and happiness, and plunge us into a tremen-dous gulf of infamy and wretchedness, from which we may never be able to emerge."[26]

In explaining the nature of this anxiety, scholars have tended to portray the Federalists simply as reactionaries: angry and bitter, but not all that constructive. In a recent comprehensive discussion of the age of Federalism, for example, Elkins and McKitrick describe the "response of Federalism" as "righteous-ness under siege" that "amounted to little more in the end than a sterile defense of constituted order."[27] Gordon Wood, in his influential study of the creation of the Constitution, portrays the Federalists as "disingenuous" in their "manipula-tion of Whig maxims." To add insult to injury, Wood then holds the Federalists responsible for fostering the breakdown of real political debate in America as they used a rhetoric of liberal-ism "to explain and justify their aristocratic system."[28] In his recent Pulitzer Prize-winning book, Wood follows up this dis-cussion by asserting that because the Federalists assumed that "most people were self-interested and absorbed in their pri-vate affairs," they were unable to provide "civic foundations for their scheme."[29] Joyce Appleby defines the "cohering prin-ciple" of the Federalists as "skeptical,"[30] and even James Ban-ner, who otherwise provides a somewhat sympathetic treatment of the Federalists, portrays the Federalists (specifically Massa-chusetts Federalists) as feeding upon "provincial illusions and fears" and appealing to those "frightened by the specter of an unparalleled revolution abroad," "frustrated by the failure of their own revolution to bear out its promise," and to those "simply unable to understand change."[31]

Federalism appears, thus, as anti-antifederalism: as fulmi-nation without foundation. Attempts to explain the basis for Federalist discontent have often been equally unsatisfactory. Several prominent scholars have argued that the Federalists appear as eighteenth-century "Court" politicians to the Jeffersonian "Country" opposition. Elkins and McKitrick see the Federalists as having to "choose one abstraction or the other," that of a Country or Court ideology.[32] Murrin, too, suggests that when Federalist and Republican faced each other, they "accurately recognized what were basically Court and Country coalitions, respectively," even though there were also Court-Country tensions operating within the Federalists.[33] Lance Banning, who agrees that the Republicans used a "Country" language, is quick to note that a "careful search of Federalist writings, both public and private, fails to uncover any systematic use of 'Court' ideas in replies to Republican attacks on corruption."[34] As Kramnick has argued quite persuasively, not only is it difficult to read the "nostalgia, hierarchism, and anticommercialism" of the "Court" into the late eighteenth-century, but there were a number of political idioms, not just two, that coexisted in American political discourse at the time.[35]

Other suggestions have been made, as well, for understanding the ideological foundation of the Federalists, portraying them as aristocrats or as "classical republicans,"[36] as dismayed revolutionary idealists or as liberal Hobbesian "realists."[37] Though these categories each capture some aspect of the Federalists, they also at important points conflict with each other, lending a further incoherence to Federalist thought.

Two scholarly contributions have been important in lending some integrity and coherence to the Federalist position. The first is Linda Kerber's *Federalists in Dissent*, which remains one of the most articulate statements about what might be called the political culture of the Federalists. Kerber identifies in the Federalists a constellation of scientific, literary, economic, and political attitudes that were consciously styled after what was seen as the golden age of Augustan England.[38] The second work is Daniel Howe's article, "The Political Psychology of *The Federalist.*" Howe argues that one can understand the Federalists as employing a faculty psychology in their construction and defense of the Constitution. Faculty psychology posits a hierarchy of "rightful precedence among conscious motives: first reason, then prudence (or self-interest), then passion," with short-term interest treated more as a passion and long-term, more collective interest as akin to reason. The problem for human action was that "these motives varied inversely in power: passion was the strongest and reason the weakest." This provided a justification for "identifying liberty with order" since "liberty of the individual's will required preventing any faculty from disturbing the harmony of the mind (especially any passion from usurping the authority of reason)." Extending faculty psychology to the body politic, the case was made for "guarding political liberty with social order" in which "parts were subordinated to the welfare of the whole, balances were struck between conflicting motives, and order was based on a rational hierarchy."[39]

Though Howe's focus is on *The Federalist* and the defense of the Constitution, we can extend this notion of the disruptive influence of passion on the social body to understand later Federalist concerns. What I will argue, in extending Kerber's argument as well, is that the Federalists looked not only to an Augustan age but to America's Puritan past. They did so to provide an historical basis for their political theory, a theory that would protect liberty through the control of human passion. The Federalists saw two significant threats to this liberty: the unrestrained impulses that remained after the Revolution and the new spirit of party, made all the more dangerous by the importation of French thought to American soil. To these concerns the Federalists would invoke the Puritans as both a force of moderation and a model of a civic body.

Reinterpreting the Revolution

The American Revolution and its aftermath would profoundly and permanently transform American society. As Gordon Wood has noted recently:

> By every measure there was a sudden bursting forth, an explosion—not only of geographical movement but of entrepreneurial energy, of religious passion, and of pecuniary desires. . . . The Revolution resembled the breaking of a dam, releasing thousands upon thousands of pent-up pressures. There had been seepage and flows before the Revolution, but suddenly it was as if the whole traditional structure, enfeebled and brittle to begin with, broke apart, and people and their energies were set loose in an unprecedented outburst.[40]

No Federalist wished to repudiate the Revolution, but they were alarmed by what they saw as an outgrowth of the Revolution, made worse by the terror in France; namely, the subjection of the social body to the convulsions of passion.

The Federalists started from an understanding of the "body politick" as a "corporeal body." This had important implications, among them that each political body contained "within itself the principles of *life* and *death*; of *preservation* and *decay*." Conceived of as a unity, "the only principles of preservation" in a republic "are the *virtue* and *wisdom* of the people who take an active part in publick affairs; as these predominate over *vice* and *ignorance*, the government will be strong and healthy."[41] This notion of an organic unity did more than justify the existence of a hierarchical differentiation of functions; it directed Federalist attention, as we will see, toward maintaining the integrity of the whole (what the Federalists would call a "national character") and toward emphasizing virtues of moderation and restraint.

In articulating this notion of a political body, though, the Federalists were met with an immediate problem. Revolutions by their nature are tumultuous, passionate, even chaotic, and thus disruptive of the body politic. Moreover, the Revolution had demonstrated to the Federalists the human capacity for "turmoil" that would undermine the fragile nature of the "experimental republic."[42] How, then, does one affirm the values of the Revolution and celebrate the revolutionary figures without, at the same time, justifying the passions that drove the Revolution? This the Federalists did by recasting the revolutionaries as heirs of Puritan moderation.

In part this appropriation of the Puritans drew upon revolutionary rhetoric and historical writings, which cast the founders as fleeing from tyranny and boldly establishing a community founded on liberty in the inhospitable wilderness. Banner, for example, argues that the Federalist "condemnation of corruption" after the Revolution contained "clear overtones of American revolutionary thought."[43] We see the invocation of something like a jeremiad by both revolutionary leaders and Federalists, but in looking at how the image of the Puritans was used by both groups we discover a change in the implications of this recounting of the past. For the revolutionaries, the Puritans, in some sense, fanned the fire of liberty, whereas for the Federalists the Puritans served to dampen these same flames.

At first glance, there seems to be nothing new in the recounting by William Tudor, a mercantilist and founder of the

North American Review, of the Pilgrims: "Our ancestors left their homes and their country, not for any infraction of their political rights, but to avoid persecution for their religious opinions. They embarked for these then unexplored regions, not in search for gold, or in pursuit of traffick; not in thirst for conquest, or through want of subsistence, but to enjoy freedom of religion." Where previous (and subsequent) recountings would lead to a discussion of the purity of Puritan motives, what Tudor emphasized, as he looked about at the "stormy season of history" in which he lived, was how, "Persevering in a steady course, [the Puritans] never lost sight of the object for which they had contended, liberty of self-government. To this point all their exertions were directed. To perpetuate this was the main object of education."[44] What distinguished the Puritans from other settlers in this case was not so much that they were more pure. Rather, they were able to control their short-term passions of "thirst" and "want" and were guided, instead, by a harmony of reason, prudence, and interest.

The Federalists, thus, could claim that the revolutionaries acted consistently with this Puritan moderation, driven not by short-sighted impulses but able to subject such passions and interests to reason. John Church, for example, noted how the enjoyment of "civil liberty, was one design of our ancestors in coming to this land." This purpose, importantly, was transmitted to "Their descendants" who "kept the same noble design in view. New-England became the residence of virtuous, enlightened freemen." In this environment, "Habits of industry, sobriety, and subjection to civil government were formed." It is this same spirit that would guide the revolutionary leaders. The Revolution "was not a spirit of opposition to government, *as such,* but a conscientious regard to our invaluable rights, which led us to oppose their arbitrary measures." What was to be admired about the revolutionary period was the "order and regularity which prevailed in the commencement of our revolution." The regard for liberty, the assertion of the "right to be free and independent," was not meant to signal the adoption of "the principles of licentiousness" but to establish forms of government that would be protective of these rights.[45] The current Federalist leaders of America—"Washington, Adams, and Ellsworth"—as well as the "departed spirits of Davenport,

Hooker, Winthrop, Wolcott, Hopkins, Haynes, and Eaton" and "a Lawrence, a Warren, a Mercer, [and] a Wooster" were remembered as part of the Federalist tradition.[46] All of these great men, consistent with the Federalist interpretation of the Revolution, had sought to restore rather than destroy; they "repaired the roof of an ancient and venerable edifice, enlarged the number of its lights, amended the style of its architecture, and cemented the rocks of its foundation" rather than seeking to "collapse its pillars" or "burn its temple."[47]

This emphasis upon the moderate temperament of the revolutionary leaders as an inheritance from the Puritans would be repeated by other Federalists. Thomas Danforth identified the revolutionary leaders as the "immediate descendants" of the Puritans who "were not less renown for their hardihood of courage, or their vigor of intellect." Like the Puritans, the American revolutionaries reacted to oppression with "the most elevated effort of magnanimity and patriotism. Slow in its rise, it exhibited the calmness of deliberation; resolute in its progress, it never departed from the regularity of system. . . ."[48] This appropriation of Puritanism would extend outside New England, as well. In an oration in South Carolina, Charles Fraser recalled how "Our common ancestors" had "braved the terrors of the Atlantic main, and sought on its western shores an asylum from oppression." These ancestors "transmitted" to the subsequent generations the "genuine integrity of virtue" acquired through their toils in the wilderness and the "dangers of enterprize." It was these same motives that served as the "impulse" in the American Revolution. For without "the impulse of these feelings," the revolutionaries "would have legitimated the title of rebellion with which the enemies of their revolution wished to stigmatize it."[49] Instead, like the Puritans before, Americans emerged from their oppressive situation with dignity rather than unrestrained passion.

This notion of the revolutionaries as inheritors of a tradition of liberty and moderation would find strong support from the revolutionary historiographies that were emerging at the time. David Ramsay, a South Carolina physician, in his widely read account of the American Revolution, would recount how the revolutionaries read not only "Cato's letters" and "the Independent Whig," but also "histories of the Puritans" which "kept alive the remembrance of their forefathers, and inspired a warm attachment, both to the civil and the religious rights of human nature."[50] The Puritans were seen as prompted by a "spirit of liberty"[51] or, in the words of John Marshall, a "spirit of republicanism."[52] Even Mercy Warren, the most anti-Federalist of historians from this era and least sympathetic in her portrayal of the Puritans, would see in these early New England settlements the "stable foundations . . . that have since spread over the fairest quarter of the globe."[53] As one contemporary historian has noted, "The [revolutionary] historians insisted that these principles" of ordered liberty and public virtue "were not new to the Revolutionary era. The conflicts of the 1760s and 1770s merely called forth the character that had energized the colonists from the beginning of settlement."[54]

The moderate temperament displayed by both the Puritans and revolutionaries arose always out of social attachments. The Pilgrim fathers, from the very beginning, "moved as social beings, like the Israelites with the tabernacle of Jehovah." They "held it to be inconsistent with man's duty, as a creature formed for society, and with the dictates of Christianity, for any family to run away into the woods, and live like wild beasts, without the means of religious knowledge, and the ordinances of publick worship."[55] For this reason, the Puritans always moved as a congregation, immediately setting up schools and churches wherever they stayed. Left on their own, "mankind would have no restraint upon their passions," particularly the venality and political ambition the Federalists saw in the Republicans. Even "political information," if "unrestrained by virtuous and religious principles, will only facilitate the practice of iniquity, and afford ability for the commission of crimes, with the greater impunity."[56] Humans were meant to live as social beings which, for the Federalists, required the "steady habits" of morality, fostered by religion and education.[57] John Quincy Adams opened his commemoration of the Pilgrim landing with such a Burkean eulogy to these forefathers. As Adams noted, "man" was "not made for himself alone"; instead, he was "made for his species" and "for all ages past by the sentiment of reverence for his forefathers." These principles "redeem his nature from the subjection of time and space: he is no longer a 'puny insect shivering at a breeze.'"[58]

Yet, Adams would not embrace completely a Burkean notion of society, for the Pilgrims were seen as entering into a "social compact" that served as the "legitimate source of government."[59] Moreover, there were a number of other Federalist references to the Puritans as entering an uncivilized, uncultivated, and unrestrained state of nature. As the most influential Federalist magazine in America wrote, the Puritans came into "a dreary, inhospitable, and dismal desert, in which nothing was to be seen but the wild products of nature, and little to be heard, save the howl of the 'tenants of the forest,' or the whoop of the rude savage."[60] One Ohio Federalist noted how the Puritans had to enter the wilderness and meet "man in a state of nature":[61] savages who, as another orator noted, were "ignorant of all social affection."[62] The Federalists, in reinterpreting Bradford's image of the "desert wilderness," did not draw upon the Biblical parallel to the Israelites, nor did they use the state of nature to highlight the individual origins of a Lockean contract, for such a contract could justify the subordination of the civic body to individual interest. What was emphasized, instead, was that even as the Puritans and Pilgrims thought about the legitimate basis of their political organization, they remained a social body: "knit together in a strict and sacred bond, to take care of the good of each other and of the whole."[63] What threatened this social body, and human social existence, was what the Federalists saw as the emergence of the party spirit, a spirit that pitted individual against individual, and tended to inflame passion over reason.

The Party Spirit

A fear of the party spirit was nothing new: it was an issue addressed by Madison, for example, in *The Federalist*. Although faction was undesirable, observed Madison, its effects could be mitigated by a citizenry of diverse interests spread over a large territory with intelligent and rational leaders speaking for an impassioned public. Such palliatives may have been soothing in the 1780s, despite Shays' Rebellion, but a number of events had transpired that made faction of grave importance in the 1790s and the first decade of the nineteenth-century. In 1794 the Whiskey Rebellion shook Pennsylvania. Even while the situation was being brought under control, an attempt was made in Maryland to seize the Fredericktown armory, and "rumblings of discontent" against such excises were heard "in Kentucky, Georgia, and the Carolinas."[64] In 1799 Pennsylvania was again home to an armed resistance against the collection of taxes, this one led by John Fries. Defiance of the national government could be seen in the Virginia and Kentucky resolutions, authored by Thomas Jefferson and James Madison, which were written in opposition to the Alien and Sedition Acts. And the French Revolution with its attendant reign of terror, as it unfolded in American newspapers, instilled a terror of its own across the new nation. The French Revolution, as many orators proclaimed, had unleashed radical philosophies of equality, rationalism, and atheism. In a time of Federalist strength, competing foreign ideas might not have been so threatening. But the Federalists had lost their privileged status, even in their previous stronghold, New York. The Republicans were in the ascendancy, revealed most clearly in the Federalists' worst nightmare, Thomas Jefferson's rise to the presidency and his overwhelming reelection victory.

There was a real change occurring in the nature of parties that underlay the Federalists' concern, as well. Although parties had existed before, they had usually taken the form of "the people against the rulers, the country against the court." But Americans were now faced with parties "among the people themselves," parties founded on interest: occupation, region, creditor or debtor status.[65] These ambitions of "very corrupt individuals," noted John Adams, were not in "the common spirit of party."[66] The factions Madison had hoped would be diffused throughout the nation had come together to create permanent national organizations. The desires of individuals had combined to become the design of party organizations. "Ambition, under the specious cover of republicanism," was now "stalking over the earth."[67]

In looking at the Federalist response to the emergence of the Republican party, scholars have been quick to portray the Federalists as "striking furiously at parties in general, in a desperate effort to turn back the clock."[68] When not flailing, the Federalists appear disingenuous, hypocritical, or outright manipulative. Their rhetoric of disinterestedness is contrasted with the protection of their own interests.[69] Or the Federalist position is seen as necessitating the "molding" of public opinion since it espoused a view to which people "were not naturally sympathetic."[70] Or, as one historian has argued, in distinguishing between older aristocratic Federalists who disdained parties and newer Federalists who accommodated themselves to and sought to build political parties, these new Federalists simply combined "the rhetoric of popular government with the hard reality of the iron law of oligarchy. In place of the happy vision of a silent multitude and a speaking elite, they substituted an uglier but more workable arrangement—a silent elite in the midst of a speaking multitude."[71] Certainly the Federalists became increasingly desperate, certainly they saw the shift in power away from them, but the basis of their anxiety lay, importantly, in a fundamentally different political theory, one whose corporate foundations were antithetical to the new equation of liberty and the passionate pursuit of one's own interests.

Rhetorically, Federalist anxiety found its expression in the form of the jeremiad.[72] There was jubilation in the past: the heroism of the revolutionary leaders, the establishment of the Constitution, the sense of security from external aggression, the growth of agriculture and commerce, and the flourishing of learning. As if on cue from Cotton Mather, though, each thought of good times carried with it a stern warning about the dangers that lay ahead. Just as prosperity had the unhappy result of love of the world, so liberty and learning had "for its companion sophistry and faction."[73] Jonathan Edwards' grandson, Timothy Dwight, warned, "'Behold,' saith the Saviour, 'I come as a Thief'—suddenly, unexpectedly, alarmingly—as that wasting enemy, the burglar, breaks up the house in the hour of darkness, when all the inhabitants are lost in sleep and security."[74] This sentiment was echoed by Samuel Fiske in a Fourth of July oration. "As venomous insects and noxious weeds are warmed into being by the vivifying rays of the sun, so a number of unprincipled and detestable paracides [parasites], have been nourished into life, by the mild influence of the American government."[75] So nourished was such a parasite that it had developed two heads. The first head spewed forth the philosophies of the French Revolution. The second head, working with the first, was the party of Jefferson, the Republicans.

The conspiracy of the *philosophes* and the Jeffersonians was a commonplace assumption of the Federalists. "From the day Mr. Genet [the French envoy] landed on this Continent 'till the poisonous, debauching diplomatic intercourse between us and France was prohibited, French emissaries and American jacobins have been constantly plotting and executing treasons against our government, which according to the laws of every well regulated society, would subject the authors to the punishment of death."[76] Speaking of the Republicans, George Sullivan suggested, "Our country nourishes in her bosom a faction, coextensive with our empire, protected by and devoted to the interest of France, which plots the destruction of our national government, and would rejoice to see it prostrate."[77] The ever-paranoid John Adams began listing names: "There is no other newspaper circulated in the back country of the southern States than Freneau's National Gazette, which is employed with great industry to poison the minds of the people."[78]

This two-headed parasite of republicanism and "philosophism" posed such a menace to the body politic, not so much because it introduced differing ideas but because, in the mind of the Federalists, it served to inflame the passions of the civic body. This, for the Federalists, would make impossible any calm deliberation actuated by reason and prudence. Those who introduce a party spirit, spoke one Federalist, "prevent a calm and candid investigation of public characters and public measures. Under their influence, many will be more actuated by passion and prejudice, than by sound judgment and national conviction. Designing men will constantly increase the popular ferment."[79] The language of the Federalists was extraordinarily graphic in depicting a civic body torn apart by passionate disagreement. The source of this passion, as Madison had noted, was property (or, more accurately, inequality of property), but it was made all the worse now by the entrance of these private interests into political life. The spirit of party "irritates the minds of the people" who are now "impelled by opposite interests, and enraged by mutual injuries."[80] There can be no discussion, no deliberation, where people are "impelled" and "enraged," where reason can no longer reign in passion.

The spirit of republicanism was seen as working its way into the populace, deluding the masses as it appealed to these passions. As one surveyed modern republics in Europe, noted one Federalist, "Dissension and party spirit" were "excited among the people, and their passions were artfully inflamed against those institutions and restraints, which wisdom had devised, and the experience of ages had sanctioned."[81] Spoke Benjamin Silliman about early days in New England, "Men were not yet intoxicated with visionary ideas of liberty, nor deluded with theories of the perfectibility of man. The delusive prospect of a *general good,* too general to be perceived or attained, had not seduced the sober yeomanry from the pursuits of industry, and the concern of domestic employment. A group of politicians was not to be seen in every tavern and at every corner. . . ."[82] The seductiveness of the "pestilential doctrines of modern philosophy" that appeared in "the form of a serpent" was seen as taking advantage of the "weaker part of the community . . . the *populace,*—in this concealed and insidious manner, with all the fawning arts of deceitful intrigue, commences his attack."[83] "Happy were it for us," spoke Chauncey Lee, "had the forbidden fruit remained untouched—had not the seeds of that noxious foreign plant, the Tree of *Liberty* and *Equality,* been sown and cultured in the midst of our political Eden, and had no tempter emerged from *Gallic Pandomonium* to seduce the virtue of our countrymen, by the poisonous fruit of that Bohon Upas of human happiness, that tree of knowledge of political good and evil (of good lost, and evil gained) which corrupts the fountain of national felicity, diffuses its poison through all the streams of social life and threatens the forfeiture and loss of all the blessings of Independence."[84]

Rather than cultivating "respect, veneration, and reverence" toward government, the Republican party spirit, in opposition to "the authority of Heaven," threatened to extinguish all respect for authority. Thomas Day noted the devolution from faction to anarchy:

Party spirit always weakens, and not unfrequently destroys, this reverence [for magistrates]. The next step is a riot, and then an insurrection. These evils the United States have already experienced. They have indeed been suppressed, but the cause remains; and unless the most vigorous exertions are made to exterminate it, our nation, bright as its prospects have appeared, will, in all probability, soon by con-vulsed with a civil war.[85]

Liberty without authority, for both the Puritans and Feder-alists, always resulted in an enslavement: to one's passions and, ultimately, to the despotic control by another's passions. In a nation divided by a party spirit, "Factions alternatively pre-vail, until one more successful than the rest, finally predomi-nates, and establishes its own private liberty, upon the ruins of that of the public."[86] It is for this reason that the "natural enemies" of the Constitution were "the spirit of sophistry, the spirit of party, the spirit of intrigue, profligacy, and corrup-tion, and the pestilence of foreign influence, which is the an-gel of destruction to elective governments," announced John Adams in his Inaugural Address.[87]

In the face of such Republican challenges that, according to the Federalists, were designed "to destroy ancient systems—ancient habits—ancient customs—to introduce a new liberty, new equality, new rights of man, new modes of education, and a new order of things," the Federalists sought to construct such a venerable past.[88] The events and institutions of America were to be "transmitted, without variation, to the latest ages" to in-sure a continued piety as in the past, and continued venera-tion of the Puritans.[89] Wrote one minister, in expressing alarm at the unraveling of the social fabric, "It is incumbent on every individual, of every order of society, to endeavour to cleave to the old paths, and use every exertion to prevent all innovation on the institutions and usages which we have received from our forefathers."[90] The Fourth of July Orations, in this vein, assumed an almost ritual and religious quality as they duti-fully recounted the important events of American history: the first Puritan settlements, oppressive actions by England, and the Revolutionary victories.

In part, the Federalists looked to the Puritan past for ex-amples of proper civic habits. One Massachusetts Federalist praised the Puritans for having imparted to the citizens of the state a "love of posterity" that allowed her members to "watch with eager, cautious, resolute eye, the wary movements of dis-organizing time."[91] Others would see the Puritans as a model for civil government in which it was "designed, not for the aggrandizement or private advantage of a few, but for the safety and welfare of the whole community."[92] The New England governments, as they had descended from a Puritan past, were seen as "the most *democratical*" because they allowed an "aristocracy of talents" to be elevated by the preferences of the people.[93]

A recurrent theme in Federalist rhetoric, and one that goes to the heart of the civic foundations of Federalism, was that of education.[94] For the Federalists, what was distinct about the philosophies of Godwin and Condorcet, and their American version found in Paine, was that they were "Unconnected with any system of faith or politics." The "language of philosophism," instead, believed in the "perfectibility" of humankind, a "primeval innocence" that was corrupted by "religion and social institutions." A new basis for society was called for by the *philosophes*, one in which "government, religion and every social institution are to be abolished, and men are to become immortal by the mere omnipotence of mind over matter." Quite in contrast, the Puritans sought not to be "theoretical philosophers" who engaged in speculative inquiry about the nature of society, but "gave credit to the voice of history" and "learned from their bible and their experience that man is naturally depraved and ignorant, constantly prone to vice and to error." Rather than leaving individuals to their primeval selves, the Puritans "believed that religious instruction, both public and private, is indispensable to the existence of a well ordered society."[95] As governor of Massachusetts, Caleb Strong would also emphasize the importance of education for civic acculturation. "Our ancestors were impressed with the importance" of widespread education "and manifested an earnest solicitude, that their children might be educated in literature and religion and moral principles." Such education was "necessary in republican governments," thought Strong, because they "depend, for their support, upon the enlightened and affectionate attachment of the people."[96]

On a far more ominous note, though, many Federalists would look to the Puritans as a justification for a politics of purity in which Republicans could be justly removed from the civic body. Timothy Dwight provided the religious rationale for such insulation. We are "eminently called," announced Dwight, "to undertake an entire separation from our enemies," including the political ones.[97] There were several reasons given for such a drastic action. First, to continue to intermingle with the unregenerate would result in the corruption of the pure. Despite one's best efforts not to adopt the practices of the degenerate, "Common sense has however declared, two thousand years ago, and God has sanctioned the declaration, that 'Evil communications corrupt good manners.'" A second reason was that God's retribution toward these sinners would rain on all those associated with the unregenerate, a reason Winthrop and Cotton had given for leaving England. "Should we, however, in a forbidden connection with these enemies of God, escape all hope, from moral ruin, we shall still receive our share of their plagues," spoke Dwight. There was no such separation between individual and communal culpability: private conduct reflected on the community and the community was consequently punished. Because "'one sinner destroyeth much good,'" the "personal conduct of no individual can be insignificant to the safety and happiness of a nation."[98]

That the enemy, republicanism, was known did not make the task of rooting out the impure any easier than it had been for the Puritans to discern the saint from the sinner. In fact, the very hiddenness of this internal foe added to the hysteria. The person to be feared was not racially or ethnically distinct, did not speak a different language, and did not act differently. That the danger appeared in a form no different from the "true patriot," spreading its insidious poison in secret, slowly "sap[ping] the foundations of our republic," made the battle all the more frenzied.[99] Anyone could be the enemy—one's friend, relative, neighbor, even possibly oneself. And since there were no obvious indicators of who was unclean, vigilance was called for. Now was not the time for complacency. "The present day, therefore, is a day for action and alarm, and not for security and sloth. It is a day which tries men's souls. It is a cause in which there are not, there *cannot* be any *neuters*. 'He that is not with us, is against us, and he that gathereth not with us, scattereth abroad.'"[100]

Purity, not pluralism, was the order of the day. Charles Paine alluded to this desire for purification when he called to his audience to "renew our solemn obligations, to venerate the memories of our fathers, to preserve their institutions, to emu-

late their virtues, to defend their inheritance, to cultivate a
national character, to glow with pride at the name of our country, to become only AMERICANS!"[101] Tradition was invoked
to create boundaries that separated "insiders" from "outsiders." Timothy Dwight was to the point: "In this country you all
sprang from one stock, speak one language, have one system
of manners, profess one religion, and wear one character. Your
laws, your institutions, your interests, are one. No mixture
weakens, no strangers divide, you."[102] Like the Jews, the American tribe was not to be infected by the Philistines, nor would
American principles be corrupted through their application
to the French Revolution. Reacting to the revolution overseas,
Charles Paine inquired, "Can that principle, which produces
order and happiness, produce also confusion and misery? Does
the same cause, which engenders the thunder to purify the
atmosphere of its noxious vapours, produce also the wild tor-
nado to desolate where it spreads?" No, indeed. "The spirit of
your fathers rises indignant at the comparison."[103]

Actions followed from these words. In an attempt to secure
God's protection from this "afflictive situation," President John
Adams proclaimed a day of national fasting in 1798 and again
in 1799. Through "solemn humiliation, fasting and prayer" the
regenerate could hopefully insulate themselves from the iniquity that abounded.[104] The Federalists, also during Adams'
administration, passed the Alien Act, the eighteenth-century
version of the Cart and Whip Act, which empowered the president (although the authority was never used) to deport without trial any immigrants who were suspected of being spies.
And throughout the 1790s the Federalists were engaged in
hostilities with France, hostilities that began to end only when
John Adams (despite the cries of betrayal by the Federalists)
sent an envoy to France to negotiate a treaty pacifying relations between the countries.

In the spirit of the best Puritans, the Federalists assumed
the task of scrutinizing the words and actions of the entire
community to determine who were the great unwashed. Thus,
we see the passage of the Sedition Act, a law whose broadness
of language revealed the extent of this anxiety as well as the
difficulty of clearly identifying the purveyors of party interest.
The Act, designed to be in force until March 3, 1801, after the

next presidential election, was directed against "any person or persons" who

> write, print, utter or publish, or shall cause or procure to be written, printed, uttered or published, or shall knowingly and willingly assist or aid in writing, printing, uttering or publishing, any false, scandalous, and malicious writing or writings against the government of the United States . . . with intent to defame the said government . . . or to bring them . . . into contempt or disrepute; or to excite against them . . . the hatred of the good people of the United States; or to stir up sedition within the United States; or to incite any unlawful combination therein for opposing or resisting any law of the United States. . . .[105]

It was a relentless search, an awesome task of casting the light of righteousness on the darkness of the heart. Numerous arrests of editors and others who dared to defy the act added to the drama of the time. In one of the most famous instances, Jedidiah Peck, who had circulated a petition calling for the repeal of the Alien and Sedition Acts, was arrested and transported two hundred miles to stand trial in New York City. Writing on behalf of the Sedition Act, Charles Lee defended these actions, depicting a nation under siege from within. "If, with impunity, the legislature and executive may be made the objects of contempt and hatred among the people by means of malicious and false stories, calculated to excite commotions and resistance to the measures of government, is it not certain that the constitution will be undermined and subverted?" The answer was obvious from within a Federalist understanding of the civic body: Government's "basis is the affection and respect of the people; take these away and the government is at an end."[106] Even with the destruction of the "viperous insect of foreign perfidy, whose cancerous tooth has blighted the foliage of our glory," true Americans had "now to cauterize the wide spreading roots of domestic faction, which have nourished their rank vegetation on the strength of our soil."[107] With the election of Jefferson there was even talk in New England about seceding from the union.[108] The exuberance of America's prospects had given way to an anxious search for the Republican enemy within.

It is in this environment that we can understand Federalist warnings about the need to establish a "national character."

The term had been used by Madison before to warn of the dangers of becoming indebted to England, for fear that such indebtedness would corrupt the national character, as it did individual character.[109] But for many Federalists in the 1790s and early 1800s, the concern was not so much with debt as much as with how to secure an American identity. Some "barrier must be erected," spoke one Federalist, "to guard against the possibility of future dangers, from the encroachments of either foreign or domestic enemies." Such a barrier was not "formed" by "our strength, our opulence or our numbers" but "by the minds of our citizens. Every nation receives the stamp of infamy or greatness, from the respective characters of the several individuals of which it is composed."[110]

Implicit in this notion of national character was the idea of an inherited tradition, for what the Federalists in part were reacting to was the "torrent" of "Gothic barbarity" unleashed by the revolutionaries in France. To craft this tradition, many Federalists would seek to link this national character back to "the simplicity of our fathers," as this connection to religion served as an integral component of character. "Americans ought to be characterized," announced one orator, "as firmly attached to the religion of their fathers" and, following this, "partial to the government of their choice; dignified in their submission to the constituted assemblies; delighted with their own country, and ambitious to be completely independent of any other."[111] Wrote one Boston writer, in addressing other more negative characterizations of the Puritans, "What a *falling off* there is at this day from the examples set us by our illustrious ancestors—we may call our present character liberality, or christen it with what name we please, but its baneful effects best tell its inutility—we may talk of the rigid manners, and the puritannical usages of our progenitors, but far better would it be for us, if we copied their frugality, their honesty, and their *reverence for laws & rulers*, which is known they possessed."[112] The Federalists, in their interpretation of the Revolution, in their assessment of the Republicans, and in their understanding of national character, stood for order and filial piety because they saw in such piety not the privileging of their position but the foundation of civic liberty. It was a liberty which had its foundation in the Federalist construction of a Puritan past.

Notes

1   [David Humphreys], "The Glory of America; or, Peace Triumphant over War: A Poem" (Philadelphia, 1783), 3, 16.

2   Ezra Stiles, "The United States elevated to Glory and Honor" (New Haven, 1783), in *The Pulpit of the American Revolution*, ed. John Wingate Thornton (Boston: Gould and Lincoln, 1860), 406, 440.

3   See Merrill Jensen, *The New Nation*, (New York: Random House, 1950), 148-9, 208-9, chapt. 6.

4   See Gordon S. Wood, *The Radicalism of the American Revolution* (New York: Vintage, 1991), especially 229-43.

5   On this sense of corruption following the Revolution, see Gordon S. Wood, *The Creation of the American Republic, 1776-1787* (New York: W. W. Norton, 1969), chapt. 12.

6   David Daggett, *An Oration, Pronounced in the Brick Meeting-House, in the City of New-Haven, on the Fourth of July, A.D. 1787* (New-Haven, [1787]), 4.

7   Daggett, *Oration*, [1787], 3, 16; John Gardiner, *An Oration, Delivered July 4, 1785, at the Request of the Town of Boston, in Celebration of the Anniversary of American Independence* (Boston, [1785]), 33; John Brooks, *An Oration, Delivered to the Society of the Cincinnati in the Commonwealth of Massachusetts, July 4th, 1878* (Boston, 1787), 7.

8   Alexander Hamilton, "Federalist Paper No. 15," *The Federalist Papers* (New York: Mentor, 1961), 107.

9   Daggett, *Oration*, 22.

10 Robert Livingston, *An Oration Delivered Before the Society of Cincinnati (sic) of the State of New-York* (New-York, 1787); Simeon Baldwin, *An Oration Pronounced Before the Citizens of New-Haven, July 4th, 1788; In Commemoration of the Declaration of Independence and Establishment of the Constitution of the United States of America* (New-Haven, 1788), 8-9.

11 Gardiner, *Oration*, 1785, 33, 34-5; Massachusetts Colony Laws (1651 and 1652) quoted in an endnote of Gardiner's *Oration*.

12 Jonathan Austin, *An Oration, Delivered July 4, 1786, at the Request of the Inhabitants of the Town of Boston, in the Celebration of the Anniversary of American Independence* (Boston, 1786), 16. On the importance of fiscal concerns to the Federalists, see Roger H. Brown, *Redeeming the Republic: Federalists, Taxation, and the Origins of the Constitution* (Baltimore: Johns Hopkins University Press, 1993).

13   Gardiner, *Oration*, 1785, 34.

14   Brooks, *Oration*, 1787, 8.

15   Daggett, *Oration*, 1787, 14.

16   Timothy Dwight, *A Discourse on Some Events of the Last Century, Delivered in the Brick Church in New Haven, On Wednesday, January 7, 1801* (New Haven, 1801), 35.

17   John Adams, "A Defence of the Constitutions of Government," in *The Works of John Adams*, 10 vols., ed. Charles Francis Adams (Boston: Charles C. Little and James Brown, 1851), 4: 290.

18   Daggett, *Oration*, 1787, 15.

19   Ibid.

20   Benjamin Rush, "Address to the People of the United States" (Philadelphia, 1787), in *Principles and Acts of the Revolution in America*, ed. Hezekiah Niles (New York: A. S. Barnes & Co., 1876), 234.

21   Joel Barlow, *An Oration, Delivered at the North Church in Hartford, at the Meeting of the Connecticut Society of the Cincinnati, July 4th, 1787. In Commemoration of the Independence of the United States* (Hartford, [1787]), 11.

22   Benjamin Hichborn, *An Oration, Delivered July 5th, 1784, at the Request of the Inhabitants of the Town of Boston; in Celebration of the Anniversary of American Independence* (Boston, [1784]), 14. See also John Treat Irving, *Oration, Delivered on the 4th of July, 1809, Before the Tammany Society* (New York, 1809), 15; Chauncey Lee, *The Tree of Knowledge of Political Good and Evil. A Discourse at Colebrook, on the Twenty-Fourth Anniversary of American Independence. July 4th, 1800* (Hartford, 1800), 30; and Charles Paine, *Oration*, 17.

23   For a discussion of a similar change in tasks in Leninist regimes, see Kenneth Jowitt, "Inclusion and Mobilization in European Leninist Regimes," *World Politics* 8 (October 1975): 69-96. For an account of this as a Federalist task, see Linda K. Kerber, *Federalists in Dissent: Imagery and Ideology in Jeffersonian America* (Ithaca: Cornell University Press, 1980), 192-212.

24   Jonathan Austin, *Oration* (1786), 17.

25   [Anonymous], "Rudiments of Law and Government Deduced from the Law of Nature" (Charleston, 1783), in *American Political Writings during the Founding Era: 1760-1805*, 2 vols., eds. Charles S. Hyneman and Donald S. Lutz (Indianapolis: Liberty Press, 1983), 1: 566.

26   Levi Frisbie, *An Oration, Delivered at Ipswich, at the Request of a Number of the Inhabitants, on the Twenty-ninth of April, 1783; on Account of the*

Happy Restoration of Peace between Great-Britain and the United States of America (Boston, 1783), 22-3.

27   Stanley Elkins and Eric McKitrick, *The Age of Federalism* (New York: Oxford University Press, 1993), 24. This perspective is an outgrowth of the historical interpretations of many of the Progressives. See, for example, Vernon L. Parrington, *Main Currents in American Thought*, 2 vols. (New York: Harvest, 1927), vol. 1, book 3, part 2.

28   Wood, *Creation*, 562.

29   Wood, *Radicalism*, 264.

30   Joyce Appleby, *Capitalism and a New Social Order: The Republican Vision of the 1790s* (New York: New York University Press, 1984), 83.

31   James M. Banner, Jr., *To The Hartford Convention: The Federalists and the Origins of Party Politics in Massachusetts, 1789-1815* (New York: Alfred A. Knopf, 1970), 22.

32   Elkins and McKitrick, *Age of Federalism*, 24.

33   See John M. Murrin, "The Great Inversion, or Court versus Country: A Comparison of the Revolution Settlements in England (1688-1721) and America (1776-1816)," in *Three British Revolutions: 1641, 1688, 1776*, ed. J. G. A. Pocock (Princeton: Princeton University Press, 1980), 422, 415.

34   Lance Banning, *The Jeffersonian Persuasion: Evolution of a Party Ideology* (Ithaca: Cornell University Press, 1978), 133.

35   Isaac Kramnick, *Republicanism and Bourgeois Radicalism: Political Ideology in Late Eighteenth-Century England and America* (Ithaca: Cornell University Press, 1990), 169, 260-88.

36   Appleby, *Capitalism*, 59.

37   See John Zvesper, *Political Philosophy and Rhetoric: A Study of the Origins of American Party Politics* (Cambridge: Cambridge University Press, 1977), 13. Zvesper contrasts the Federalist "realists" to the Jeffersonian "idealists."

38   See Kerber, *Federalists*, chapt. 1.

39   Daniel W. Howe, "The Political Psychology of *The Federalist*," *The William and Mary Quarterly*, 3d series, 54 (July 1987), 491-2.

40   Wood, *Radicalism*, 232.

41   Elnathan Pope, *An Oration . . . in Rochester* (New-Bedford: Lindsey, 1809), 7-8. For a discussion of the relationship between faculty psychology and the political body, see Howe, "Political Psychology," 496-99.

42   See Kerber, *Federalists*, 192-202.

43   Banner, *Hartford*, 36. See also 40.

44   William Tudor, *An Oration Pronounced July 4, 1809* (Boston: Belcher, 1809), 6-7, 14.

45   John Hubbard Church, *Oration, Pronounced at Pelham . . . July 4, 1805* (Haverhill, Mass.: Gould, 1805), 3, 16, 4.

46   David Daggett, *Sun-Beams may be Extracted from Cucumbers, but the Process is Tedious. An Oration Pronounced on the Fourth of July, 1799. At the Request of the Citizens of New-Haven* (New-Haven, 1799), 27-8.

47   Charles Paine, *An Oration, Pronounced July 4, 1801, at the Request of the Inhabitants of the Town of Boston, in Commemoration of the Anniversary of American Independence* (Boston, 1801), 12.

48   Thomas Danforth, *An Oration, Pronounced July 4, 1804* (Boston: Russell & Cutler, 1804), 10-11. For Danforth, the "ardor" and "zeal" of the Puritans "converted the frightful wild of the forest into fields and vallies, into towns and cities, into states and empire" (10).

49   Charles Fraser, *An Oration, Delivered in St. Michael's Church, Before the Inhabitants of Charleston* (Charleston: J. Hoff, 1808), 7-8.

50   David Ramsay, *The History of the American Revolution*, 2 vols. (Lexington, Ky.: Downing and Phillips, 1815, orig. published 1789), 1: 43-4.

51   Ramsay, *History of the American Revolution*, 1: 32.

52   John Marshall, *The Life of George Washington . . .*, 5 vols. (Philadelphia: Wayne, 1804 [-07]), 1: 106.

53   Mercy Warren, *History of the Rise, Progress and Termination of the American Revolution*, 3 vols. (Boston: Manning and Loring, 1805), 1: 9. See also William Gordon, *The History of the Rise, Progress, and Establishment of the Independence of the United States of America*, 3 vols. (New York: Hodge, Allen, and Campbell, 1789), which opens with an extended discussion of the Puritans, and John Lendrum, *Concise and Impartial History of the American Revolution* (Boston: I. Thomas and E. T. Andrews, 1795).

54   Lester H. Cohen, "Creating a Usable Future: The Revolutionary Historians and the National Past," in *The American Revolution: Its Character and Limits*, ed. Jack P. Greene (New York: New York University Press, 1987), 318.

55   Ezra Stiles Ely, *The Migration of the Pilgrims* (Philadelphia: U.S. Gazette Office, 1818), 14-5.

56   Mackie, *Oration*, 1804, 14-5.

57   Ely, *Migration*, 21.

58   John Quincy Adams, *An Oration, delivered at Plymouth* (Boston: Russell and Cutler, 1802), 6.

59   See Adams, *Oration*, 6, 17-20.

60   *The Port Folio*, New Series, 4 (Nov. 28, 1807), 344.

61   Thomas Henderson, *An Oration, Delivered in the Court-House, Cincinnati* (Cincinnati: Browne, [1807]), 4.

62   John Mackie, *An Oration, Delivered in the Meeting-House in Wareham* (New Bedford: Shearman, 1804), 8. See also Adams, *Oration*, 13, and Joseph Otis Osgood, *An Oration Commemorative of American Independence, Pronounced at Salisbury* (Newburyport: Gilmans, 1810), 8.

63   Adams, *Oration*, 15. This image makes it down to Georgia, as well. See John McPherson Berrien, *An Oration, Commemorative of the Anniversary of American Independence* (Savannah, [Ga.]: Seymour and Woolhapter, 1808), 9-10. This argues directly against Zvesper's suggestion that the Federalists held a Hobbesian view of the state of nature. See Zvesper, *Political Philosophy*, 14.

64   John C. Miller, *Alexander Hamilton and the Growth of the New Nation* (New York: Harper & Row, 1959), 406.

65   Wood, *Creation*, 402-3.

66   John Adams to his wife, December 19, 1793, in *Familiar Letters of John Adams and His Wife Abigail Adams, During the Revolution*, ed. Charles Francis Adams (New York: Hurd and Houghton, 1876), 134.

67   Noah Webster, *An Oration Pronounced Before the Citizens of New-Haven on the Anniversary of the Independence of the United States, July 4th, 1798* (New Haven, [1798]), 12.

68   Elkins and McKitrick, *Age of Federalism*, 701.

69   See Wood, *Radicalism*, 264-70.

70   Richard Buell, Jr., *Securing the Revolution: Ideology in American Politics, 1789-1815* (Ithaca: Cornell University Press, 1972), 123.

71   David Hackett Fischer, *The Revolution of American Conservatism: The Federalist Party in the Era of Jeffersonian Democracy* (New York: Harper & Row, 1965), 33. Kerber, *Federalists*, and Banner, *Hartford Convention*, both provide an important corrective to the notion that Federalist ideology, in Banner's words, was simply a "strategy of rationalizing upper-class rule" (*Hartford Convention*, 61).

72   For an important discussion of the Federalist jeremiad, see Sacvan Bercovitch, *American Jeremiad* (Madison: University of Wisconsin Press,

1978), chapt. 5, though Bercovitch overstates the extent of consensus, particularly "the free-enterprise values of their culture" (137).

73   Charles Paine, *Oration*, 18.

74   Timothy Dwight, *The Duty of Americans, at the Present Crisis, Illustrated in a Discourse, Preached on the Fourth of July, 1798* (New Haven, 1798), 30. See also 21.

75   Samuel Fiske, *An Oration Pronounced at Claremont, on the Anniversary of American Independence* (Windsor, 1799), 13-4.

76   Daggett, *Sun-Beams*, 20.

77   George Sullivan, *An Oration, Pronounced at Exeter on the Fourth Day of July 1800, in commemoration of the Anniversary of American Independence* (Exeter, N.H., 1800), 12.

78   John Adams to his wife, January 14, 1793, in Adams, *Familiar Letters*, 119.

79   Church, *Oration*, 1805, 18-9.

80   Mackie, *Oration*, 1804, 17. See also Fisher Ames, "The Dangers of American Liberty" (1805), in *Works of Fisher Ames* (Boston: T. B. Wait & Co., 1809).

81   Church, *Oration*, 1805, 20.

82   Benjamin Silliman, *An Oration, Delivered at Hartford on the 6th of July* (Hartford, [Conn.]: Hudson and Goodwin, 1802), 32.

83   Cushing Otis, *Oration*, 16; Chauncey Lee, *Tree of Knowledge*, 10.

84   Chauncey Lee, *Tree of Knowledge*, 4.

85   [Charles Lee], *Defense of the Alien and Sedition Laws, shewing their entire consistency with the Constitution of the United States, and the principles of our government* (Philadelphia, 1798), 22; Thomas Day, *An Oration on Party Spirit, pronounced before the Connecticut Society of Cincinnati, convened at Hartford, for the Celebration of American Independence, on the 4th of July, 1798* (Litchfield, [1798]), 7, 9.

86   Mackie, *Oration*, 1804, 17. Church concludes, in surveying modern republics, that factions result in despotism (*Oration*, 1805, 20).

87   John Adams, "Inaugural Speech to Both Houses of Congress," March 4, 1797, in *The Works of John Adams*, 10 vols., ed. Charles Francis Adams (Boston: Little, Brown and Co., 1854), 9: 109. These concerns replay earlier Federalist rhetoric which expressed their enthusiasm for the Constitution. In restoring order, wrote John Jay after reciting a litany of America's ills, the Constitution "should be sufficiently energetic to raise us from our prostrate and distressed situation. . . ." (Jay, *Address*,

75). In Simeon Baldwin's Fourth of July oration, after recalling how the Puritans sacrificed their comforts for religious and civil liberty, he looked to the Constitution as restoring authority that would return to America the "glory" that had been "tarnished by the consequences of a confederation totally deficient" in its ability to make and enforce laws (Simeon Baldwin, *An Oration Pronounced Before the Citizens of New-Haven, July 5th, 1788* [New-Haven, 1788], 9). The Constitution was seen by some as the means of redemption to a distressed people. S. B. Webb commented that Jay's pamphlet "had a most astonishing influence in converting anti-federalism to a knowledge and belief that the new Constitution was their only political salvation" (Written on April 27, 1788. Quoted in Jay, *Address*, 67).

88   David Daggett, *Sun-Beams*, 27-8. See also James D. Hopkins, *An Oration Pronounced Before the Inhabitants of Portland, July 4th, 1805, In Commemoration of American Independence* (Portland, 1805), 12.

89   Samuel Thacher, *An Oration, pronounced July 4, 1796, at the Request of the Inhabitants of the Town of Concord, in Commemoration of the Twentieth Anniversary of American Independence* (Boston, 1796), 5.

90   Thomas Robbins, *An Historical View of the First Planters of New-England* (Hartford: Peter B. Gleason & Co., 1815), 294.

91   Danforth, *Oration*, 1804, 18.

92   Church, *Oration*, 1805, 10.

93   Silliman, *Oration*, 1802, 30.

94   For an excellent discussion of Federalist views of education, see Kerber, *Federalists*, chapt. 6.

95   Silliman, *Oration*, 7, 9, 28, 25-6.

96   Caleb Strong, "Speech, Delivered Jan. 4, 1801," in *Patriotism and Piety* (Newburyport: Blunt, 1808), 40-1. See also Silliman, *Oration*, 28.

97   Timothy Dwight, *Duty*, 19.

98   Ibid., 21, 16.

99   Cushing Otis, *Oration*, 12. See also George Sullivan, *Oration*, 1800, 12-3.

100   Chauncey Lee, *Tree of Knowledge*, 30.

101   Charles Paine, *Oration*, 24.

102   Timothy Dwight, *Duty*, 46.

103   Charles Paine, *Oration*, 22.

104 John Adams, "Proclamation for a National Fast," March 23, 1798, and March 6, 1799, Adams, *Works*, 9: 169-70, 172-4.

105 *The Alien and Sedition Laws, and Virginia and Kentucky Resolutions* ([Boston], [1798]).

106 [Lee], *Defense*, 22.

107 Charles Paine, *Oration*, 17.

108 G. M. Stephenson, *The Puritan Heritage* (New York: Macmillan, 1952), 89.

109 See Elkins and McKitrick, *Age of Federalism*, 92.

110 Mackie, *Oration*, 13-4.

111 Whitman, *Oration*, 32, 29-30.

112 [Boston] *Independent Chronicle*, Sept. 7, 1786, quoted in Brown, *Redeeming*, 156-7. See also Fisher Ames, "The Dangers of American Liberty," (Boston, 1805), in *American Political Writings*, eds. Hyneman and Lutz, 2: 391.

Chapter 5

The Whig Rhetoric of Founding

In looking to the politics of the opening decades of the nineteenth-century, scholarly attention has often been drawn to the self-destruction of the Federalists, the ascendancy of the Jeffersonian Republicans, or the emergence of the Jacksonian Democrats. What gets lost in the way scholars view this political drama is the coalescing of an American Whig identity, one that was forged in the decade of the 1820s.[1] At least part of this inattention to the formation of a Whig identity can be explained by scholarly appraisal of the Whig party as intellectually incoherent, politically cynical, and ultimately unsuccessful.

The Whig position was, indeed, a curious one. The Whigs heralded the growth of the modern capitalist market, which would unleash the forces of entrepreneurial individualism, yet they decried the loss of the pre-commercial values of deference, virtue, and hierarchical community; they embraced the prosperity brought about by commerce, yet they feared the corruption of virtue that resulted from the pursuit of interest; and they looked forward to a capitalist economy while glancing back at an anti-democratic Federalism and Puritan moralism. In assessing these positions, scholars have taken a variety of tacks, oftentimes tending to caricature rather than characterize the Whigs. For some, the Whigs were but a fragile amalgam of Federalists, conservative or disgruntled Democrats, National Republicans, and Antimasons who were brought together out of a spirit of political opportunism rather than ideological identification.[2] Others have seen the Whigs as representatives of an evangelical moralism who discussed other issues only to broaden their appeal and win elections.[3] A widely argued view is that the Whigs were a conservative, anti-democratic reaction to Jacksonian democracy; their principles, when not cynical, were inconsistent.[4] Some have portrayed the Whigs as heralds of the positive liberal state who would play a major role in promoting industrial development[5] while others, seemingly in direct contradiction, have depicted the Whigs as drawing upon a classic republican tradition, distrustful of the state.[6]

It is only recently, spurred in large part by the work of Daniel Walker Howe, that our understanding of the Whigs has been broadened: we can view them not simply as being a political party but as embodying a coherent "political culture."[7] Howe understands "culture" as "an evolving system of beliefs, attitudes, and techniques for solving problems, transmitted from generation to generation and finding expression in the innumerable activities that people learn," including politics.[8] In the previous chapter we undertook an examination of Federalist political culture, looking at invocations of the Puritans to help us understand the political anxieties of that group. This chapter continues this inquiry by examining the cultural referents used by early Whigs. My primary focus will be on Whig political speeches, though I will place these speeches against the backdrop of other cultural expressions, including sermons, periodical articles, historiographies, and literary works. For the Whigs, these referents served to authorize a vision of the political and economic future and convey a sense of cultural identity.[9]

Whig rhetoric, and political rhetoric in general, has been treated with some suspicion, seen as manipulative of the public[10] or unreflective of the actual views of the people.[11] We cannot fully appreciate the value of these orations in our contemporary society, in which speeches are captured in sound bites and given a political "spin." Orations in the nineteenth-century were seen as a highly valued literary form. By the nineteenth-century, America was applauded as a "speech-making country" with New England at its center.[12] In the hands of the Whigs, orations and histories served not just to convey information but to construct an identity. In an essay on George Bancroft's *History of the United States*, for example, the *North American Review*, the most prominent Whig journal in America, applauded Bancroft's work, even though he was a Democrat, because it reflected more than the "accumulation of facts" in a "timid adherence to what is erroneously called truth," but involved the recalling of the "actual presence" of the past, to make immortal the "enduring zeal, the open-handed liberality, the fortitude, and the heroism, with which, in the day of small beginnings, the first foundations were laid."[13] Such great Whig orators as Edward Everett "meant to create a tradition that would inspire as well as inform. Like the Attic orators—and dramatists," Everett "knew the power of symbols to create a people's political identity."[14]

One such referent that appeared in Whig speeches, particularly but not exclusively those in New England, was the Puritans. By invoking the Puritans, the Whigs drew upon a legacy that, as we have seen, was already prominent in American historiography and literature as well as in American political discourse. James Savage, for example, had published Winthrop's *History of New England* (1825-26), complete with notes about what lessons might be gleaned from this Puritan past. On the frontispiece to both editions of the *History*, Savage quotes the Roman historian Sallust: "Often have I heard that Quintis Maximus and Publius Scipio, as well as the most renowned men of our state, were accustomed to say that when they had contemplated the images of their ancestors, their minds were most vehemently inspired toward courage."[15] Benjamin Trumbull's *A General History of the United States of America*, as one example of the prominent place given to New England, opens with a celebration of a now quite familiar depiction of the Puritan settlement as a "vast wilderness, a land not sown, replete with savage beasts and more savage men" and closes the second chapter with a call to venerate the "selfdenial (sic), industry, economy, and greatness of mind" and "perpetuate this glorious inheritance."[16] The memory of the Puritans was furthered by an ever-expanding number of Fourth of July celebrations, commemorations of the Pilgrim landings, the spread of New England Societies to the south and west, and a growing interest in historical fiction, with New England maintaining its dominance in these writings, as well.[17]

At issue in many of these recollections was how this Puritan past would be interpreted. Orthodox Congregationalists, writing through such Calvinist journals as the *Panoplist*, extolled the virtues and religious purity of the Puritan founders, often using the Puritans to point to the backsliding of contemporary society. Among those works that expressed unqualified admiration for the Puritan founders was Timothy Dwight's posthumously published reflections, *Travels in New England and New York* (1821-2). Dwight, grandson of Jonathan Edwards, Congregationalist minister, and president of Yale College, used his numerous travels across the region to reflect on the transformation, started by the Puritans, of the wilderness into a civilized country. Dwight was unabashedly enthusiastic about the intellectual and spiritual contributions of his grandfather and equally admiring of the strength of the New England character, one that was and still is well-mannered, industrious, civil, grave, and enterprising. Moreover, Dwight continually emphasized the spirit of progress that seemed to animate New England, be it in education, manufacturing, or religion. But Dwight presented himself as more than a New England partisan: in concluding his reflections, he sought to connect this spirit of progress with the creation of a national and transatlantic Christian union that would usher in the new millennium.[18] The work was widely read and admired by many, including such non-Calvinists as Ralph Waldo Emerson, Henry David Thoreau, and Nathaniel Hawthorne.[19]

On the opposite end were many liberals speaking for a new spirit of religious toleration, including a growing number of Unitarians, who saw not purity but rigidity, intolerance, and hypocrisy as the hallmark of the Puritan temperament. An important portrayal of this aspect of Puritanism could be seen in one of the earliest works of historical fiction, Catharine Sedgwick's *A New-England Tale; or, Sketches of New-England Character and Manners* (1822). Calvinism, for Sedgwick, who was herself raised in a Puritan New England village, appears as a religion in which people "[assume] the form of godliness, without feeling its power." The Calvinist clergy, furthermore, come across as zealous and rigid. At a funeral sermon, for example, the Puritan minister in her *Tale* chooses "for his text, 'The wages of sin is death,' instead of using the occasion to illustrate the "tenderness" of the Lord. More than anything else, Sedgwick contrasts the hypocrisy of those who believe themselves to be God's elect with a Unitarianism that celebrates diverse religions united by universal and genuine virtues.[20]

Rather than rejecting the Puritan past, many writers not necessarily sympathetic to contemporary forms of Calvinism romanticized the Puritan past, often portraying it as a source of a liberal spirit. This past was sometimes made more palatable to liberals by distinguishing the Pilgrims from the Puritans, since the Pilgrims did not carry the same historical baggage of persecution and intolerance.[21] But this was not always the case. The transcendentalist Emerson, for example, in his commemoration of the founding of Concord, would talk about both the Pilgrims and Puritans. In recalling the hardships and struggles of these early settlers, a conception that was by now axiomatic in describing the Puritans and Pilgrims, Emerson suggested that "The Puritans, to keep the remembrance of their unity one with another, and of their peaceful compact with the Indians, named their forest settlement CONCORD." The Puritan spirit, for Emerson, was the expression of the universal longing for community that resides in the spirit of all humanity. The Puritans, though, more than exemplars of the transcendental spirit, were also politically important. The "first recorded political act of our fathers, this tax assessed on its inhabitants by a town," was singularly important for Emerson because it established a principle of sovereignty that served as a blueprint for the development of future towns and, ultimately, the "thirst for liberty" that ignited the revolutionary clergy.[22] Emerson, in a later address, would suggest that the greatness of the Puritans did not lie "in what they designed" as the Whigs would argue, but in "what they were." What they were, for Emerson, was a reflection of the Divine which places all of us in service to others.[23]

George Bancroft, a Democrat, Unitarian, and prominent historian, credited the Puritans—and not just the Pilgrims—with planting "the undying principles of democratic liberty."[24] Bancroft was even able to praise both Roger Williams, for his adherence to the principle of a free conscience and intellectual liberty, and the Puritans (who had banished Williams), in whom he could see a "mildness" of character in all subjects but religion. Even their religious intolerance could be understood as the result of a laudable zeal for a purity of spirit. And

Jeremy Belknap, a Congregationalist minister who began as a theological conservative but became, later in his life, a critic of Puritan dogmatism, would give prominence to the "frugality, decency and temperance" of the early Puritans in his *American Biography*, a series of extended essays on explorers and statesmen.[25]

It was from this historical milieu that the Whigs would craft their interpretation of the Puritan past. The Whigs treated the Puritans and Pilgrims as "essentially . . . the same sort of men," conflating them in recollections of the past.[26] They also lent to the Puritans the liberal spirit to which Bancroft referred. But in the hands of Whig orators, the Puritans were much more: they were made into a founding legend that demonstrated how the commercialization of the economy and the central role of government in promoting this development could invigorate a sense of community and restore order to a fragmented American population. The Whigs (more than the Jeffersonians, Jacksonians, or Van Buren Democrats) drew upon the Puritans to explain and authorize their vision of a future economic and political order.[27] Somewhat appropriately, in doing so they looked to a rhetorical legacy in the Puritans that was in many ways as conflicted as what they sought to explain.

The Rise of Commerce

The first decades of the nineteenth-century were a time of accelerating social change as farmers entered into commerce, household economic relations were replaced by wage labor, merchant capitalists supplanted the local artisans, and stable class relations were torn asunder by a new ethos of social mobility and individualism. The result was widespread anxiety as those affected struggled to make sense of the individual and communal implications of the changes. The economic transition of the early nineteenth-century, driven initially by a commercial boom that ended only with the 1807 embargo, had become a (if not *the*) central issue of American politics by this time.

The Hamiltonian Federalists had already politicized the market interests of the commercial elite as they fought for the centrality of the state in promoting economic development.

The emerging commercial class began to look to the government to "guarantee property; to enforce contracts; to provide
juridical, financial, and transport infrastructures, to mobilize
society's resources as investment capital; and to load the legal
dice for enterprise in countless ways."[28] Thomas Jefferson similarly politicized the opposition, riding to office on a democratic tide while calling for the maintenance of a rural republic of farmers and mechanics. Early in his career Jefferson
depicted the "Cultivators of the earth" as "the most valuable
citizens" and artisans as the "panders of vice."[29] The reason
for this grew out of a republican belief that a virtuous and
moral people were necessary for a healthy democracy, virtue
having "its roots in nature and in an image of pristine simplicity in the agrarian republic."[30] Agriculture, in its tie to nature,
promoted a purity born of simplicity. In "those places, where
formerly sprang the thorn and the nettle," spoke one republican orator, "now shall grow the *rose* and the *lilly*—'the moun-
tains shall rejoice and be glad, the little hills shall clap their
hands with delight.'"[31] Agriculture, it was argued, worked to
refine an untamed nature. "Our trackless wilds shall soften
under the hand of cultivation; the desart and the silent place
shall rejoice, and the 'wilderness shall blossom like the rose.'"[32]
An American democracy premised on the agricultural refinement of nature would lead, as one republican exclaimed, to
the creation of "a second Eden."[33]

Even as radical Jeffersonians remained true to this agrarian
vision and decried the steady commercialization and urbanization of society, the moderates, including Jefferson himself,
moved toward a synthesis of commerce and agriculture, unified under a banner of democracy. By Jefferson's First Inaugural Address he elevated commerce to the "handmaid" of
agriculture.[34] Commercial development, as it made people
dependent on the capriciousness of the market for their own
survival, would threaten the virtue, if not the livelihood, of
the people. But it could be made a part of a democratic ethos
by subsuming it into a greater agrarian cause.[35]

The Jacksonians picked up on these Jeffersonian strands at
a point at which commercialization and its consequences (seen
dramatically in the Panic of 1819) were much more pronounced. The Jacksonians, too, feared the growth of manufac-

turing as the rise of large capital threatened the independence of the small laborer.[36] By creating a system of dependence of the laborer on the employer and by threatening the existence of the small farmer and mechanic, big capital undermined the fundamental equality necessary for democratic government. In the words of the Jacksonian orator Theophilus Fisk, the past paints a picture of prolonged struggle between the laboring classes and "the omnipotent power of Capital." The "warfare" will end only when "all are placed upon the broad tableland of perfect political equality. The sellers of labor will yet wrest from the unholy grasp of the apostles of Mammon the right to govern themselves, to make their own laws, and to select their own agents to execute them."[37] The Jacksonian fusion of commerce with democracy pitted large manufacturers against the united interests of farmers, laborers, and small business.

A Commercial Republic

Quite fearful of the unbridled pursuit of individual interest, the Whigs desired the creation of a virtuous people, a people defined by individual self-discipline, industriousness, and an orientation to the public good. Though appearing as classic republicans in this regard, Whiggery posed a challenge to republicanism in two ways. First, by promoting a government role in commercial ventures, the Whigs altered the republican assumption that civic virtue would be undermined once private commercial ends were allowed to intrude into the public realm. Second, by embracing the prosperity that arose out of a commercial society, they had to respond to a traditional republican concern that the allure of such wealth might turn the individual from a concern with virtue to material greed. The Whigs would continue to declare their allegiance to republican principles. Yet, it was not a Jeffersonian republicanism they drew upon; rather, in formulating a republicanism suitable to a commercial world the Whigs looked to the Puritans.[38]

In recalling the Puritans, the Whigs drew on a legacy, as we saw in chapter one, noted for its ambivalence toward prosperity and commerce.[39] Lyman Beecher, a former student of Timothy Dwight and, later, the head of the Lane Theological Seminary in Cincinnati, revealed some of this ambivalence as he used the occasion of the commemoration of the Pilgrim landing to call for an extension of religion as "the only means of reconciling our unparalleled prosperity with national purity and immortality." America's "rapid increase in wealth will be the occasion of our swift destruction," continued Beecher. The Puritan tradition within which Beecher spoke, though aimed at promoting a revival spirit, was one that had become reconciled to a Whig constituency of businessmen, professionals, and commercial farmers who were interested in the growth of manufacturing and commerce. We can get some sense of this merging of traditions when Beecher listed as the first step necessary for moral renovation the elimination of monopolies since "*the earth must be owned by those who till it.*" Combining a political with a religious lesson, Beecher suggested that "Nearly all the political evils which have afflicted mankind have resulted from the unrighteous monopoly of the earth. . . ."[40]

Although the Puritans had seen commerce and prosperity as antagonistic to purity and to a corporate ethic, the Whigs, invoking the memory of the Puritans, placed commerce and manufacturing in the service of community. The Whigs accomplished this in several ways. Often, they drew upon contemporary historical and fictional portrayals of Puritan frugality by speaking of the Puritans as having established habits of enterprise.[41] Like recollections of revolutionary statesmen who saw the Puritans as imbuing the American character with a love of liberty, the Whigs added to this the spirit of enterprise. Such accolades to the Puritan spirit were so commonplace in orations that, at times, the references appeared almost perfunctory. Other orators focused on the role of the Puritans in acquiring legal right to property. This right, which had been invoked in revolutionary discourse as a basis for colonial rebellion, was now seen as providing a contractual basis for property ownership central to Whig economic theory. The Puritans, went the claims of the Whigs, had gained title to their land fairly through agreements with the Indians who had occupied the lands. This view not only allied the Puritans with the Whigs, but placed both in opposition to the Jacksonian policy of forcible removal of the Indians from western land.[42] What gave the Puritans true title to the land, though, was not simply these agreements but the purposeful transformation of the land through their labor. In explaining the extraordinary work of the Puritans, the Whigs depicted these founders as confronting not an Edenic paradise as portrayed by some republicans but a "desolate wilderness" or a "dismal forest" that was made productive only through the application of their labor.[43]

Jefferson, too, would argue for private property based on this transformation of land by labor. But he saw such ownership, when combined with abundant American lands, as providing the basis for economic equality consistent with his political egalitarianism. Private property remained for Jefferson very much an agrarian ideal. The Whigs, on the other hand, sought to read into the human purpose of labor the emerging commercial spirit. Speaking on the occasion of the commencement of work on the Chesapeake and Ohio Canal, John Quincy Adams, in words reminiscent of Locke, justified government involvement in promoting internal improvements: "To subdue the Earth was therefore one of the first duties assigned to man at his Creation; and now in his fallen condition it remains among the most excellent and virtuous of his occupations. To subdue the Earth is preeminently the purpose of the undertaking, to the accomplishment of which the first stroke of the spade is now to be struck."[44] One of the most famous Whig orators, Edward Everett, spoke of a second settlement of American lands: the first by the "husbandman" who "reclaimed" the land from the unproductive "state of nature" through "the hard labor of the human hands"; the second by "the manufacturer, the engineer, and the mechanic" who would settle the land "by machinery, by the steam-engine, and by internal improvements." Heralding the rise of this new commercial society, Everett proclaimed, "We must, in every direction, have turnpike roads, unobstructed rivers, canals, rail-roads, and steamboats."[45]

Internal improvements, the canals and roads promoted by the federal government that made this commercial prosperity possible, held out the promise of harnessing the vast wilderness. What was called for was nothing less than "a conquest over physical Nature such as has never yet been achieved by man." John Quincy Adams, speaking less like Locke and more in the cadence of biblical prophecy, announced, "May they [internal improvements] increase and multiply 'til, in the sublime language of Inspiration, 'every valley shall be exalted, and every mountain and hill shall be made low—the crooked straight—the rough places plain. . . .'"[46] These extraordinary achievements could be traced to the Puritans who laid "the foundation of a great, prosperous, and growing republic."[47] By zealously pursuing opportunities to prosper, spoke Adams, America would "convert . . . prophecy into History."[48] Edward Everett echoed these same sentiments. An "organized, prosperous state," spoke Everett in capturing this Whig spirit of economic providence, is the "way that we are to fulfill our destiny to the world."[49]

Important in Everett's statement was the term "organized." The Puritans, though motivated in part by "commercial speculation (itself liberal and praiseworthy)," were not guided by an individualistic and unrestrained pursuit of self-interest, according to Everett. Instead, they acted in accordance with a "self-denying enthusiasm" in which they sacrificed their immediate interests for the good of the community.[50] For the Puritans, this enthusiasm was directed toward religion, a spirit that was handed down to "our fathers in the revolution, assuming then the form of the passion for civil liberty." It "is the same principle, which, in every age, wars against tyranny, sympathizes with the oppressed, kindles at the report of generous actions, and, rising above selfish calculation and sensual indulgence, learns 'to scorn delights and live laborious days;' and is ready, when honor and duty call, to sacrifice property, and ease, and life."[51] It is instructive to trace the course of this speech, as Everett merged two seemingly incompatible motives into the actions of the Puritans: a desire for commerce on the one hand and a republican concern with the public good on the other. These founding motives were to animate, as they did with the revolutionary leaders, the spirit of the new commercial republic. Commerce, in this formulation, became less a private endeavor and more an action consistent with civic responsibility. In this way the Whigs could justify government involvement in commerce, not as a promotion of private interest but of civic ends.

The Bonds of Commerce

Almost from the first days of the Puritan landing, the communal ideal enunciated by John Winthrop, the governor of the Massachusetts Bay Colony, was threatened by migration to the

American frontier and the pursuit of economic interest. Individuals and families challenged the integrity of a community knit together as they pushed westward to better their condition, search for more fertile land, or escape the repressiveness of the town. The individual pursuit of gain that accompanied the new American prosperity posed a grave threat to this communal ethic. Republicans and Whigs would later express similar fears that, in this time of prosperity, "ignoble, self ambition" might take "the place of patriotism."[52] Fred Somkin has noted that, during this time, Americans faced the "agonizing and finally unsuccessful attempt to retain the esprit of a sacred society, a family brotherhood, within a framework of conceptual and institutional constructs based upon freedom of contract."[53]

Though Somkin overstates the extent of a family brotherhood that united Americans, it was certainly the case that the Whigs sought to combine the rise of commerce and manufacturing, as it was based on respect for property, with a spirit of mutuality and interdependence that bound the nation together. The Whigs became the party of the Union, struggling to preserve the nation in the face of increasing sectional animosities. The Whigs looked to the Declaration of Independence and the Constitution in arguing for unity, elevating the documents to almost sacred status. To understand the Whig vision of a proper functioning community in a commercial republic, however, it is helpful to look once again, as did many of the Whigs, to the Puritans.

In characterizing the Whigs as aristocratic elites, it is often assumed that they thereby sought to defend unequal distributions of property. Certainly Jacksonian Democrats depicted the Whigs as defenders of unequal property (and thus power).[54] The Jacksonians, on the other hand, argued on behalf of egalitarian property relations. In a brief mention of the Pilgrims in an otherwise lengthy oration that covered the sweep of history, the Massachusetts Jacksonian Robert Rantoul, Jr. saw the Pilgrims as "setting out on the principle of an entire equality of rights" that they sought to "encourage, promote, and preserve" in their laws. Importantly, Rantoul's interpretation differed from those of the Whigs in that he did not ascribe American success to the Pilgrims; instead, he saw the Pilgrims as succeeding because of these egalitarian principles.[55]

The Whigs carried no such egalitarian pretensions, but they did consider broad-based property ownership as essential. They did so not for reasons of natural right nor for pursuit of individual interest but for political stability. This stability, so the Whigs argued, had its origins in the Puritan founding. The Puritans "left behind" a feudal system of property and maintained no significant disparities of wealth among them. This condition "demanded a parcelling out and division of the lands" that *"fixed the future frame and form of their government."* The laws respecting property "determined" the character of the political institutions, which was transmitted subsequently to current generations. Departing from his earlier reactionary Federalism, Webster, in an early statement of this Whig view, saw such wide distribution and protection of property as preventing both the plundering of the powerful and the impoverishment and dependence of the mass of people.[56] With so many people having a stake in the system through the ownership of property, government became less ruled by passion and more by a sentiment for stability.

While property ownership provided an important stabilizing influence on the republic, economic specialization and commerce would replace the Jeffersonian ideal of small, self-sufficient towns with a national community knit together by the market. As the "transportation revolution" pushed the market further into the countryside, the outlying areas were transformed as they were integrated into a capitalist division of labor.[57] "As transport gave areas comparative advantage in more specialized production, diverse manufactures developed around the port cities, the adjacent countryside specialized in perishable vegetables, fruits, and dairy products for urbanites, grain and livestock were produced at successively greater distances, and interior towns processed lumber, hides, and grain."[58] The intrusion of the market upset traditional patterns of rural life, providing a powerful base for Democrats to assail the emergent bourgeoisie and commercial establishment as disruptive (to those who wanted to keep the market out) and exclusive (to those who wanted to share in the opportunities for profit). The Whigs, whose political strength was, not surprisingly, concentrated in commercial areas and along transportation routes, depicted this new division of labor not as a cause of fragmentation but as the foundation for a new communal ethic.

Edward Everett, speaking in Plymouth on the anniversary of the Pilgrim landing, spoke of the communal implications of this commercial penetration. "The substantial clothing of our industrious classes is now the growth of the American soil, and the texture of the American loom; the music of the water-wheel is heard on the banks of our thousand rural streams; and enterprise and skill, with wealth, refinement, and prosperity in their train, having studded the sea-shore with populous cities, are making their great 'progress' of improvement through the interior, and sowing towns and villages, as it were, broadcast through the country." The result would be the creation of "a new bond of mutual dependence" rendered by this new division of labor.[59] John Shaw would pick up on this same theme in a later commemoration of the Pilgrims. The North needed "the agricultural and mineral productions of the middle and the South;—the South, the assistance of the navigation and manufactures of the North." The entire nation would profit from the fertile plains of the West, but the West relied on a naval force to secure shipping on the Mexican gulf. The result was the creation of the "bonds of union" even as each region pursued its own interests.[60] A Whig review of Joseph Story's influential *Commentaries on the Constitution of the United States* pointed to the first "internal improvements" undertaken by the Puritans in 1644. The colonists "'agreed that it be left to Mr. Hopkins,'" the governor of the Connecticut colony, "'to take care for providing some man or men to find and lay out the best way to the Bay, and the charge to be borne by the whole.'" Even at this early time, the internal improvements were seen as guided by "the early instinct of necessity, as a great natural object to a confederation of States." It is to "this primitive plan of Confederation," went the Whig interpretation of Story, that "the great constitutional compact of the present day" could be traced.[61]

The vision of community enunciated by the Whigs, though at times premised on contractual relations, looked as well to a Puritan model of harmony and order. It is this model that helps to explain what some have seen as the "preposterous" Whig position equating liberty with obedience to laws.[62] For the

Puritans, liberty was not the license to do as one wanted. Instead, the liberty the Puritans spoke of was a moral liberty, a freedom that depended on restraint, discipline, and obedience to good laws.[63] As portrayed in the nineteenth-century, this aspect of the Puritan character was a two-edged sword. In Sedgwick's account, as well as later in Nathaniel Hawthorne's *The Scarlet Letter*, the more unsettling aspects of the Puritan character were emphasized. But we really have to wait until the twentieth-century for the unrelenting negative portrayals of the Puritans to become intellectually fashionable. Puritan intolerance may have been ridiculed, as it certainly was in the early nineteenth-century, but for the most part this intolerance was seen as an unfortunate historical byproduct of the moral soundness of the Puritan character.[64] Numerous historiographies, including those of Bradford, Bancroft, Trumbull, Belknap, Pitkin, and Palfrey, attested to the fortitude of the early Puritans: the "love of liberty and undefiled religion," "courage and self-denial," and the "spirit of industry" as they transformed a desert wilderness.[65] Dwight's *Travels* confirmed the continuation of these virtues in contemporary New England in which "the active spirit" that led to not only a subduing of the wilderness but the "unceasing succession of inventions" in agriculture, manufacturing, and "the mechanic arts" was balanced by "a quiet, orderly, and obliging deportment" to "submit readily to lawful authority, and to obey even the recommendations of their rulers."[66] The Whigs could support the rehabilitation of Roger Williams by the likes of Bancroft as heralding the principle of "'intellectual liberty.'"[67] But this new liberal spirit for the Whigs was one tempered necessarily by self-control. Dwight, thus, would applaud the spread of "freedom, intelligence, and Christianity" in America as encouraging gentle manners in "the middle and inferior classes." The Whigs, therefore, spoke for obedience to laws that were designed to aid in the self-mastery necessary for attaining a "higher" form of civilization.[68] The nature and extent of these laws were widely debated among the Whigs, encompassing everything from temperance laws (which Daniel Webster opposed) to provisions for public education.

The Whig argument for self-restraint had a philosophic foundation: an individual was not born into a state of nature without attachments, free to pursue his or her own self-interest, but was "a member of a well-ordered family."[69] To that extent, society was not premised on the contractual relations of liberty-seeking individuals. But there was also a practical dimension to this argument. Self-control and discipline provided the link for the Whigs between individual and communal responsibility. An indulgence in one's own passions would result in the dissolution of society; self-control, on the other hand, would lead to the continual progress, both moral and material, of the community. Speaking on the anniversary of the landing of the Pilgrims, Webster pointed to "the mercantile classes, the great commercial masses of the country, whose affairs connect them strongly with every State in the Union" as working to "preserve the union" and providing "the stability of the free government under which we live."[70] Everett saw in the rise of manufacturing and commerce both dangers and possibilities. On the one hand the emerging laboring class, often portrayed by the Whigs as ignorant and lacking in self-discipline, posed a threat to the stability of the community. On the other hand, the spread of manufacturing in America thus far had demonstrated the possibility of the widespread dissemination of "enlightened moral public sentiment" that would act as a "watchman at our doors."[71] It is through the diffusion of knowledge brought about by technological innovation and communication that such widespread sentiments were made possible. As Everett explained, "A discovery results in an art; an art produces a comfort; a comfort, made cheaply accessible, adds family on family to the population; and a family is a new creation of thinking, reasoning, inventing, and discovering beings. Thus, instead of arriving at the end, we are at the beginning of the series, and ready to start, with recruited numbers, on the great and beneficent career to useful knowledge."[72] Although the family brotherhood that Somkin spoke of was gone, commerce and social organization were again conjoined, as they had been in Puritan New England.

A Whig social experiment in Lowell, Massachusetts, drew on this same corporate idea. Formed around the Merrimack Manufacturing Company, the town was to be a model of the moral virtue of industrialism. The company housed its employees and provided a school, hospital, and libraries and sought to instill virtue through the establishment of churches, a bank for promoting savings, and the supervision of the private lives of the workers. The society created at Lowell was hierarchical, with its harmony based on the fulfillment of one's role within a functionally differentiated and unequal society. Though there were a number of intellectual currents that informed the Lowell experiment, "the model that influenced the founders of Lowell most of all was the preindustrial New England village, with its traditional patterns of deference made more rigid by a corporate table of organization."[73] In a Fourth of July oration at Lowell, Edward Everett spoke of the redemptive potential of manufacturing as it was incorporated into a moral community. The invisible hand of the commercial market did not by itself engender a public good. One had only to look to the "industrial system of Europe" which "requires for its administration an amount of suffering, depravity, and brutalism, which formed one of the great scandals of the age." The Whig model was not the European city divided between an exploitative bourgeoisie and an uneducated laboring class but the New England town characterized by a sense of civic virtue (now called patriotism by the Whigs) and moral enlightenment. Unlike the oppressive European system, "for physical comfort, moral conduct, general intelligence, and all the qualities of social character which make up an enlightened New England community, Lowell might safely enter into a comparison with any town or city in the land."[74]

The great contribution of Lowell, according to Everett, was that it revealed the possibility of a "holy alliance" between labor and capital. What Everett meant by this, it would seem, is that, through careful education and supervision, labor had acquired the proper habits of deference. The Lowell community had "rolled off from the sacred cause of labor the mountain of reproach of ignorance, vice, and suffering under which it lay crushed" and realized a vision of social life governed by the conversion of labor into capital. The "foundations" for this new age of commerce and manufacturing, exemplified by the Lowell experiment, were laid, according to Everett, by Governor Winthrop and his company.[75]

Such a model was duplicated in other areas of the country, as in the creation of "Prattville" by Alabama manufacturer and

Whig Daniel Pratt. Pratt used the example of his hometown of Temple, New Hampshire, to introduce southern "whites" to "the positive New England virtues of sobriety, thrift, and hard work." Like the Lowell factory, Prattville was a small community in which workers lived in cottages that were "neatly painted and a uniform size" set in a bucolic setting. The workers were to be provided with technical skills and were to follow a regimen of education, religious instruction, and temperance. Such a form of economic and social organization, in turn, served as a model for the expansion of cotton factories across Alabama and would be replicated in North Carolina.[76] A new commercial age, rather than robbing America of community, would forge the Winthropian bonds of harmony and affection as it extended into all regions of the country and all segments of society.

The Puritan Basis of Whig History

Central to the difference between a Whig outlook and a Jeffersonian or Jacksonian one were their respective understandings of the role of history in the formation of both individual and national identity. Both the Jeffersonians and Jacksonians posited an essentially ahistorical understanding of American democracy. In Jefferson's assertion that "the earth belongs in usufruct to the living; that the dead have neither powers nor rights over it," he explicitly rejected any prescriptive force of the past over the present.[77] Nor was any such tradition necessary for a Jeffersonian ideology; democratic habits were not founded in a distant past but were grounded in a material present. When the Republican orators did invoke the past, they did not do so to suggest a bond to this past as much as to point to a common connection to nature. In reacting to the rise of manufacturing, the Republican John Davis, for example, yearned for a return to a simpler time, a "recurrence to this primitive age" of the founding Puritans.[78] So, too, Andrew Dunlap in a Fourth of July oration in Fanueil Hall suggested that "it was the desire of [the Pilgrims'] hearts, that their feelings and manners should be transmitted in their simplicity and vigour, as the best legacy which they could leave to their posterity."[79] In this case, the Puritans were not part of a tradition of American democracy as much as a reminder of the connection of virtue to simplicity. Jacksonians saw individual virtue as possible only with the elimination of artificial inequalities resulting from "unjust positive institutions," such as the Bank of the United States. The Jacksonian virtues of industry and frugality, seen as impossible under a Whig system that "corrupt[s] one part of the community and debase[s] the other," would be promoted when individuals were allowed to engage in and be rewarded accordingly for their enterprises.[80]

The Whigs, on the other hand, saw an essential connectedness of individuals to the past and future which served to elevate human morality and temperament. "It is a noble faculty of our nature," spoke Daniel Webster, "which enables us to connect our thoughts, our sympathies, and our happiness with what is distant in place and time." Through this alliance with history, individuals could escape an "insulated" existence and be inculcated with traditions, civility, and morality essential, it was argued, for an enlightened community. The desire was, in the words of Webster, to see "ourselves being but links in the great chain of being, which begins with the origin of our race, runs onward through its successive generations, binding together the past, the present, and the future, and terminating at last, with the consummation of all things earthly, at the throne of God."[81] The Whigs saw history as an unfolding of some greater design, decipherable by listening to "the voice of our history," according to Everett.[82] In recalling the Pilgrims, Rufus Choate exclaimed that "Our past" should "announce, should compel, should spontaneously evolve us from a germ, a wise, moral, and glorious future." By "gazing" at the past, and the Puritans specifically, "we may pass into the likeness of the departed,—may emulate their labors, and partake of their immortality."[83]

This Whig interpretation of history has received ample scholarly attention. What has been less discussed is how the Whigs looked to the Puritans in constructing this history. In seeking to "preserve the worth of our forefathers from forgetfulness," the Whigs looked to the Puritans not simply as historical figures who have something to teach us but also as prophets of the American future.[84] Their prophecy, though at times invoking sacred terms, was fundamentally secular. The Puritan legacy was not, as is usually argued, that Puritan providentialism would wend its way into Americans' sense of themselves as

God's chosen people. Rather, the Puritan contribution to American destiny for the Whigs was in providing a founding that endowed America with institutions and principles that would give it an identity unique among nations.

In peering into the past, the founding of other governments was seen by American Whigs as "shrouded in impenetrable darkness." In contrast, American traditions and "political forms" could be traced unquestionably back to Puritan origins.[85] As in their attempts to trace union principles back to the Puritans, so the Whigs also identified in the Puritans the republican principles of a nation founded on the consent of the governed. The historiographies of the day provided ample material for this Whig appropriation. Trumbull's important *History of Connecticut*, for example, gave prominence to this idea when, in his second paragraph, he describes how "In an age when the light of freedom was but just dawning," the founders of Connecticut, "by voluntary compact, formed one of the most free and happy constitutions of government which mankind have ever adopted." In this government, the Puritans encouraged a "mildness of its laws" and "the general diffusion of knowledge, among all classes of its inhabitants."[86] The Whigs would elaborate on this republican theme. The Pilgrims, for example, were seen as moving from their "disconnected" and "unorganized social existence" to an organized, republican community "deliberately conferred together" by "their original compact." The Puritans under Winthrop, as well as the settlers in Salem, in securing their communities, also established a principle of independence from "foreign dominion" and "of all other bodies of men, both ecclesiastical and political." So too with the New Haven settlement.[87]

The Puritans as founders, according to this Whig interpretation, uniquely endowed America with its commercial and patriotic course. Rufus Choate listed "Ward, Parker, and Saltonstall, and Wise, Norton, and Rogers, and Appleton, and Cobbet, and Winthrop" as "the founders of a race of freemen." In describing the founding, Choate did not speak about the Puritans (or colonists) as chosen; instead, he described how the Puritan "spirit of liberty" combined with the fervor of "republicanism" and was "strengthened and reinforced, until at length, instructed by wisdom, tempered by virtue, and influenced by injuries, by anger and grief and conscious worth and the sense of violated right, it burst forth here and wrought the wonders of the Revolution."[88] In a later speech Choate saw the Puritans as constituting a heroic age. The Puritans were accorded this status as founders because, according to Choate, they were able to impart permanent virtues and institutions and "to kindle and feed the moral imagination, move the capacious heart, and justify the intelligent wonder of the world."[89]

The American founding was seen as historically special. Asia and Africa never felt freedom, suggested Choate, even though their "history begins ages before a ray of the original civilization of the East had reached to Europe." The great civilizations of Greece, Rome, and Venice, though having republican forms of government, could not make those governments endure. Besides America, only England, Holland, and a dozen Swiss Cantons built enduring republics. What explained this success was that the Puritans, imbued with a spirit of liberty, faced hardships and struggles upon their arrival. The result, according to Choate as he gave to the Puritans the virtues of republican founders, was the creation of "a truly strong, masculine, commanding character" that would allow liberty to endure.[90]

Webster, in transporting his audience back to the founding of Plymouth, gave to the Puritans the voice of American prophecy: "'If God prosper us,'" spoke Webster as he assumed the voice of a Puritan founder, "'we shall here begin a work which shall last for ages,'" a work that would include the subduing of the wilderness, westward expansion, "'prosperous commerce,'" and the growth of "'a hundred cities.'"[91] Reading forward from this Puritan birth, the Whigs looked to the present age of new inventions, new products, growing cities, an expanding nation, and new economic opportunities as the culmination of history. So rapid was this change that in "speaking of future advancement," suggested Joseph Willard, "the future becomes present with the completion of all that we had expected. Time has as it were changed this mode of computation; days stand for months, and a few years answer all the purposes of an age."[92] Time had, indeed, changed. America, so it seemed, was entering the political millennium; the ravages of time and the threats of enemies would no longer imperil the republic. America would be eternal.

The political millennium occurring in America was to extend to the whole world. America's victory meant the end of tyranny and misery and the opening of a new age of moral purity and prosperity. Just as "the posterity of Abraham were set apart to preserve a knowledge of the Great First Cause, so, we believe, was this western world to be the dwelling-place of liberty." Without fear of "any adversary," liberty will go forth "silent and resistless as the course of nature, to bless and regenerate the world."[93] Already, as orators were quick to point out, the spirit of reform had spread across the globe—to France, South America, the German states, Prussia, Spain, Greece, and Italy.[94] America represented the departure of the world from the "history of human nature in ruins." This nation would, as promised in Revelation, "make all things new." In a time when the Second Great Awakening was gathering steam, Lyman Beecher saw in the revivals "the purpose of God to employ this nation in the glorious work of renovating the earth."[95]

America promised to be a model of virtue and an asylum of freedom. The eyes of all the nations were on America, orators from across the country told their listeners, invoking Winthrop's now familiar words. "The eyes of an anxious world are fixed upon us. We are to exhibit the effects of republican institutions; the influence of freedom upon the human mind and character."[96] The rest of the world was watching "to learn whether institutions so free as ours can be permanent," a question that had been resolved satisfactorily in the American mind.[97] America was "as a beacon light in the broad pathway of nations—by our example, giving lessons of freedom to the world; but carrying dismay and rebuke to the bosom of despotism."[98] The hope was that "the influence of our revolution may induce all nations to demand their rights with decision and firmness and to pursue them with zeal and unabating stedfastness" without the United States having to "descend from the lofty station we hold."[99] Until this universal reformation was complete, America would offer her shores to refugees of tyranny. "The unhappy European, driven by persecution, religious or civil, from his native land, finds in America an asylum, where the 'wicked cease from troubling, and the weary are at rest.'"[100] Caleb Stetson combined timelessness with the theme of America as a haven for the oppressed when he repeated the following verse: "'There is no other land like thee,/ No dearer shore;/ Thou art the shelter of the free;/ The home, the port of Liberty/ Thou hast been and shalt ever be/ Till time is o'er.'"[101] By invoking a Puritan birth, the Whigs could claim for America a life eternal.

More than eternity, though, the Puritans at root provided a sense of identity for a group that saw in history the manna of cultural sustenance. The opening of a Whig review of Webster's address commemorating the Pilgrim landing evoked this quest for identity. "Americans have been repeatedly charged . . . with being deficient in that patriotic attachment to the land we spring from, in that filial and pious regard for the ashes of our forefathers, which the people of other countries feel proud to cherish."[102] The review pointed to the shifting population and the desire for adventure as resulting in a lack of sentiment for any one spot. Webster's speech, as did so many other Whig orations, attempted to fill this void, to provide a foundation steeped in a Puritan tradition for both an American and Whig identity.

More than being an ineffective political force, the Whigs provided a powerful reinterpretation of America's Puritan past. In a history-conscious age, the Whigs fashioned for the nascent commercial republic a founding legend that gave America a voice in the conversation of history. The Whigs read into the American past the moral basis for their economic and political vision, a vision in which the individual remained closely tied to a corporate order. At a time in which an individualist ethos was penetrating American economic, social, and political life, the Puritans served as a reminder for the Whigs that the individual does not exist apart from the community nor the community from history. The Whigs, somewhat ironically as they so much valued historical remembrance, have been forgotten in America's consciousness. But their crafting of a founding legacy that gave to the United States a moral identity has endured in the American conscience.

Notes

1   This discussion of Whiggery follows the work of Daniel Walker Howe. See *The Political Culture of the American Whigs* (Chicago: University of Chicago Press, 1979). For an analysis of Whiggery in the South, see Charles Grier Sellers, Jr., "Who Were the Southern Whigs?" *American Historical Review* 59 (Jan. 1954): 335-46.

2   See Lynn L. Marshall, "The Strange Stillbirth of the Whig Party," *American Historical Review* 72 (Jan. 1967): 445-68, who argues that the "key element in the formation of the Whig party was party organization, not ideology" (445). Charles Sellers, *The Market Revolution: Jacksonian America 1815-1846* (New York: Oxford University Press, 1991), 360, refers to the "noncommittal politics of White and Harrison" as successes upon which the Whigs chose to build. See also Glyndon G. Van Deusen, *The Jacksonian Era 1828-1848* (New York: Harper & Row, 1959), 96.

3   Ronald P. Formisano, *The Birth of Mass Political Parties: Michigan, 1827-1861* (Princeton: Princeton University Press, 1971). His chapter on the Whigs deals exclusively with their moralistic aspects.

4   See Rush Welter, *The Mind of America 1820-1860* (New York: Columbia University Press, 1975), who can barely contain his revulsion for the Whigs; Arthur M. Schlesinger, Jr., *The Age of Jackson* (Boston: Little, Brown, 1945), who depicts the Whigs as Federalists in a new guise; and Marvin Meyers, *The Jacksonian Persuasion: Politics and Belief* (Stanford: Stanford University Press, 1960), 257-8, who discusses what appears as an almost pathetic attempt by the Whigs to master a democratic rhetoric.

5   See Lee Benson, *The Concept of Jacksonian Democracy: New York as a Test Case* (Princeton: Princeton University Press, 1961).

6   See Thomas Brown, *Politics and Statesmanship: Essays on the American Whig Party* (New York: Columbia University Press, 1985).

7   Howe, *Political Culture*, introduction. See also Lawrence Frederick Kohl, *The Politics of Individualism: Parties and the American Character in the Jacksonian Era* (New York: Oxford University Press, 1989) and Major L. Wilson, "The 'Country' Versus the 'Court': A Republican Consensus and Party Debate in the Bank War," *Journal of the Early Republic* 15 (Winter 1995): 619-647. Wilson, in arguing against "dismissing Country-Court language as rhetoric puffery," notes that though "Democrats and Whigs were both liberal," the "political language of republicanism enabled them to illuminate contrasting visions of the good society" (621).

8   Howe, *Political Culture*, 2.

9   The chapter focuses on early Whig rhetoric in an attempt to under-
    stand the process of identity formation as the Whig culture began
    expressing itself politically. Many of the speeches I have identified as
    Whig occur before the actual formation of the Whig party in 1834. I
    see the formation of the party not as the beginning of American
    Whiggery but as one expression of a Whig culture that was becoming
    identifiable in American politics in the preceding decade. This is con-
    sistent with Howe, who draws upon speeches and writings of Whigs
    in the years before the naming of the Whig party. See Howe, *Political
    Culture* and Howe, *The American Whigs: An Anthology* (New York: John
    Wiley & Sons, 1973). This is also consistent with statements by the
    Whigs themselves. For example, in an 1842 speech before the Massa-
    chusetts Whig convention, Daniel Webster declared, "I am a Whig, I
    always have been a Whig, and I always will be one." He furthermore
    saw himself as having battled the Whig cause for "five-and-twenty years"
    (Daniel Webster, "Reception at Boston, September 30, 1842," in *The
    Papers of Daniel Webster: Speeches and Formal Writings, Volume 2, 1834-
    1852*, ed. Charles M. Wiltse [Hanover, N.H.: University Press of New
    England, 1988], 341).

10 Meyers, *Jacksonian Persuasion*, 257, refers to the "mock conversion" of
    the Whigs to democracy in the 1840 election. Also see Sellers, *Mar-
    ket*, 350, 362.

11 See Benson, *Concept* and Formisano, *Birth*. There is much I am sympa-
    thetic to in what has become known as the ethno-cultural interpreta-
    tions of voting behavior, including the importance these historians
    place on the role of symbols in mobilizing the electorate. I would be
    reluctant, though, to separate symbolic politics from the substantive
    concerns of the electorate to the extent done by ethno-cultural inter-
    pretations. For a discussion of ethno-cultural interpretations, see Ri-
    chard L. McCormick, "Ethno-Cultural Interpretations of Nineteenth-
    Century American Voting Behavior," *Political Science Quarterly* 89 (June
    1974): 351-77. Kohl, *Politics*, is a notable exception to the tendency to
    ignore rhetoric.

12 "The New England Character," *North American Review* 44 (Jan. 1837),
    138.

13 "Bancroft's *History of the United States*," *North American Review* 40 (Jan.
    1835), 117, 101-2. This view of history helps to explain the Whig ap-
    preciation of the Democrat Bancroft's *History* and the Whig's corre-
    sponding dislike for English historian James Grahame's *The History of
    the United States of North America* (London: Longman, 1833).

14 Garry Wills, *Lincoln at Gettysburg: The Words That Remade America* (New
    York: Touchstone, 1992), 51.

15   John Winthrop, *History of New England*, 2d ed., 2 vols., ed. James Savage (Boston: Little, Brown, and Co., 1853). Translation of Sallust quote in James G. Moseley, *John Winthrop's World: History As a Story; The Story As History* (Madison: University of Wisconsin Press, 1992), 127-8.

16   Benjamin Trumbull, *A General History of the United States of America from the Discovery in 1492, to 1792* (Boston: Farrand, Mallory, & Co., 1810), 1, 113.

17   Buell, *New England*, 195. For a discussion of the role of a Puritan past in literary expressions after 1830, see Jan C. Dawson, *The Unusable Past: America's Puritan Tradition, 1830 to 1930* (Chico: Scholars Press, 1984).

18   Timothy Dwight, *Travels in New England and New York*, 4 vols., ed. Barbara Miller Solomon (Cambridge: Belknap Press, 1969), 4: 369, 372-3.

19   Perry D. Westbrook, *The New England Town in Fact and Fiction* (London: Associated University Presses, 1982), 26.

20   [Catharine Sedgwick], *A New-England Tale; or, Sketches of New-England Character and Manners* (New York: Bliss and White, 1822), 31, 13.

21   Hannah Adams seems to favor the character of the Pilgrims over the Puritans, largely because of the Puritan zealousness in their persecutions of dissenters. Even then, though, Adams minimizes these "imperfections" by pointing to the "wise and benevolent principles" that guided them. *A Summary History of New-England* (Dedham: Mann & Adams, 1799), 21-2, 36. Adams quotes from John Adams' "Canon and Feudal Law" in justifying Puritan excesses.

22   Ralph Waldo Emerson, "Historical Discourse, at Concord . . . Sept. 12, 1835," *The Works of Ralph Waldo Emerson*, 14 vols. (Boston: Houghton, Mifflin, & Co., 1883), 11: 42, 44, 75.

23   Emerson, "The Method of Nature, 1841," *The Collected Works of Ralph Waldo Emerson*, 5 vols. (Cambridge: Belknap Press, 1971), 1: 135.

24   George Bancroft, *History of the United States of America, From the Discovery of the Continent*, 6 vols. (New York: D. Appleton and Co., 1888), 1: 322, 320. See Sacvan Bercovitch, *The Rites of Assent: Transformations in the Symbolic Construction of America* (New York: Routledge, 1993), chapt. 6, for a discussion of Bancroft's role in constructing "the myth of American revolution" (174).

25   Jeremy Belknap, *American Biography*, 2 vols. (Boston: Thomas & Andrews, 1798), 2: 341. Belknap is writing about John Winthrop but also expresses his dissatisfaction with the persecutions conducted by the Massachusetts Bay Colony.

26 "The New England Character," *North American Review*, 238.

27 I would tend to agree with Buell, who sees the invocation of the Puritans more as "a mood inspired by special occasions than a constant, indwelling magnetic force." See Buell, *New England*, 195.

28 Sellers, *Market*, 32.

29 *The Life and Selected Writings of Thomas Jefferson*, eds. Adrienne Koch and William Peden (New York: Modern Library, 1972), 377.

30 See John Ashworth, *'Agrarians' and 'Aristocrats': Party Political Ideology in the United States, 1837-1846* (New Jersey: Humanities Press, 1983), 27.

31 Joseph Bartlett, *An Oration, Delivered at Biddeford, on the Fourth of July, 1805* (SACO, Maine, 1805), 14.

32 John Treat Irving, *Oration Delivered on the 4th of July, 1809, Before the Tammany Society* (New York, 1809), 23.

33 Augustus Alden, *An Address, Delivered at Augusta, on the Thirty-Fourth Anniversary of American Independence, July Fourth, 1809* (Augusta, 1809), 8.

34 Koch, *Life*, 324.

35 Ashworth, *'Agrarians'*, 135. See also Sellers, *Market*, 35.

36 Ashworth, *'Agrarians'*, 30-1.

37 Theophilus Fisk, "Capital against Labor. An Address delivered at Julien Hall before the mechanics of Boston on Wednesday evening, May 20, 1835," in *Social Theories of Jacksonian Democracy: Representative Writings of the Period 1825-1850*, ed. Joseph L. Blau (Indianapolis: Bobbs-Merrill, 1954), 201.

38 Rufus Choate draws this exact connection in an 1834 address ("The Colonial Age of New England," in *The Works of Rufus Choate with a Memoir of His Life*, 2 vols., ed. Samuel Gilman Brown [Boston: Little, Brown, 1862], 1: 353-6. For a discussion of how evangelical Christianity was an important component of a Whig political culture, see Richard J. Carwardine, *Evangelicals and Politics in Antebellum America* (New Haven: Yale University Press, 1993), chapt. 2, and Daniel Walker Howe, "The Evangelical Movement and Political Culture in the North during the Second Party System," *The Journal of American History* 77 (March 1991): 1216-1239. In part, Howe's interest is to examine the relationship between evangelical social reform and the emergence of capitalism. By looking at the invocations of the Puritans, we can get some insight into how for the Whigs this relationship was articulated.

39 There is a long and illustrious debate on this subject, beginning with Max Weber's *The Protestant Ethic and the Spirit of Capitalism* (New York:

Charles Scribner's Sons, 1978). For important contributions to this debate, see David Little, *Religion, Order and Law: A Study of Pre-Revolutionary England* (New York: Harper & Row, 1969); Sacvan Bercovitch, *The American Jeremiad* (Madison: University of Wisconsin Press, 1978); Darrett B. Rutman, *Winthrop's Boston: A Portrait of a Puritan Town, 1630-1649* (Chapel Hill: University of North Carolina Press, 1965); and Michael Walzer, "Puritanism as a Revolutionary Ideology," *History and Theory* 3 (1964): 59-90. For an extension of this discussion into Connecticut, see Paul R. Lucas, *Valley of Discord: Church and Society Along the Connecticut River, 1636-1725* (Hanover, N.H.: University Press of New England, 1976).

40   Lyman Beecher, *The Memory of our Fathers, a Sermon Delivered at Plymouth, on the Twenty-second of December, 1827* (Boston, 1828), 21, 8.

41   William Bradford's chronicle of the early struggles of the Pilgrims, *Of Plymouth Plantation 1620-1647*, new ed. (New York: Alfred A. Knopf, 1966), was already well known. Contemporary histories that portrayed the enterprising nature of the early settlers include Bancroft's *History*; James Grahame, *The History of the United States of North America, till the British Revolution in 1688* (Boston: Russell, Odiorne, and Co., 1833); Timothy Pitkin, *A Political and Civil History of the United States of America*, vol. 1 (New Haven: Hezekiah Howe and Durrie & Peck, 1828); John Gorham Palfrey, *History of New England during the Stuart Dynasty* (Boston: Little, Brown, and Co., 1858), x; and Trumbull, *General History*, 106-7.

42   See "The New England Character," *North American Review* 44 (Jan. 1837), 237-8, and Edward Everett, "The Settlement of Massachusetts, delivered at Charlestown Lyceum on June 28, 1830," in *Orations and Speeches on Various Occasions*, 2d ed., 4 vols. (Boston: Little and Brown, 1850), 1: 237-9.

43   Choate, "Colonial Age," 365; Everett, "Settlement of Massachusetts," 1: 244. For similar statements, see Everett, "First Settlement of New England, delivered at Plymouth, December 22, 1824," in *Orations and Speeches*, 2d ed., 1: 46 and Edward Everett, "Fourth of July at Lowell, delivered on July 5, 1830," in *Orations and Speeches*, 2d ed., 2: 58.

44   John Quincy Adams, "Address held at the Little Falls, near Georgetown, District of Columbia, July 4, 1828," in *Trumpets of Glory*, ed. Henry A. Hawken (Connecticut: The Salmon Brook Historical Society, 1976), 116-7.

45   Edward Everett, "A Discourse on the Importance to Practical Men of Scientific Knowledge, and on the Encouragement to its Pursuit," compiled by Everett in 1836 from speeches made in 1827, 1829, and 1830, in *Orations and Speeches, on Various Occasions*, ed. Edward Everett (Boston: American Stationers', 1836), 248.

46 John Quincy Adams, "Address held at the Little Falls," 116, 118 (quoting Bishop Berkeley).

47 Edward Everett, "The Settlement of Massachusetts," 1: 243. See also Hadduck, "Elements," 271.

48 John Quincy Adams, "Address," 118.

49 Edward Everett, "Principle of the American Constitutions," an oration delivered at Cambridge, on the 4th of July, 1826, in *Orations and Speeches*, 2d ed., 1: 129.

50 Everett, "Settlement of Massachusetts," 1: 233.

51 Everett, "Settlement of Massachusetts," 1: 235.

52 William Powell Mason, *An Oration Delivered Wednesday, July 4, 1827* (Boston, 1827), 13.

53 Fred Somkin, *Unquiet Eagle: Memory and Desire in the Idea of American Freedom, 1815-1860* (Ithaca: Cornell University Press, 1967), 7.

54 See Robert Rantoul, Jr., "Oration at Scituate, Delivered on the 4th of July, 1836," in *Memoirs, Speeches and Writings of Robert Rantoul, Jr.*, ed. Luther Hamilton (Boston: John P. Jewett & Co., 1854), 252-3, 288.

55 Rantoul, "Oration at South Reading, delivered . . . on the Fourth of July, 1832," in *Memoirs*, 173.

56 Webster, "First Settlement of New England, delivered at Plymouth, on the 22d of December, 1820," in *The Writings and Speeches of Daniel Webster*, 18 vols. (Boston: Little, Brown, and Co., 1903), 1: 211, 214, italics in original. Webster invoked this same sense of a Puritan legacy in his speech on the basis of the Senate delivered December 15, 1820. For a discussion of the importance to Webster of wide distribution of property, see Melvyn Dubofsky, "Daniel Webster and the Whig Theory of Economic Growth: 1828-1848," *The New England Quarterly* 42 (Dec. 1967), 556-8.

57 The term is from George Rogers Taylor, *The Transportation Revolution, 1815-1860* (New York 1951).

58 Sellers, *Market*, 43.

59 Everett, "First Settlement of New England," 1: 54.

60 John A. Shaw, *An Oration Delivered Before the Citizens of Plymouth, July 4, 1828* (Boston, 1828), 11.

61 "Story's Constitutional Law," *North American Review* 38 (Jan. 1834), 69. Story writes that, though early efforts as forming confederacies were "abortive," these efforts "prepared their minds for the gradual reconciliation of their local interests, and for the gradual develop-

ment of the principles, upon which a union ought to rest, rather than brought on an immediate sense of the necessity, or the blessings of such a general government" (*Commentaries on the Constitution of the United States*, abridged edition [Boston: Hilliard, Gray, and Co., 1833], 74-5). The argument that the "confederation of the four New England colonies served as the basis of the great confederacy afterwards formed between the thirteen states of America" is also made by Pitkin, *Political*, 52.

62   See Rush Welter, *Mind*, 206-7.

63   For a clear statement of this, see John Winthrop, *The History of New England from 1630 to 1649*, 2 vols., ed. James Savage (New York: Arno Press, 1972), 2: 229-30.

64   David Ramsay, for example, notes that though "the religion of many of the first settlers was tinctured with enthusiasm," a euphemism for bigotry, "it is equally true, that, without a portion of that noble infirmity, no great enterprize was every accomplished." See *History of the United States* (Philadelphia: Carey, 1816), 54.

65   Trumbull, *General History*, 108.

66   Dwight, *Travels*, 4: 328.

67   Quoting Bancroft, in "Bancroft's *History*," *North American Review*, 111.

68   Dwight, *Travels*, 4: 371-2.

69   Everett, "Principles," 130.

70   Daniel Webster, "The Landing at Plymouth, delivered on Dec. 22, 1843," in *Writings and Speeches of Daniel Webster*, 3: 205.

71   Everett, "Practical Men," 250.

72   Ibid., 257.

73   Howe, *Political Culture*, 102-4.

74   Edward Everett, "Fourth of July at Lowell," 2: 63-4.

75   Ibid., 63-65.

76   Randall M. Miller, "Daniel Pratt's Industrial Urbanism: The Cotton Mill Town in Antebellum Alabama," *Alabama Historical Quarterly* 34 (Spring 1972), 11, 22, 9. Also see Richard W. Griffin and Diffee W. Standard, "The Cotton Textile Industry in Ante-Bellum North Carolina Part II: An Era of Boom and Consolidation, 1830-1860," *The North Carolina Historical Review* 34 (April 1957): 131-64. Somewhat ironically, these factory communities, while New England in their origin, were often justified as a way for the South to free itself from dependence on the North.

77   Jefferson, *Life and Selected Writings*, 488.

78   John Davis, *A Discourse Before the Massachusetts Historical Society, Boston, December 22, 1813. At the Anniversary Commemoration of the First Landing of our Ancestors at Plymouth, in 1620* (Boston, 1814), 16.

79   Andrew Dunlap, *An Oration, Delivered at the Request of the Republicans at Boston, at Fanueil Hall, on the Fourth of July, 1822* (Boston, 1822).

80   William M. Gouge, "Principles and Effects of the Banking System," in *Social Theories of Jacksonian Democracy*, ed. Joseph L. Blau (New York: Bobbs-Merrill, 1954), 190, 188.

81   Webster, "First Settlement," 181-2.

82   Everett, "First Settlement of New England," 1: 53.

83   Choate, "The Age of the Pilgrims the Heroic Period of Our History: An Address Delivered in New York before the New-England Association, December, 1843," in *Works of Rufus Choate*, ed. Brown, 1: 392-3.

84   Everett, "Settlement of Massachusetts," 1: 216.

85   "Kingsley's *Historical Discourse*," *North American Review* 47 (Oct. 1838), 480-1.

86   Benjamin Trumbull, *A Complete History of Connecticut* (Hartford: Hudson & Goodwin, 1797), 2. Daniel Webster, too, would contrast the clearness of American Puritan origins with the foundings of other countries that are "obscured in the darkness of antiquity" ("First Settlement," 1: 198).

87   "Kingsley's *Historical Discourse*," 481-3. Though the nation was born of an "original compact," it was not a contract of individuals pursuing their own interests but a compact to forge the bonds of community. The Whigs, thus, like the Federalists, sought to combine more modern notions of consent with traditional organic images of community.

88   Choate, "Colonial Age of New England," 352-3. See also Lyman Beecher, *A Plea for the West* (Cincinnati, 1835), in *The American Whigs: An Anthology*, ed. Howe, where he states that "the puritans . . . laid the foundations of the republican institutions of our nation" (142).

89   Choate, "Age of the Pilgrims," 374. In this speech, Choate refers to the Puritans as "an authentic race of founders" (374). In his famous speech at Plymouth later repeated before the Senate, Daniel Webster compared the Puritans favorably to other founders. Ancient Greek settlers, as an example, did not possess sufficiently elevated principles or purposes to motivate them, as did the Pilgrims in their desire for civil and religious liberty. Roman settlements were based on "power and dominion" with no sustaining principle independent of Rome.

Asian colonies were based solely on trade and, thus, rarely attained the status of self-governing political entities. And in the West Indies, as commerce was built on slavery, the owners of capital never developed attachments to the land or the country (Webster, "First Settlement," 193-4, 196).

90   Choate, "Age of the Pilgrims," 360-1. See also George Cheever's oration in New York in which he identifies the "inheritance of liberty through trials" from our Pilgrim ancestors as essential to our "National Greatness." "Address" (1842), in *New England Society Orations*, eds. Brainerd and Brainerd, 291.

91   Webster, "First Settlement," 186.

92   Joseph Willard, *An Oration Delivered at Lancaster, Mass. in Celebration of American Independence, July, 1825* (Boston, 1825), 7.

93   John Shaw, *Oration*, 22.

94   See, for example, Alexander Everett, *An Oration: Delivered at the Request of the City Government, Before the Citizens of Boston, on the 5th of July, 1830* (Boston, 1830); Charles Loring, *An Oration, Pronounced on the Fourth of July, 1821, at the Request of the Inhabitants of the Town of Boston, in Commemoration of the Anniversary of National Independence* (Boston, 1821); and Theodore Lyman, Jr., *Oration*.

95   Lyman Beecher, *The Memory of Our Fathers. A Sermon Delivered at Plymouth, on the Twenty-second of December, 1827* (Boston, 1828), 2, 6-7, 15. The Second Great Awakening, through its emphasis on moral responsibility, accountability, individual grace, and collective redemption, is important in providing the moral impetus behind Whig ideology. See Howe, *Political Culture*, 9. This millennialism also served as an important impetus behind the colonization movement. See David Brion Davis, "Reconsidering the Colonization Movement: Leonard Bacon and the Problem of Evil," *Intellectual History Newsletter* 14 (1992): 3-16. Davis quotes President John Tyler as stating, "Monrovia will be to Africa what Jamestown and Plymouth have been to America" (12). Other Whigs would draw on the Puritans to call for America to cleanse itself of the sin of slavery. See, for example, Daniel Webster, "First Settlement," 221-2.

96   Thomas Brackenridge, *Oration*, 17.

97   Thomas G. Cary, *An Oration Delivered at Brattleborough, Vermont, July 4, 1821* (Brattleborough, 1821), 7.

98   Caleb Stetson, *An Oration Delivered at Lexington, on the Fourth of July, 1825*, (Cambridge, 1825), 11.

99   Rev. John Bisbe, *Oration*, 22.

100 Thomas Brackenridge, *Oration*, 14.

101 Stetson, *Oration*, 18.

102 *North American Review*, 36, New Series, No. 11 (July 1822), 22.

Epilogue

Rhetoric Without Meaning

The English philosopher Edmund Burke, in describing attempts by revolutionaries in France to strip away tradition, lamented that:

> All the pleasing illusions, which made power gentle, and obedience liberal, which harmonized the different shades of life, and which, by a bland assimilation, incorporated into politics the sentiments which beautify and soften private society, are to be dissolved by this new conquering empire of light and reason. All the decent drapery of life is to be rudely torn off. All the super-added ideas, furnished from the wardrobe of a moral imagination, which the heart owns, and the understanding ratifies, as necessary to cover the defects of our naked shivering nature, and to raise it to dignity in our estimation, are to be exploded as a ridiculous, absurd, and antiquated fashion.[1]

What Burke observed as occurring politically two hundred years ago in France we can now observe occurring rhetorically in contemporary American culture. Words, and the invocation of these words in political rhetoric, no longer appear clothed in shared meanings that we have inherited from our past. Rather, the rhetoric of meaning has been replaced by a rhetoric of suspicion in which we seek to expose how each word is used to advance a particular agenda or disguise our hegemonic desires. Writes Andrew Delbanco, in talking about contemporary literary criticism, "We have turned literary texts into excretions through which, while holding our noses, we search for traces of the maladies of our culture."[2] What is revealed in the end is not the pleasure of language but a costume worn to mask our nakedness.

This study has sought, somewhat unfashionably, to resist this deconstructive tendency. It has done so not by clinging to a Burkean notion of tradition but by locating the meaning of a Puritan past in its rhetorical construction as a founding tradition. Tellingly, our contemporary invocations of the Puritans betray little of this multivocality. What has taken its place, in the words of Rochelle Gurstein, is "'Puritanism' as Epithet."[3] Certainly, the Puritans were not always portrayed in the most positive light, as we saw in the writings of Catharine Sedgwick or Nathaniel Hawthorne. But now to accuse someone of "Puritanism" is to take a stand between "enlightenment and superstition, candor and hypocrisy, free speech and censorship, sexual emancipation and prudery, democracy and elitism, urbanity and provinciality—in short, a choice between the modern and the old-fashioned."[4] How much has changed from when John Adams posed exactly this set of tradeoffs in his "Dissertation on the Canon and Feudal Law."[5] Only for Adams, the Puritans were on the side of enlightenment and democracy and, in fact, had been the forebears of these ideas on colonial soil.

It is not difficult to trace the narrowing of the historical meaning of the term "Puritanism." We need only look to the turn of this century to witness what appears now as nothing less than an attempted exorcism of this Puritan past from America's soul. Whether we speak of H. L. Mencken's withering criticism of the American Puritan spirit that subjects all aesthetic sensibility to moral approbation[6] or of Randolph Bourne's characterization of "The Puritan" as "a case of arrested development"[7] or of Emma Goldman's condemnation of Puritanism as "killing what is natural and healthy in our impulses,"[8] we refer to a Puritan past that came to be viewed as opposed to a new valuation of desire. Puritanism came to stand for moral repressiveness, a repressiveness given expression in a variety of reform movements aimed at legislating against, among other activities, drinking, prostitution, and forms of sexual emancipation. The equation of Puritanism with moral regulation in general, and sexual repressiveness in particular, made a "sudden, explosive appearance in the opening decades of the twentieth-century when an angry generation of feminists, birth-control champions, anarchists, free-speech lawyers, cultural critics, realist novelists, and Greenwich Village bohemians attacked their forebears for willfully evading what they considered to be the most pressing issue of life—sex."[9]

Historians of the period lent further evidence to the barrenness of this Puritan past, emphasizing not only the oligarchic aspects but the cultural emptiness of a Puritan theocracy. Vernon Parrington, for example, wrote that "It is not pleasant to linger in the drab later years of a century that in its prime had known able men and accomplished notable things. A world that accepted Michael Wigglesworth for its poet, and accounted Cotton Mather its most distinguished man of letters, had certainly backslidden in the ways of culture." Parrington, continuing on this bleak note, suggested that in the latter half of the seventeenth-century, "Not a single notable book appeared; scarcely a single generous figure emerged from the primitive background. A thin soil and the law of Moses created a capable but ungainly race, prosaic and niggardly." Speech had lost its English grace as "the Puritan middle class had substituted asceticism for beauty."[10] For Parrington, there was little reason to look to the Puritan past, particularly since the dreary provincialism would give way to the liberalism of the colonial mind. Parrington would identify the foundations of an American culture, instead, in the "undistinguished years of the early and middle eighteenth century" when the "forgotten men and women" who "wrote little, debated little, very likely thought little" created a "psychology of democratic individualism" as they brought new land under the plow. The Puritans could be ignored because the eighteenth century farmer and worker were engaged in "uprooting ancient habits of thought" and "destroying social customs that had grown old and dignified in classridden Europe."[11] In scarcely a century after Daniel Webster's celebration of the Puritans as giving to America a founding not lost in the darkness of a European past, Parrington had made the Puritans into a last relic of feudalism.

It is in reaction to these depictions of the Puritans that we can understand the importance of Perry Miller's work. For what Miller did was lend a vibrant intellectual coherence to the Puritans that was political, literary, and social.[12] So powerful was Miller's work that it gave rise to a whole generation of scholars who, perhaps in the enthusiasm of giving color to a past that had been painted in broad strokes of gray, saw in Puritanism everything from the origins of an American democratic ethos and civility to the foundation for American exceptionalism and sense of purpose.

This scholarly exuberance, which (much like the Puritans) has since come under suspicion by current trends in cultural criticism, never really entered the mainstream of American culture. Instead, on the one hand we witness a sanitizing of the Pilgrims as founders of the first Thanksgiving who, if nothing else, got along with their neighbors. On the other hand, we see the demonizing of the Puritans as a way of "discrediting" any efforts to impose both "authority and morality."[13] More specifically, as moral issues have come to be seen as self-legislating, any attempt to call for rules or restrictions about moral behavior is, in itself, viewed as an illegitimate assertion of authority and subject to the label "Puritan."

This has led to some interesting twists-and-turns in whom we now describe as "Puritan." The term has been used by the columnist Sidney Blumenthal, for example, to describe Paul Tsongas, a candidate in the 1992 Democratic presidential primaries. Recalling Randolph Bourne's description in 1917 of a "true Puritan" as "at once the most unselfish and the most self-righteous of men," Blumenthal saw in Tsongas' "self-efface-ment" a "form of domination" achieved by holding out and enforcing on others "the illusion of the hard truth."[14] For other commentators, true to the critiques of Puritanism at the turn of the century, the "neo-Puritans" are those "humorously imposing on others arbitrary (meaning their own) standards of behavior, health and thought." Where we saw such Puritan intolerance played out against the backdrop of McCarthyism in Arthur Miller's "The Crucible," in contemporary society this brand of righteousness appears as attempts to restrict "life-style" choices: smoking, drinking, and eating high-cholesterol foods, most notably.[15] The religious sobriety of the Puritans has been transformed into a purity of the body: a purity honed in the gym, cleansed "of everything but organically raised broccoli," and enforced with a "smugness" and "grim superiority."[16] *New York* even devoted its cover story to the "deprivation chic" of the "New Puritans" who "pursue self-denial as an end in itself, out of an almost mystical belief in this purity it confers."[17] On a similar note, the *New Republic* allowed John Winthrop to speak (in his Puritan script) to the issue of the proper balance between "worldly delights" and "graces of the spirit." Not surprisingly, Winthrop fails to strike the proper balance. The reason, it seems, lies in the notion of "Christian libertie." Such "'libertie,'" suggests the columnist, "would allow each of us to make mistakes, to find this acceptable balance—for ourselves and on our own." But "'Christian' modifies this liberty with a moral code to be honored, if not followed." Given the choice between "'libertie' or its qualifier," the author chooses "liberty."[18] It is a liberty, importantly, that can admit of no authority, Christian or otherwise.

Puritanism has been invoked, as well, to decry the feminist left's crusade against pornography. Alan Wolfe, for example, notes that though there is "little redeeming social value" in pornography, it nonetheless "speaks to needs within the self" and provides "outlets for our imaginations, relying on our power to give meaning to representations of fantasies buried deep within the self, even if the pictorial representations of those fantasies involve, on the surface, harm to others."[19] John Irving reminds us that the "Puritans are not dead and gone" but are alive and, now in the guise of "formerly liberal-thinking feminists," are "as dangerous to freedom of expression as the old Puritans ever were." So dangerous are they, in fact, that anti-pornography feminists and Puritans get grouped together with "fascism" which, for Irving, "usually amounts to banning something you dislike and can't control."[20] More generally, but related to this reaction to the anti-pornography movement, is a sense that the new feminism represents a neo-Puritan sexual repressiveness. Speaking in reaction to the Clarence Thomas hearings, the Harvard sociologist Orlando Patterson criticizes "American feminists" and "politicians manipulating the nation's lingering Puritan ideals" for making moral offenses into absolutes rather than placing such offenses in the cultural context in which they occur.[21]

Puritanism has been used as well to warn of the "exaggeration of the virtue of tolerance" which, at that point, makes "political correctness" into "a form of Puritanism."[22] And it has been used to label a conservative attack on enlightened values of freedom.[23] So, for example, in response to attempts to cut funding for the National Endowment for the Arts (as a result of some highly publicized uses of the grant money to fund what some saw as obscene projects), Anthony Lewis begins one column, "A small band of religious zealots and right-wing political opportunists is trying to show the world that America is an intolerant country, contemptuous of artists."[24] Similarly, in an article reminiscent of Emma Goldman's assault on Puritanism, Robert Brustein suggests that "despite its political form," current attacks on the NEA reflect more a "spiritual" problem. What one sees in the American soul is a Puritanism of both the right and left. The Puritanism of the right is a moralism that attacks "anything that deviates from the purity and sanctity of some pre-lapsarian ideal." And the Puritanism of the left is a utilitarianism that demands that artistic works "demonstrate their usefulness to the body politic."[25]

Read culturally, what all of these assessments have in common, in linking the perceived "wrong" with Puritanism, is a notion of freedom that is radically suspicious of any expression of restraint, whether that restraint is expressed as the "censorial" desires of anti-pornography crusaders,[26] the "lectures" that networks give on the "merits of old-fashioned puritanism" by not showing people enjoying themselves having sex,[27] the "terrorizing" of those who choose to be unhealthy,[28] or even the self-restraint of those who pursue healthy lives.[29] The desire to unmask born of a suspicion of sin, which Richard Sennett traces to a Puritan past, has been replaced by a desire to unmask born of a suspicion of authority, pursued not by Puritans but by self-proclaimed anti-Puritans.[30] Tellingly, Roland Joffé's 1995 film, "The Scarlet Letter," ends with Hester Prynne's daughter, Pearl, asking "Who is to say what is a sin in the eyes of God?" Absent an answer, there can be no sin.

This suspicion of authority takes an ironic twist in one historian's understanding of the Republican "Contract with America" as an anti-modernist "Puritan Covenant." For Hatheway, the congressional elections of 1994 represented "the victory of a conservative, anti-modernist mentality that has deep historical roots in the American experience," an experience that he traces back to the Puritans. "Rather than accept the modernist propensity to understand human behavior within its cultural context, the anti-modernism mentality extols the truth of an autonomous self informed by Christianity and faithful to antebellum republican ideals of gentility, prudence, and virtue."[31] Specifically, the Puritan's contribution to this antimodernist outlook was to reject an Enlightenment notion of reason and articulate, instead, a view of both individual and social sins that were "less a consequence of impersonal, evolutionary, and interdependent forces as much as they were the results of the human propensity to give in to temptation and sin" that "only God could help the individual overcome."[32] What this leads to in Hatheway's account is the rejection by the antimoderns of the "interdependent self" for two reasons: first, a notion of interdependence would seem to "deny autonomy and the truths of Christianity"; and second, a scientific view of social development would undermine the claims that the United States was "God's unique providence."[33]

This anti-modernism is now being used by supporters of the Republican contract, suggests Hatheway, to establish "order and authority based upon the cultural hegemony of a relatively small elite informed by the late-eighteenth-century republican ideals of hard work, prudence, sobriety, and gentility, which derived from a white, middle-class New England-based 'aristocracy of merit.'" The problems of modernity are placed on those who are actually its victims: the poor, immigrants, gays and lesbians, women, Native Americans, and other "'multiculturals.'" In actuality, though, the "anti-modernist discourse about less government, personal autonomy, and moral responsibility mask[s] an intrusive social agenda which will be initiated under the rubrics of God, republican virtue, and states' rights and facilitated by federal legislation in support of a very narrow social, cultural, political, and economic elite."[34]

What is striking in this rather sweeping indictment of America's Puritan past is how at odds a contractual basis of human society is with what even Hatheway recognizes as the covenant basis of Puritan society. For though the covenant for the Puritans was initiated by God to a fallen people, as Hatheway observes, the covenant occurs among an already constituted community. What is so important about the covenant in this regard, and is lost in Hatheway's commentary, is that the covenant arises out of, and in turn confirms, a sense of community responsibility that presupposes some authority that stands outside the immediate community. Where contractual obligations arise out of the arbitrary agreement between two or more parties, the covenant does not create obligations as much as provide a way for the fulfillment of already felt responsibilities. This is why Winthrop, in his lay sermon pronounced before landing on American soil, would speak of the promise of the "city upon a hill" as resting upon "charity" toward others.[35] If the people failed in this task, the community, and not just the individual, would perish. This is why in subsequent generations, as well, and we can see this happening through Lincoln, there were continual calls to renew this covenant as a way for the community to remember its responsibilities.[36]

The loss of the acknowledgment of human interdependence that Hatheway so decries is a result not of a Puritan past but, ironically, of exactly Hatheway's brand of rationalism that exposes the superstition of tradition and frees us from our past. The issue is not that we should accept an uncritical stance toward our past, nor is the point that the past can tell us how we should live. What a language of tradition does provide is a vocabulary that emerges from, and to that extent shows, the possibility of defining a life together. That we do not want to be Puritans is understandable. But in casting something as Puritan, we are doing more than denouncing a Puritan past. We are using the Puritans to cast suspicion on anything that binds us, whether the nature of the binding is external (through laws, traditions, or moral opprobrium) or internal (through the guilt of our conscience or the pursuit of a regimen of ascetic self-denial). And we embrace, in its place, a vocabulary of freedom whose very essence is that it has no grounding or direction beyond, to use Michael Oakeshott's term, the "felt need" of the moment.[37] The freedom that emerges from giving direction to the future as it engages the past has been replaced by a freedom without memory and a direction born of desire.

Notes

1   Edmund Burke, *Reflections on the Revolution in France* (Garden City: Dolphin Books, 1961), 90.

2   Andrew Delbanco, "A Losing Battle?" *Salmagundi*, Nos. 101-102 (Winter-Spring 1994), 117-8.

3   See Rochelle Gurstein, "'Puritanism' as Epithet: Common Standards and the Fate of Reticence," *Salmagundi*, Nos. 101-102 (Winter-Spring 1994): 95-116.

4   Rochelle Gurstein, "A Discussion: 'The New Puritanism' Reconsidered," *Salmagundi*, Nos. 106-107 (Spring-Summer 1995), 196.

5   John Adams, "A Dissertation on the Canon and Feudal Law," originally printed in the *Boston Gazette*, August 1765, in *The Works of John Adams*, 10 vols., ed. Charles Francis Adams (Boston: Little, Brown, & Co., 1865), 3: 448-64.

6   H. L. Mencken, "Puritanism as a Literary Force," in *A Book of Prefaces* (Garden City, New York: Garden City Publishing Co., 1927).

7   Randolph Bourne, "The Puritan's Will to Power," *The New Republic* (April 1917).

8   Emma Goldman, "The Hypocrisy of Puritanism," in *Anarchism, and Other Essays* (Port Washington, New York: Kennikat Press, 1969), 174.

9   Gurstein, "'Puritanism as Epithet," 101. See also Christopher Lasch, *The New Radicalism in America, 1889-1963: The Intellectual as a Social Type* (New York: W. W. Norton, 1965), 109.

10 Vernon L. Parrington, *Main Currents in American Thought: The Colonial Mind 1620-1800*, 2 vols. (New York: Harvest, 1927), 1: 85.

11 Parrington, *Main Currents*, 1: 133.

12 For discussions of how Miller recast Puritanism into a usable, perhaps "mythical," past, see James Hoopes, "Art as History: Perry Miller's *New England Mind*," *American Quarterly* 34 (1982): 3-25; Francis T. Butts, "The Myth of Perry Miller," *American Historical Review* 87 (1982): 665-694); Stanford J. Searl, Jr., "Perry Miller as Artist: Piety and Imagination in *The New England Mind: The Seventeenth Century*," *Early American Literature* 12 (1977-1978): 221-233.

13 Elizabeth Fox-Genovese, "Beyond Individualism: The New Puritanism, Feminism and Women," *Salmagundi*, Nos. 101-102 (Winter-Spring 1994), 81.

14 Sidney Blumenthal, "The Puritan: Paul Tsongas's will to power," *The New Republic* (March 23, 1992), 11-12.

15 John Elson, "Busybodies: New Puritans," *Time* (August 12, 1991), 20.

16 Allan Fotheringham, "The Dangerous New Puritans," *Maclean's* (April 10, 1989), 80.

17 Dinitia Smith, "The New Puritans: Deprivation Chic," *New York* (June 11, 1984), 24-5.

18 Jefferson Morley, "Our Puritan Dilemma: Life, libertie, and earthly delightes," *The New Republic* (Dec. 1, 1986), 14.

19 Alan Wolfe, "Dirt and Democracy: Feminists, Liberals, and the War on Pornography," *The New Republic* (Feb. 19, 1990), 30-31.

20 John Irving, "Pornography and the New Puritans," *The New York Times Book Review* (March 29, 1992), 24-5.

21 Patterson, "Race, Gender and Liberal Fallacies," *The New York Times*, Oct. 20, 1991, E 15. See also Orlando Patterson, "The New Puritanism," *Salmagundi*, Nos. 101-102 (Winter-Spring 1994): 55-67. For a discussion of the difficulty of finding a feminist vocabulary that can address sexism without ending with sexual repression, see Ellen Willis, "Villains and Victims: 'Sexual Correctness' and the Repression of Feminism," *Salmagundi*, Nos. 101-102 (Winter-Spring 1994): 68-78.

22 Richard A. Schweder, "Puritans in High-Top Sneakers," *New York Times*, Sept. 27, 1993, A17.

23 See, for example, Jay Hatheway, "The Puritan Covenant II: Anti-Modernism and the 'Contract with America,'" *The Humanist* (July/August 1995): 24-33.

24 Anthony Lewis, "Fight the Philistines," *New York Times*, June 8, 1990.

25 Robert Brustein, "The NEA Belly Up," *The New Republic* (June 18, 1990), 33.

26 Irving, "Pornography," 1.

27 George V. Higgins, "TV Puritans: Who killed J. R.'s sex life?" *Harper's* (Oct. 1985), 73.

28 Fotheringham, "Dangerous," 80.

29 Smith, "New Puritans."

30 See Richard Sennett, "A Republic of Souls: Puritanism and the American Presidency," *Harper's* (July 1987), 41-46.

31 Hatheway, "The Puritan Covenant," 24.

32 Ibid., 28.

33 Ibid., 28-9.

34 Ibid., 32.

35 Winthrop, "Modell," 195-9.

36 For a discussion of Lincoln's use of the sacred in his political language, see John P. Diggins, *The Lost Soul of American Politics: Virtue, Self-Interest, and the Foundations of Liberalism* (Chicago: University of Chicago, 1984). Interestingly, President Bill Clinton has recently invoked a notion of a "New Covenant," both in the primaries and as a response to the Republican "Contract With America." See Bill Clinton, "The New Covenant: Responsibility and Rebuilding the American Community," Speech at Georgetown University, Oct. 23, 1991; Clinton, "A New Covenant for Economic Change," Speech at Georgetown University, Nov. 20, 1991; Clinton, "Values," Speech at University of Notre Dame, Sept. 11, 1992; and Clinton, "Responsible Citizenship and the American Community," Speech at Georgetown University, July 6, 1995. Downloaded from <http//nuinfo.nwu.edu:70/1ftp%3Awhit>.

37 See Michael Oakeshott, "Rationalism in Politics," in *Rationalism in Politics and Other Essays* (Indianapolis: Liberty Press, 1991).

Index

Adams, Abigail, 114
Adams, John, 94, 110, 111, 112, 114, 138, 150, 152, 155, 202
Adams, John Quincy, 146, 176
Adams, Samuel, 103, 104
Alien Act, 155
Alien and Sedition Acts, 156
American Revolution, and civic republicanism, 97, 105–115; and liberalism, 97, 98–105, 115–121; and Locke, 97, 98–105; and republicanism, 115–121; and space of discourse, 107, 115, 120; and view of authority, 116; and Whigs, 107
Anabaptists, 18
Anderson, Virginia, xvi
Andros, Sir Edmund, 16, 71, 99
Antinomianism, and Jonathan Edwards, 65
Antinomian Affair, 21–23
Appleby, Joyce, 140
Arminianism, and Jonathan Edwards, 60, 64–66
Augustine, and Puritanism, 29
Aurelius, Marcus, 112
Austin, Jonathan, 121, 137
authority, contemporary conceptions, 201–208; and Puritanism, 2–29; and Jonathan Edwards, 66–70; and American Revolution, 115–121; and

Federalists, 142–147; and Whigs, 174–184

Backus, Isaac, 77
Bailyn, Bernard, 97, 105–106, 116
Baltimore, Frederick Calvert, Earl of, 77
Bancroft, George, 168, 171, 181
Banner, James, 140
Banning, Lance, 141
Baptists, 19; and historiography, 77
Barlow, Joel, 139
Barnwell, Robert, 75
Beecher, Lyman, 174, 175, 188
Belknap, Jeremy, 172
Bellah, Robert, xix
Bercovitch, Sacvan, xii, 9, 17, 95
Body of Liberties, 15
Bolingbroke, Henry St. John, Viscount, 105, 107–108
Boorstin, Daniel, 97
Bourne, Randolph, 202
Bozeman, Theodore Dwight, 7–8, 16
Bradford, William, 10, 50, 51, 73, 147
Bradstreet, Simon, 25
Buell, Lawrence, 80
Burgh, James, 105, 107, 109
Burke, Edmund, 146, 201
Burr, Aaron, 70
Bushman, Richard, 7
Byrd, William, 79

Caner, Henry, 78

Cart and Whip Act, 18, 155
Catholics, historiography, 77
Cato's Letters (Trenchard and
       Gordon), 108, 145
Chesapeake, as developmental
       model, xiii
Child, Robert, 25
Choate, Rufus, 185, 186, 187
Church, John, 144
Church of England, historiogra-
       phy, 80
Cicero, Marcus Tullius, 105
civic republicanism, xviii, 105–
       115
civil millennialism, 71–2
Constitution of Massachusetts
       (1780), 118–119
Cooper, Samuel, 119–20
Cotton, John, 4
covenant of grace, 5, 21
covenant of works, 5
cultural theory, 38 (fn 15, 19), 39
       (fn 25)
culture, and Puritan legacy, xi,
       49, 54; and Federalists,
       141–142; and Whigs,
       168; see also political
       culture
Cushman, Robert, 50–51

Daggett, David, 136
Daggett, Naphtali, 70
Danforth, John, 26, 28
Danforth, Thomas, 145
Davies, Samuel, 70
Dawes, Thomas, 112, 115
Day, Thomas, 151
Day of Humiliation, 114
Dedham Covenant, 11
Delbanco, Andrew, 12, 201
Dickinson, John, 74
Downer, Silas, 104
Drummer, Jeremiah, 102
Dudley, Thomas, 14, 30
Duffield, George, 74
Dunbar, Samuel, 72
Dwight, Timothy, 138–139, 149,
       153–154, 170

Edwards, Jonathan, 58, 59, 60–70;
       and aesthetics, 68; and
       Antinomians, 65, 66; and
       Arminians, 60, 65, 66;
       and George Bancroft, 68;
       and grace, 61–63, 64, 66;
       and hierarchy, 68; and
       the insular individual,
       63, 65, 66; and love, 67–
       70; and Puritan founding
       (legacy), 67–8; and the
       Separates, 67; and sin,
       60–63; and social
       organization, 66–70; and
       virtue, 67; and the will,
       63, 64
Elkins and McKitrick, 140
Emerson, Ralph Waldo, 53, 170–
       171
Episcopalians, historiography, 78,
       79
Everett, Edward, 169, 176, 177,
       180, 182–183

The Federalist, 147
Federalists, and the American
       Revolution, xviii, 142–
       147; and education, 153;
       and faction, 147–157;
       and hierarchy, 143; and
       jeremiad, 149; and
       liberty, 141–142; and
       national character, 143,
       156, 157; and Puritan
       legacy, xviii, 143, 144,
       145, 146, 147, 152–157;
       and purity, 153, 154, 156;
       and Republicans, 148–
       157; views, 140, 141; and
       view of nature, 147
Finley, Samuel, 70
Fiske, Samuel, 149
Foster, Stephen, xii, 13–14, 18
Foster, William, 74
Franklin, Benjamin, 53, 75–76,
       93, 94, 115
Fraser, Charles, 145
French and Indian War, 70

Frisbie, Levi, 139

Galloway, Joseph, 77
Gardiner, John, 137
General Court, 10, 14, 15, 17, 18, 22–25
Georgia, historiography, 76
Goldman, Emma, 202
Goodwin, George, 5
Gordon, Thomas, 72, 105, 107–108
Great Awakening, xvii, 58–70, 99; and Puritan influence, 58, 59
Greene, Jack, xiii
Greenstone, J. David, xvi

Habermas, Jürgen, xv
Hamilton, Alexander, 136, 172
Hartz, Louis, 97
Hatch, Nathan, 95
Hawthorne, Nathaniel, 53, 170, 181, 202
Heimert, Alan, xi, 95
Hichborn, Benjamin, 139
Higginson, John, 28
Hooker, Thomas, 4
Howe, Daniel Walker, 141, 168
Howgill, Francis, 35
Hubbard, William, 73
Humphreys, David, 135
Hutchinson, Anne, 12, 13, 18, 19, 21–23
Hutchinson, Thomas, 73, 102

Innes, Stephen, xvi

Jackson, Andrew, 167, 172, 175, 178, 184; and commerce, 173–174; and the Great Awakening, xi–xii, 58
Jamestown, 79
Jefferson, Thomas, 75, 94, 115, 140, 148, 150, 167, 172, 184; and commerce, 173; and the Great Awakening, xi–xii, 58
jeremiad, xii, 29, 31–32, 46 (fn 108), 62–3

Johnson, Edward, 24, 52

Kentucky, historiography, 75
Kerber, Linda, 141
King George's War, 70
Knight, Janice, 2
Konig, David, 15
Kramnick, Isaac, 109, 141

Langdon, Samuel, 70, 113
Laud, William, 72
Lee, Chauncey, 151
Lee, Richard Henry, 75, 121
Livingston, John Henry, 74
Livingston, William, 74
Locke, John, xviii; and American Revolution, 98–105, 115–121; and Federalists, 176
Locke, Samuel, 70
Lovell, James, 102

Machiavelli, Niccolò, 97, 105
Madison, James, 147–148, 157
Marshall, John, 146
Marshall, Christopher, 120
Mason, Jonathan, 114
Massachusetts Bay Charter (1684), 71
Massachusetts Constitution (1780), 118
Mather, Cotton, 24, 27, 29, 30, 53, 71
Mather, Increase, 3, 30, 32, 61, 71
Mather, Moses, 101
Mather, Richard, 28
Mayhew, Jonathan, 93, 99, 100, 115
Mencken, H. L., 202
Middlekauff, Robert, xvi
Miller, Perry, xi, 95, 203; and declension thesis, xi, xiii
Moore, Maurice, 75
Murrin, John, 141

Neal, Daniel, 53, 101
New Divinity, 58
New Jersey, historiography, 75
New Lights, 59, 63

New Netherlands, historiography, 73

New Side Presbyterians, 70, 86 (fn 76)

New York, historiography, 74

Niles, Nathaniel, 113–114, 118

North Carolina, historiography, 75

Old Lights, 59

Old Side Presbyterians, 70, 86 (fn 76)

orations, xviii; Boston Massacre, 96, 101–105; Fourth of July, 96; Pilgrim landing, 96; see also rhetoric

Otis, James, 104

Paine, Charles, 154–155

Paine, Thomas, 153

Parrington, Vernon, 203

Patterson, Orlando, 205

Peck, Jedidiah, 156

Pennsylvania, historiography, 74

Pilgrims, xiii, 144, 147, 171–172, 178, 186

Plymouth, 10

Pocock, J. G. A., xviii, 97–98, 106

political culture, xiv, 141, 168

preparationism, 5, 6, 45 (fn 96)

Price, Richard, 105

Priestly, Joseph, 105

Prince, Thomas, 53–54

Puritanism, and art, 206; and bourgeois capitalism, xii, 1, 9, 17; church membership, 19–21; conception of self (or selfhood), 3–6; conversion, 33–35; definition, xi, xiii, xvi, xvii, xx–xxi (fn 6); and discursive space, 2, 22; and education, 56, 57; and economic prosperity, 23–29; and egalitarianism, 6–7, 10, 11, 12; founding legend, 50–54;

as founders, xvii, xviii, 49, 50–54, 72–80, 96, 101–105, 110–115, 143–147, 152–157, 172, 184–189; and grace, 29, 30, 31, 32, 33, 34, 35; and hierarchy, 6, 7, 8, 9, 12–18; historiography, 57, 72, 73, 76–80; and the insular individual, xvi, 3–6, 19–29; legacy, xi, xiii, xiv, xv, xvi, 1, 49, 72, 73, 76–80; and liberty, 71; and Locke, 99–105; and migration, xvi, 6–7, 50; ministerial strength, 54, 55; and modernity, 17; and primitivism, 1; printed material, 56; and purity, 155; and republican virtues, 110; self-definition, xvi–xvii, 9–10; sin, 29, 30, 31, 32, 33, 34, 35; and social ethic, xii; and social organization, 6–18, 6–29, 40 (fn 41); and space of discourse, xv–xvii, 21, 36, 59; and state support of churches, 55; and Whigs, xviii, 71; world view, 1, 2

Puritan legacy, and the American Revolution, xvii, 98; contemporary interpretations, 201–208; and Federalists, xviii; and feminism, 205; as founders, xvii, xviii, 49, 50–54, 72–80, 96, 101–105, 110–115, 143–147, 152–157, 172, 184–189; and Great Awakening, xvii, 67–68; rhetorical invocations, xv; and Contract with America, 206–8

Quakers, 8–9, 14, 18–19, 33–35, 75; historiography, 76

radical Whigs, 105–110
Ramsay, David, 121, 145
republicanism, 105–121
rhetoric, and invocation of Puritan past, xv; and political orations, xvii, xxii (fn 19), 96–97, 168–169; see also orations
Rousseau, Jean-Jacques, 19
Rush, Benjamin, 120, 138
Rutledge, John, 121

Savage, James, 169
Second Great Awakening, 188
Sedgwick, Catherine, 170, 181, 202
Seligman, Adam, 8–9
Sennett, Richard, 206
Seven Years' War, 70
Sewall, Samuel, 34
Shain, Barry, 95, 112
Shays' Rebellion, 147
Shepard, Thomas, 24
Sherwood, Samuel, 117
Silliman, Benjamin, 151
Smith, John, 78, 79
Smith, Samuel, 75
Somkin, Fred, 178, 182
South Carolina, historiography, 76
space of discourse, defined, xv; and interpretations of Puritan past, xvii
Stamp Act, 110–111
Stetson, Caleb, 188
Stiles, Ezra, 135
Stoddard, Solomon, 20–21, 43 (fn 70)
Story, Joseph, 180
Stout, Harry, 59, 95
Stowe, Harriet Beecher, 53
Strong, Caleb, 153
Sudbury, 10
Sullivan, George, 150

Taylor, John, 60
Thanksgiving, 114
Thoreau, Henry David, 170
Tillinghast, George, 77
Trenchard, John, 105, 107–108
Trumbull, Benjamin, 169, 186
Town Act, 15
Tudor, William, 143–144

United States Seal, 93–4

Van Buren, Martin, 172
Virginia, historiography, 75, 78–79
Virginia and Kentucky resolutions, 148

Walzer, Michael, 6
Warren, Joseph, 102, 112
Weber, Donald, 95
Webster, Daniel, 179, 181–182, 185, 187, 189, 203
Webster, Samuel, 113
Wheelwright, John, 22
Whigs, xvii, xviii; and commerce, 172–184; and community organization, 177–184; and development of a founding legend, xviii; Fourth of July orations, 169; and internal improvements, 180; and liberty, xvii, 181–182; and Lowell, Massachusetts, 182–3; and political culture, 191 (fn 9); political rhetoric, 168, 169; and Prattville, 183–4; and property, 178, 179; and Puritan legacy, 169–172, 172, 174–184, 184–189; and social organization, 177–184; and view of history, 184–189; view of nature, 172–174; views, 167, 168
Whiskey Rebellion, 148

Whitefield, George, 58
Whiting, John, 26
Wigglesworth, Samuel, 28–29
Willard, Joseph, 187
Williams, Abraham, 116–117
Williams, Elisha, 101
Williams, Roger, 181
Winthrop, John, 12–14, 16, 17,
     23, 25, 30, 31, 40 (fn 41),
     51, 52, 73, 100, 112, 120,
     177, 205
Winthrop, Margaret, 31
Wise, John, 99
Wittgenstein, Ludwig, xiii, xiv
Wolfe, Alan, 205
Wood, Gordon, 95, 140, 142
Woolman, John, 34

Zubley, John, 76
Zuckerman, Michael, 8–9

Major Concepts in Politics and Political Theory

This series invites book manuscripts and proposals on major concepts in politics and political theory—justice, equality, virtue, rights, citizenship, power, sovereignty, property, liberty, etc.—in prominent traditions, periods, and thinkers.

Send manuscripts or proposals, with author's vitae to:

Garrett Ward Sheldon
General Editor
College Avenue
Clinch Valley College
University Virginia
Wise, VA 24293

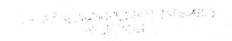